The Reluctant Innkeeper

The Reluctant Innkeeper

Geraldine Sylvester

MILLCITY
PRESS

Mill City Press, Inc.
212 3rd Avenue North, Suite 570
Minneapolis, MN 55401
612.455.2294
www.millcitypress.net

ISBN - 978-1-934937-14-3
ISBN - 1-934937-14-2
LCCN - 2008929772

Cover Design and Typeset by James/DZYN Lab

Printed in the United States of America

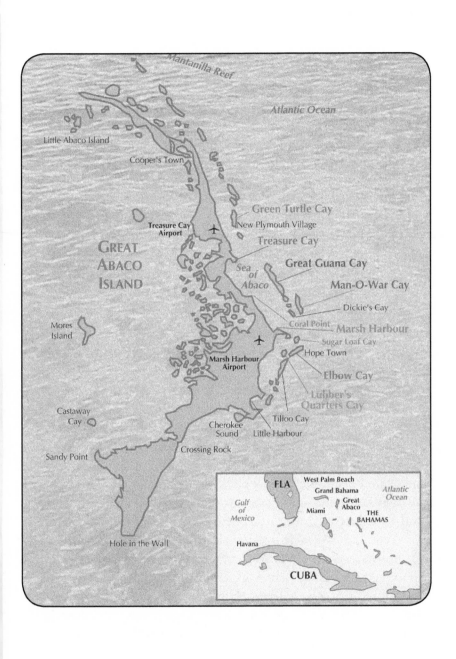

CHAPTER 1

Definitely Not York Beach

I'm sitting here wondering how many of you at one time or other acted spontaneously—just did something on the spur of the moment without giving it a lot of thought. Maybe you said something before you even put your brain in gear. Well, that's a habit of mine. That is my history. But the last time I said something before I realized I had said it, my husband Bob and I ended up being innkeepers.

We were finally retired. We sold the business that Bob had started and operated for twenty-four years—a business that manufactured high quality electronic parts. It had started out in our family room with only two employees—Bob and me—and ended up with over 150. And I had retired after a career in politics and state government as a director of two agencies. We were free and clear to relax and do as we pleased.

Summers, we sailed our 40.2-foot Sabre sloop *The Yankee Cowboy* all around the coast of Maine. Occasionally we'd head a little south to Massachusetts or Rhode Island, but, we would quickly return back to Maine, and always wonder why. Sometimes it was cold, even in the summer; and many, too many times, it was foggy. But we loved it with all the wonderful inlets and harbors it had to offer. In the fall, after the insurance company deemed there was little chance of hurricanes, we would really head South—to Florida and beyond.

I loved traveling the Intercostals Waterway, and even though we had traveled it many times, it always seemed to be just a little different. We picked out favorite marinas along the way, and after a couple of weeks on the water we would just leave the boat docked there and fly home. My Mom was still alive, so I didn't want to leave her for too lengthy a time. She was doing just fine but I knew that she got lonely. She missed her "little girl" and said she even missed Bob.

Once we finally reached Florida, it was time to cross over the Gulf Stream and head for Marsh Harbour in the Abacos. I actually did the crossing by boat twice and swore never to do it again. Even when the weather reports claimed the Gulf Stream was ideal for a smooth trip across, I thought differently. I didn't enjoy unexpected wind, waves and a lot of bouncing around. Guess I am just not really much of a sailor. I informed Bob that the next crossing he could take a friend—perhaps JO White, or a couple of our sons, or whoever—but not me. From then on I would fly over and meet them at the Marsh Harbour Marina. The first time across I got on a tiny airplane and the pilot shut the door on all four of the passengers and proceeded to climb into his window to get to his pilot seat. I wasn't too damn sure I hadn't made a big mistake. Afterward I took several other trips on small planes, not the four-passenger types, but six- and nine-seaters. Then, lo and behold, I found airline carriers that could take up to nineteen folks. They even had a host or hostess that brought around water or soft drinks, and right up next to the 'cockpit was a toilet—a tiny one, but it was there. Even though the flights across from Florida to the Marsh Harbour "INTERNATIONAL" Airport only takes about an hour, I was often grateful for the luxury of that little amenity.

We always ended up in Marsh Harbour. It is the largest town in the Abacos, exceeded in size only by Nassau and Freeport. The population is about 5,000. They had three grocery stores until two burned down. Now they are building another couple and all of them are owned by the same people. They have a couple of liquor stores, a hardware store, other shops, and recently opened up—not a Bed Bath and Beyond like we have in the states—but a tiny place called Bed Bath and Between. There is also one traffic light—the only one in all of the Abacos. Most didn't like it, and when hurricane Floyd blew it down, no one complained that it took a couple of years to get up again.

We always docked at the Marsh Harbour Marina on the north side of the harbor. It is owned and operated by Boo and Tom Laffler, who not only treat you like royalty, tending to your every need, but they were great caretakers who carefully watched over *The Yankee Cowboy* when we left her there for lengthy periods of time. They also operate a restaurant named the Jib Room, where they often have special affairs for all their boaters. It was at the Jib Room that we met Penny Turtle, who graciously offered to sponsor us as a member of the Royal Marsh Harbour Yacht Club. At the time it only cost $25 to join, but you couldn't get in without a sponsor.

I am not sure exactly when I suggested to our kids that I might like to buy a cottage at York Beach, Maine, but they practically laughed me out of the house. "What in the world are you thinking"? one said. "York Beach is only a hop and a skip away, every one of us can get there in twenty or twenty-five minutes, and for the last fifteen years you have rented us a place there. Each of the seven of us got our own week, and that worked out perfectly since summer here is only SEVEN WEEKS LONG anyway." "Why don't you look for a place we can share that is WARM in the winter?" another offered.

So it was those bright kids of mine that planted the idea and got the whole show rolling. Bob and I both loved the Bahamas, so that's where the search would begin—we would check out the islands, or "cays" as they are called, right there in Abaco.

We did quite a bit of looking around. We checked out Marsh Harbour, then went on to most of the Cays—Green Turtle, Man 'o War, Treasure Cay, Hopetown—and found nothing of interest. We came across a nice cottage, but it was far inland and on a rocky cliff-like shore. We found a great spot on the beach, but the house was falling down. And so it went. Then we met some friends from home, Ned McIntosh and Lee Spencer. They questioned why we hadn't checked out Guana Cay. They both had homes there and absolutely loved it. When I mentioned the only thing I knew about Guana was Nippers Bar they certainly filled me in on what else Guana was all about and gave it rave reviews.

CHAPTER 2

Check Out The Charm

Ned was one of the first Americans to settle there. He bought his cottage, which he delightfully refers to as *Termite Terrace,* back in 1968 for $4,000 The location couldn't be better. His little blue place sits next to Milo's,(the little fruit and vegetable stand in the heart of town, right across from the harbor, with only a small strip of land between him and the beautiful Sea of Abaco.

When he first arrived, there were no streets, no power, no anything. If you wanted to go from one place to another, you had to push bushes aside and follow little paths. And often you could only get there by boat. In those days there were chickens running all around and, as Ned recalls, just one loud and randy rooster. Two large families lived on either side of Ned. One had thirteen children, the other only eleven. He described watching those kids grow up in a way that let you know that those families' lives certainly weren't easy. Neither family had a cistern to catch the fresh falling rain, so the kids had to walk up a steep path and carry water home from a spring. It was mostly brackish water but they seemed somehow to manage. Most all of the families had outhouses—only a very few relied on the dense native vegetation—and

Ned traded in his two-holer for a marine toilet he could operate from his second floor with buckets of water with the help of good old gravity. Ned reminisced with me about those families' struggles to survive and how great it was to see most of them as adults, still on Guana, raising their own families, and doing well. A few left Guana as they got older but amazingly enough most have remained there.

He said at first there were only the local residents. Then people began to discover, as he did, just how delightful Guana is. New homeowners came in little groupings. There were some from Kansas, some from Colorado, some from New Jersey, some from Maine, some from New Hampshire, and other locations too. It seems that once someone discovers this Cay, they let their friends in on the secret. Lee Spencer and his wife Shirley are there because of Ned, his first wife Alice (who passed away) and new wife Terry. Mickey and Elaine Hashem are there because of the Spencers, at least that's how I think it went. I do know that Lee Spencer came to visit Ned at his *Termite Terrace,* fell in love with Guana, and wanted to buy a place of his own. Fortunately for Lee, his brother was on a boat out in the harbor when he learned of a place that was for sale. He actually saw the sign go up. He contacted Lee at once, who in turn got back to the sellers in rapid time. There were two families interested in the purchase, but at least one of them was trying to talk the owner into selling at a lower price. Lee, being most astute, offered even more than the asking price and closed the deal in the nick of time. It was quite a while before the Spencers were forgiven or accepted there, but I think since years have passed, it's all better now—or mostly better. Now they had let us in on the secret—and now we were ready to explore Great Guana Cay.

Bob and I, along with our friends JO and his then-wife Carlene, boarded *The Yankee Cowboy,* left the Marsh Harbour Marina and sailed the seven miles across the Sea of Abaco until reaching our destination. As we moored in the harbor we could clearly see the Settlement, which here at home we might call the "downtown." However, the Settlement was just too small for such a grand title. Lining the narrow little front street, right across from the harbor, were quaint little homes—most of them originals. We spotted a large fig tree that we were soon to learn was the gathering place for picnics, bake sales, special events or just plain gatherings. We could see a vegetable and fruit stand, next to it was *Termite Terrace,* a few houses down we spotted the Spencer place called *The Anchorage*, then *Sea Fan*, which belongs to Mickey and Elaine, and beyond that was a small church and grocery store, and that was it. That was the Settlement.

All of us, including Wally and Janet Johnson, who are also from New Hampshire and were visiting the Spencers, trudged up to Donna's Cart Rentals and secured enough golf carts to hold us all. We were joined by Edmund Pinder, the real estate guru, and started our search. We had been bouncing around in those golf carts exploring the Cay from one end to the other. We thought it would be a nice place for that dream cottage we had envisioned because the pace was slow, the people friendly, and there are miles of unspoiled beaches. We were also told that there were beautiful sunsets. But with all of the amenities we dreamed of, we didn't find that "perfect cottage."

It was a hot day and it seemed like we had been on this search for hours. Now we were more than a little tired, hot and dusty, and some of us were on the brink of becoming downright cranky. All of a sudden, out of nowhere, we spotted a little Inn with a courtyard bar. It didn't take long for us to abandon those golf carts and claim bar stools. Now we would just relax and wait to see what the bartender could brew on our behalf.

While I was waiting for some kind of bar creation, I gazed at this pretty little eight-room Inn—the pool and the flowers in the courtyard—when all of a sudden out of my mouth came the words, "Wow, this is just the kind of place I'd love to own!" That without my even having one sip of their famous drink called a *Columbus Colada*. The real estate agent who had been showing us around said it wasn't for sale. He didn't have it listed, and he knew the owner wasn't interested in selling. In fact he had only owned it for four years and surely wasn't ready to give up his new business adventure. So that was that, or at least that's what we thought.

The Courtyard Bar

CHAPTER 3
∂⃝

Lucky Break or Big Mistake?

We finished our drinks and headed back to the Settlement. Before we climbed aboard *The Yankee Cowboy*, our friends painted a different picture. They couldn't understand why the real estate agent gave us that information, because they knew for a fact that the owner DID want to sell. He had told our friends that he was getting a divorce and that selling the Inn was part of the agreement. He really had no choice. They gave us his phone number and e-mail address in Hilton Head, South Carolina, so just for the fun of it we contacted him. Three weeks later we went down to meet him for lunch, and the next thing I knew we were in negotiations. And I'm still not sure how it all happened.

You would think that IF Bob and I were determined to be innkeepers, which of course we NEVER were, we would have settled on a bed and breakfast, perhaps on the coast of Maine, close to home. It certainly would have been easier to manage. But no, that would have been too easy. We must have thought it was better to be 1,200 miles from home, in a foreign country, where nothing happens the way you think it should, or where perhaps the things you expect should happen today or tomorrow, may not happen for a month or two, or may not even happen at all. Sure is hard to get used to the slow pace unless you are just here for the fun of it. Or perhaps, as I said, we didn't think at all—our brains were not "in gear."

It took forever to finalize the purchase. The first contract sent to us by our attorney in Nassau needed several changes. They weren't massive changes, but certain areas did need some correcting. We marked up what we wanted and shipped it back to Nassau. As soon as the changes were taken care of we'd be on our way. We waited, waited, and waited some more. Of course during this time there were many phone calls, some e-mails, and a fax or two. There were several different stories used to excuse the delay. First the young lady who was taking care of our contract got pregnant and quit. The person hired to cover her position had only been aboard for a few weeks and was trying to get her bearings, and of course the next time we called she had gone on vacation.

Finally we got the contract.

"What in God's name is this?" Bob shouted. "Come and take a look!"

I couldn't believe what I was reading. It was a contract that had absolutely nothing to do with Guana Seaside Village. It was a completely different contract. The property description wasn't even close. It was as if someone just grabbed some other contract, used some Wite-Out to make a few changes, then added our names as the buyers and the names of the sellers wherever the spaces called for it. Needless to say the next phone call to the attorney was not one that could really be described as warm and fuzzy. We were not offered any excuses, just a promise that the right contract would be in the mail the following day. Well it wasn't exactly the following day, but two weeks later it finally arrived.

Once we received it we were right back where we started. We had in our hot little hands the very first original contract, without a single change we had requested. The only choice now was for Bob to fly to Nassau and camp on the attorney's doorstep until this mess got straightened out. So off he went. In retrospect I am wondering why it hadn't dawned on two supposedly intelligent people that this fiasco was not a fluke, but probably an augur of things to come.

After ten months of negotiations, we signed the final papers on June 28, 2000 and became owners of little Guana Seaside Village. At least we thought we were, and acted like we were. We hadn't received the deed, if there is such a thing in the Bahamas. As a matter of fact we had no paperwork at all from our attorneys in Nassau. But don't for a single minute think that slowed us down.

If I were a guest I could be thinking about a nice long walk on the beach, collecting shells, or a trip to Baker's Bay, or maybe a visit to Nippers, the local bar/restaurant just a mile away, famous for its Pig Roast. Instead my thoughts were consumed with what we needed most. Should I first be looking for some new fancy dinner plates, or would it be better to invest in a good set of screwdrivers, a high-speed drill, or a chain saw? Our daughter Janet and her husband Scott were there with us at the Inn, ready to pitch in with things that needed to be done. Janet is the second youngest of five girls and the one I might describe as a little hyperactive. (Interesting, but I never noticed that about her as a child, but it sure is plain to see now that she is an adult.) First we decided to clean up the beach—the one that was right there at our front doorstep. We raked and hauled, raked and hauled, only to eventually realize that, with the wind blowing even slightly in our direction, the seaweed kept coming right back in, filling the places we had already so carefully cleaned.

I was a little discouraged, but not really concerned because my husband always has an answer for everything. This is sometimes good and sometimes—well, never mind that part. Let's just say that this time it was good. He suggested we could simply hire someone with a backhoe to come in, push tons of sand back, and make a buffer so we would have a nice clean beach. And, he was right. That is exactly what we did, and ended up with—a pretty little beach that came up right next to the swimming pool.

It didn't take Bob very long to realize that the well wasn't deep enough or the water maker big enough to ensure us an adequate water supply. He also noticed almost at once that the water maker was not only too little but was also falling apart. He found a supplier in the states that not only had the type of water maker we needed but also was partners of sorts with a Bahamian gentleman who would dig our well. Once the well was dug, the water maker could be installed so that by reverse osmosis the salt would be removed and we would have nice fresh water.

So we needed to dig the well, but had no idea of the magnitude of our request. "We will be there next week," was the first and repeated answer as time went by. We heard the words "next week" from the end of October until after the New Year. In the meantime we had to buy freighter loads of water at $750 a load. It was clearly taking a toll, not only on our pocketbook but on my husband's sanity as well.

When Bob gets upset he roars like a lion and his ears turn red. After he made about 130 phone calls to the well digger and was told "relax a little—after all, this is the Bahamas, Mon," I could see the color rising. I just got the heck out the way, and so did the staff. They sure were quick learners.

Arthur is the name of the gentleman who was to do the digging, but everyone knew him as "Dirty Daddy." I decided all on my own that we had to find a different way to get his attention. Since he actually was the Bahamian representative for a U.S. water maker company, and we couldn't install their water maker until the well was dug, perhaps a word or two or three with them directly might do the trick.

"Don't bother," said my irate husband. "It won't do a damn bit of good."

"I think I'll try anyway," I responded

"Be my guest," came the quick reply.

I called the company and started out nice and friendly, like a lady should.

"Good Morning. I believe you have a gentleman named Arthur or 'Dirty Daddy' who represents you here in the Bahamas."

"Yes we do," came the equally polite response.

"Is he actually on your payroll?"

"Why, yes he is."

"Is he the one who will be paid for digging our well here at Guana Seaside?"

"Yes he will!"

"Well you had better hold up his pay because he hasn't done anything and it looks like he doesn't intend to—at least not in the near future."

"Oh lord, it is a little late for that. He has already been paid."

"Well, just so you know it, what you have paid for is months of promises, promises,and promises–from October until now. Months and months of promises."

"Well, we are really sorry about that, but I'm not sure if there is anything we can do."

"Not even prompt him a little to get over here?"

"Well, that would be a little difficult because he is very busy."

Now I can tell you quite honestly that my polite attitude began to slip just a little bit. "Well now, I am really sorry you don't think there is anything you can do. I was only looking for someone to light a fire under his backside, but since you can't do anything, I'll tell you just what we are going to do. We are going to charge you directly for every single freighter load of water we have to have hauled in until that damn well is dug and the water maker is up and running."

The very next morning at 7:00 a.m. there was one "Dirty Daddy" with a helper perched on a heavy piece of equipment with the digging already underway. That's when I decided I had earned an early morning swim in the sea or ocean. I didn't care which because I knew the water in either place would be over 70 degrees. I am really trying to explain more than complain, because in spite of it all, owning this piece of paradise was well worth the struggles. Our goal was to condition ourselves to go with the flow, to understand just how things were. Besides, there were other little things to dwell on, like double bookings, a paddle boat that broke loose and floated away, a sunken boat, feral cats and duck attacks—just to mention a few.

I am not going to bore you with how long the beach project took. If we still had no papers, and if it took six months to get someone to dig us a well, you can just imagine for yourself. Relating this hassle would surely give me another chance to say to myself, "What the hell were you doing owning an Inn over a thousand miles away from home?"

I think it was when we were sitting there in the sand and seaweeds that Jan raised the question of how the prior owner transported guests the two miles from the Settlement ferry dock out to the Inn. I know the old brochures and Website described it as a ten-minute walk, but believe me, you couldn't walk it in thirty-five minutes if you were an Olympic walker. (That only reminded me that we'd better get started on some new brochures and a new Website.)

We decided one staff member would know the routine—the one that was right there hanging around watching us while we were doing all that hard work on the beach. "Glenn, how did you folks transport the guests from the ferry dock to the Inn?" I asked.

"We just used the golf cart," came his mumbled answer.

"Great," I thought. "They must not have had very many guests, certainly not coming in off the same ferry. Maybe they just picked up a couple at a time, or maybe three, if all they had were backpacks and no other luggage. Wonder if they just drove back and forth over that bumpy dirt road making pick up after pick up? Maybe we should think about an alternative."

Glenn interrupted my thoughts by informing me that it probably didn't matter anyway because the golf cart was currently up on blocks, completely beyond repair. I realized then that an alternative was not a maybe, but a must.

"No big deal," said Jan. "Let's just buy a van." And with that pronouncement she headed to the telephone to set a deal in motion.. That child is so impulsive and I have no idea where that comes from. Now we brushed ourselves off and headed for the courtyard to order breakfast. I couldn't believe what was happening. It was not even nine o'clock and we had, without success, raked the beach, ordered a van, and now were ordering beers to go with our great Bahamian toast. You would think that buying a new van and having it shipped directly from Nassau wouldn't take all that long. But we learned it would take at least a month to reach us and because we had the foolish idea that we wanted our logo on the side, it would delay the delivery date a month. I really am not complaining. At least when the van arrived it was the right one, and even the logo was correct.

As soon as we finished breakfast it was time to head across the bay to Marsh Harbour. If the beach had to wait, at least we could start redecorating the rooms. That was another thing that was rather misleading in the brochures. It described the rooms as being decorated in lovely Bahamian pastels. But the present decorating motif would have been better described as "just plain old fashioned faded."

CHAPTER 4

Diving In and Trying to Stay Afloat

Is it at all conceivable that we bought an Inn on the spur of the moment, yet I spent over three hours staring at paint chips to decide on the color for our first efforts at redecorating? We had already thought yellow would be nice, so those chips I stared at were just various shades of yellow—every one they had on display. There actually weren't very many; it just seemed like a lot because I kept running outside to check them in the sunlight. Finally I got it, a nice pale shade of yellow, rather like light sunshine. Now for the trim, and that was easy. It only took about an hour for me to decide on a sweet-colored peach.

Not being a painter, I wasn't sure what else was needed, but I filled a cart with brushes, rollers, and other neat little things. I wasn't sure what some of neat things were, but if they were in the paint department we'd probably need them. The only things I forgot were drop cloths, rags for wiping up spills, and scrapers. It was warm and sunny, and the pool was just begging me to come in for a dip. I tried not to look its way as I dragged paint cans and all the other goodies to the first room we would attack. I suppose you might think that using the word attack is a little inappropriate, but believe me it is the best imagery possible.

Jan and I were about fifteen minutes into the painting when she suddenly shouted, "OH MY GOD, MA! WHAT WERE YOU THINKING?" I just sat on the floor looking around in disbelief, not only at the paint on the floor, the windowsill and in Janet's hair, but also at the color I had so carefully chosen. It wasn't the light sunshine yellow I thought it was going to be. Instead it was the loud, screaming yellow you see on every yield sign all over the good old USA.

"Not to worry," I said. "The sweet colored peach trim will tone it down."

Surely that would have been the case if the peach trim had turned out to really be peach instead of the "Pepto Bismol Pink" we were facing. There was no thought of changing anything. It would take an hour over the Bay to Marsh Harbour and another hour back, and who knows what I would come back with. Janet really didn't trust me and I sure didn't trust myself, so we just kept right on painting.

It went slowly because we'd stop every once in a while to see what the other guy was swearing about, to wipe up messes with some towels I found, and also to laugh a lot. It was a mess, but we'd fix it somehow. I could buy some new towels—we needed them anyway. And the one saving grace was that at least the first couple of rooms no longer looked faded. Believe me, THEY NO LONGER LOOKED FADED!

Having some experience behind us, and not wanting the rooms to all look alike, we decided to pretend we were experts and use a whole lot of new and different color combinations. The beautiful pale lavender I chose for the walls turned out to look like gray, but the purple trim sure was purple. Some combinations worked really well, others just worked. The painting efforts went slowly. Man, was that a lot of work. It became clear other help was needed—not real painters, because we didn't know where to find any, what they would charge, or more importantly when they'd show up. But among my seven kids, surely at least one would know how to paint.

Our daughter P.J. was anxious to pay us a visit to find out about our great adventure. She flew all the way from Denver, and the first thing I showed her was a paintbrush. Next, our son Scott joined in. He is the younger of two sons and the family perfectionist—something I DID recognize in him as a child. At first he followed behind me checking for streaks and wiping up my numerous spills. I am not sure how it happened that I stepped in the paint, but he even cleaned up the footprints without a grumble. Then he gave up or gave in, depending how you want to look at it, and began slopping around just like the rest of us. After all, there were eight rooms we needed to put our creative touches to, so no time for dallying.

I really didn't want any guests checking in until we had fixed up everything. Of course that wasn't exactly Bob's idea of running an Inn. He thought we should have paying guests in at least a couple of the rooms as soon as possible. I decided that Bob had a point, so we devised a scheme to have Scott take reservations from home. It really would be a temporary situation, but at least it would be a beginning. He managed to book our very first wedding and really got into the communicating bit. Before the whole deal was finalized, he had become "best" friends with the groom. He was invited to attend the wedding and there was even a suggestion that he could be part of the wedding party.

Bride on the Inn Walkway

The Wedding Party

Much to Scott's grief, that wasn't possible. He felt the overwhelming responsibility to stay at home and man the "reservation" "desk." It was probably a good thing that this scheme was only temporary because everyone Scott contacted became a pen pal. He spent God only knows how many hours getting to know the prospective guests. They shared stories, told jokes, and had lengthy conversations. If you didn't know better, you might have thought that he was running for political office.

The going was painfully slow, but that was probably a good thing because we had to cut holes in all the walls to install new air conditioners. It really seemed like common sense for each room to have its own unit. The old ones were all in the ceilings, somehow interconnected, and worked off sea water. If you wanted to cool one room, you'd have to cool them all. And if one of them didn't work, then none of them worked. Maybe the problems only happened at low tide, but I was too tired to try and figure it out.

Bob and my son-in-law Scott, the one we call "the other Scott," were taking care of the air conditioning details and trying to stay ahead of the painters, something they managed to do without much of a problem. The one thing I found very interesting working on that paint brigade was all the bad words my kids knew. We just trudged along, made mess after mess, laughed a lot, and ended up really proud of our efforts. Well, maybe I can't say for certain that we were really proud, but for amateurs we didn't do too badly, and the rooms did look better. I can sure say for certain that we were glad when it was over.

While we were slopping around with paint, our oldest daughter Bonny was home struggling to make all the corrections necessary to the existing Website and then develop a brand new one. I viewed the task as one that was not only critical but also surely overwhelming. Nonetheless Bon just jumped in. First, the corrections were completed. Each of us was concerned about misleading information, so the pressure was on to do something quickly, and that she did. But as she began the task of designing a brand new and different Website, we remembered the need for some new brochures. So we added that to Bonny's to-do list.

"And, oh by the way, Bon. We will need some business cards, letterheads, and envelopes. And don't forget price sheets to include with the brochures. When you come down, we will need you to take some new pictures of the place . . . and perhaps since you are the family's landscape artist, maybe you could check out the courtyard. It needs a little help." It seemed to me that we were sure piling it on. But she was off and running.

Bonny is somewhat of a perfectionist also. She pays very close attention to detail and wants everything to be just right. All our demands, with the exception of the Website, were accomplished in record time. It's a good thing she wasn't working on Bahamian time or we would still be waiting.

The Website was very comprehensive. It not only showed who we were, where we were and what we were all about, it did so truthfully. She described Guana Cay, how to get there and what other attractions guests would find. There were links to just about everything. If you wanted to dine at one of the other restaurants, go diving, island hopping, fishing, or take advantage of any special we might be running, it was all there.

She included the new pictures she had taken. There were pictures of the courtyard bar, the pool, the rooms and the cottages, inside and out. It was absolutely great, but I had one small concern—the background color she had chosen. It was yellow—a rather vivid yellow. One might call it yield sign yellow. Maybe after painting with that first color I had chosen for the rooms, I was just plain sick and tired of it. We sat together at the computer trying all kinds of different background colors while Bob hovered right behind us shouting for us to get on with it.

"Damn it, would you two stop the nonsense? We need that Website."

"We have a Website, Bob. So just relax," I answered.

"I know we have one, but we need the NEW one."

"Bon has worked real hard, so give her a break."

"I know she has, but I want this new one up and running. Sorry if I seem like a hard-ass!"

To which Bonny replied, "You are a hard-ass, Dad. But we have all learned to live with it."

From that point on we just ignored him and continued reviewing all the possible choices, and ended up with—you guessed it—yellow. It was obvious that she knew better than I what would work, and what would work well.

When we finished all the basic cosmetic changes to the rooms I began struggling to find appropriate pictures to hang. "What about Nicole?" I asked Bob. "Do you think she would like to come down during her summer break and paint a few things on the walls for us?"

"It sure wouldn't hurt to ask," he answered.

So ask we did, and down she came during from her vacation from Cornell. She stayed for only two weeks and during that time managed to paint delightful scenes in six of the eight rooms. She painted a hibiscus border around the upstairs dining room and a mural downstairs that depicted the Sea of Abaco, the Inn, the dock and the two boats moored there. One boat belonged to a delightful family who came ashore to join us for meals or just to lounge around the pool. Their boat was a catamaran named *Cool* Breezes, and the younger members of that family were pleased as punch that there was a picture of their boat on our wall for all to see.

The other was her grandfather's pride and joy—his sailboat named *Yankee Cowboy*. Painting that was the only time I saw Nicole struggle a little. For her grandfather, that part of the scene had to be accurate—absolutely accurate. I was in awe of her talent, her creativity and her energy.

Every morning before beginning her task, she ran seven miles to the end of the island and back. The only problem we had with Nicole was her refusing to sign the work she did. We eventually convinced her with a variety of arguments. She signed, but her name is so teeny-tiny that you actually have to really hunt to find it. She certainly added a nice touch to this old Inn, and not a person passes through without commenting on her work or asking where we found the artist. Of course we aren't humble at all when we announce it was our granddaughter.

Both Bob and I understood that although there were many critical issues to be addressed if we wanted Seaside Village to be successful, one of the most important was that we try to pace ourselves. Well let me just say "try is try, but do is do." Even at the very end we hadn't moved beyond the try part. Bob was always up by 5:30 a.m. I was usually not far behind him, and then our day began. He tended to major upheavals like a water maker that wasn't working, our e-mail being frozen somewhere in cyberspace, a paddle boat that had floated away, a ladder missing from the dock, a beer cooler warm as toast, or flat tires on the van. (Speaking of the van, when it was only about two-and-a-half years old it looked like it was from the 1960s—always dirty from the dusty road, beginning to show rust here and there, and both outside handles missing from the front doors. As long as the sliding door for the back still worked, we could manage to get in. But because we were getting a little wiser, and somewhat more knowledgeable, we left at least one window rolled down just in case. But it sure was better for transporting guests than a golf cart, especially one still up on blocks.)

My days were filled with many different things. Perhaps there would have been fewer of them if I hadn't been such a control freak. I never did learn to accept the Bahamian way of doing things—slow and easy. One of my daily duties was to inform anyone who was listening to Cruisers Net on VHF 68 what we were offering for the day. All the owners of restaurants, inns or resorts were given that opportunity without charge. They weren't called commercials, but "invitations."

The Net was started years ago by Patty and Bob Toler and became a very valuable aid to cruisers as well as to other tourists. The section of the Net that was called *Open Mike* provided the opportunity to ask for all kinds of help: where to find a dentist or a doctor, where to leave your buckets of used oil, when church services would be held, how to find someone to re-cover your seat cushions or clean your bottom (your boat bottom, silly!). It was where you could announce birthdays, anniversaries, thank someone for a kind deed, try to locate a friend, or simply to say ""hello or goodbye". Most all communications go out over the VHF shortwave radio Channel 16 is used for hailing anyone you want to contact, and once you make that contact you move on to a different channel to carry on your conversation. Channel 16 is also used to hail Guana Fire and Rescue, which puts them right at your fingertips. Mostly the fishermen use channel 71 when they are out to sea; channel 6 is used to hail a taxi; and channel 22 is used in emergencies to contact Bahamas Air and Rescue. However, every morning at 8:15 most folks turn to channel 68 for the Cruisers Net. I could go on and on, but I guess this brief description gives you a reasonable picture.

The section in the very beginning called "Invitations" was the time when those in business would call in and tell the listening world just what they had planned for the day. They would list their menu items, explain that their pool was clean for swimming, or that they would have an extra long happy hour with $3 beers, or any number of other things that might entice tourists and cruisers to come their way. It was a wonderful opportunity for all of us in business to make ourselves known. It was also a fun thing to race to the VHF, sign in and hope to be first on the list. When our housekeeper Nora Mae was on duty, she delighted herself by being "quick on the draw."

"Guess what, Boss?" she'd say, "WE ARE NUMBER ONE! We beat out Nippers and the Jib Room!" Those two were usually either first or second, so she felt beating them to the punch was a major accomplishment.

For some reason I decided that after I told the world what our specials were going to be, I would end with a "Seaside Thought for the Day,"

Charlie and Yaya Sitting at the Inn

hoping it would set us apart from all the others. Some thoughts were serious, some were silly, and some were who the hell knows what. At first it was great fun. I was never sure who heard it or who cared. Then people started to comment.

"We heard what you said yesterday and we loved it."

My next thought was, "What did I say yesterday?"

Then folks stopped by and offered what they thought were great quotes for my thoughts. One "yachtsman" even handed me a printout of things I could use every morning. Some of the quotes had possibilities; others were far beyond the pale.

"Your quote was good yesterday, but not as good as some of the others."

Again I had to think, "What in God's name did I say yesterday?" Then someone told me they only listened to the Net until they heard my quote, then they tuned out. What had started as just a fun thing I now began to think of as a responsibility. Every morning when I woke up my first thought was, "What in hell do I say this morning?"

The only time I was off the hook was when Janet and Lisa came to give us a hand. Janet took over the Cruisers Net slot and provided the "Thought of the Day." She always introduced herself as "Bob and Gerry's favorite daughter." Interesting, but no matter. Wherever we were, people would look at the girls and ask, "Okay which one is 'the favorite daughter?'"

When Jan wasn't here, Lisa really balked at picking up the mike and taking a turn. All of this added to some fun as well as some island identity. People were always trying to figure out who was who. There were some that took the "favorite daughter" comment to heart and felt sorry for Lisa, and all of us played along. Nevertheless, providing an interesting thought of the day really took some thinking. The only times that thoughts were somewhat serious were on Sundays, just in case some of the natives who are religious happened to be listening. Thoughts like, "If you don't feel as close to God as you used to, ask yourself 'Who moved?'" There were other times when I tried to make the thoughts coincide with holidays or special events—not easy, but always a sense of relief when I hit a "home run."

CHAPTER 5

It Could Have Been Worse

Early one morning there came some loud banging on our door. It was Glenn, and the fact that he was out of bed before Bob indicated trouble of some sort. "Mr. Bob! Mr. Bob"!" shouted Glenn, "I hate to wake you but your boat sank!"

Our first thought was of *The Yankee Cowboy*, our sailboat anchored at one of the moorings right outside the Inn. Thankfully when we ran to check, she sat right there safe and sound. It was our little 21-foot runabout that was sitting on the bottom.

We had deemed it necessary to purchase that boat for a number of reasons. There were times when we needed things in a hurry, like spare parts for this or that, supplies that hadn't been delivered, someone stranded who needed to be *carried*, or whatever—you just never knew. Now there she sat with the engine deep in salt water. Guess everyone knew (except me) that you just couldn't haul her out and rinse her off and dry her with a hair dryer. "No question," Bob kept mumbling, "we'll need a whole new engine."

"Don't get discouraged, Dad. Wait and see what they have to say at the Marsh Harbour boatyard."

"Oh, I know what they'll say at the boatyard. Now the problem is how in the hell can I get it there!"

Well, Bob managed, but it sure wasn't easy. Just picture a 6,000-pound outboard being towed seven miles by a sailboat, while the Sea of Abaco pounded away. If the seven miles wasn't enough of a challenge, he then had to try and figure out just how to get it close enough to either a dock or a ramp so the boatyard workers would be able to retrieve it. Sometimes he absolutely amazes me. Not only was he able to pull off that stunt, he was also right about our needing a new engine.

Three weeks later, and minus a small fortune, we were back in business with a brand new engine. Too bad it didn't last very long. A little over two months went by and our brand new engine wasn't functioning. The boatyard apologized and informed us that all it needed was one little part. Of course they didn't happen to have that one little part. We weren't to worry, they assured us. They would call the distributor in the states and have one shipped over immediately. They did that, but the part that came was the wrong one. So they tried again.

Now we were assured that the right part had been shipped, but shipped to whom or where no one could determine. They sure didn't have it and trying to follow the tracking number for some reason didn't give them a clue. You have to realize that this 'wasn't some little fly by night operation we were dealing with, this was YAMAHA! Since it has been over four months now and we still didn't have our boat back, I was thinking they should change their name from YAMAHA to HAHAHA!

Another couple of months went by. There were numerous apologies, but still no boat part. Since it was obvious that they just couldn't figure out how to fix it, we decided they should give us a new engine, hopefully one that would last more than a month or two. Amazing, but everyone involved agreed that was the only solution. However, there would be a slight delay.

The manager of this Marsh Harbour boatyard had to get approval for the new engine from the parent organization in Japan. All we had to do was hang in there a little longer since he was planning a trip in the near future. Guess it was something that had to be authorized in person, and the way the phones work I can almost understand that. He did travel to Japan and on his return we got the good news. Not a new engine, but the part that would do the trick. All the way from Japan he carried this little rubber *thingy* of some sort that cost all of $27.50. A day later we finally had our boat. I guess the really good news is that Bob claimed it ran better than ever.

I scrapped the idea of changing Yamaha's name and started to think about changing the name of Seaside Village Inn to the Duck Doo-Doo Inn. Hard to imagine that a small group of adorable ducks could cause so much mess or cause us such frustration.

Where these ducks came from no one seems to know, and although we weren't fond of them, we had neighbors on both sides of the Inn who loved them dearly and fed them daily. And, from all the signs they left behind, they feed them well. After hearty meals the only place they could find fresh drinking water was at our swimming pool. That meant that every morning some one of us had to be out there with a heavy bristle push broom, a spray hose, soap and bleach, just to clean up the not so little "gifts" they left us on the pool deck.

Bob turned down the offer of some locals who were willing to come with guns, hide in the bushes and shoot away. And I turned down Bob's offer to poison the G-D things. I thought maybe we could rig up an automatic recording machine so, when they came waddling in, sounds like dogs barking would scare them off—shows you how brilliant I am. However, it did prompt people to think about sensor lights, so we made the investment, set them up and were delighted when it sent them swimming away. But after two nights they figured the lights weren't a danger, so they just ignored them. They were pretty smart ducks.

Next came the idea of putting containers of fresh water on the beach, well away from the pool. Maybe that would keep them away. Forget that; they just splashed around a bit then came in for their drinks.

Our cook Sandra's grandchildren, Stichy, Leechy, and DJ, who came to spend the summers with her, volunteered to catch them. They wanted to get their hands on those ducks and take them home for pets, or at least that's the reason they gave us. They were going to sit guard and watch the ducks come in, but because most of the duck activity happens after dark and the kids were a little afraid of the dark, that didn't work. Nor did it work when they pleaded with their grandmother to get out of bed and help.

"Grammy, get up, get up, and go catch the ducks for us!"

For Sandra, who is short and a little round, chasing ducks in the dark could perhaps be good for a sit-com plot, but surely not good for the results we wanted.

The neighbor on the right of us was so concerned that we might actually do something to harm these poor creatures that she was determined to build a pond and keep it filled with fresh water. God bless her, she was hoping it would attract the ducks to her side. I was also hoping it would, but 'feared it would attract mosquitoes as well.

In the meantime we took to barricading all the entrances to the pool. Each night we turned the chaise lounges upside down and stacked them side-by-side. We also had a large net on poles to cover the opening where we couldn't fit the furniture. Quite a task, but it seemed to work and was also better than cleaning up you know what! I really consider myself a kind and gentle person, but I decided that the first time I saw those ducks scooting under, climbing over, or finding a way around that barricade, I would call the locals myself.

After Hurricanes Francis and Jean, we no longer had any pesky ducks. We thought perhaps they had gotten blown away or somehow just couldn't survive storms of that magnitude. But that wasn't really what happened, and weeks went by before we learned the truth. We were told that not all of them came back. In fact only three managed to show up. It was when none of us was around, and before we had a chance to see them for ourselves, that one of the local guys decided to camp out until they came to the pool for a drink, then shoot them. I'm not sure if it was for dinner or merely for sport, but I was not a happy camper. I know they were somewhat of a nuisance, but I had really gotten used to them, and believe it or not I probably was going to miss them. More to the point, I was thinking if they had managed to survive Mother Nature's wrath, what right did this creep have to do them in? It surely didn't seem fair and I didn't dare tell the girls what really happened. They would still be out there searching for the culprit, and Lord knows what would happen if they ever caught him.

We had a few water toys here for our guests to enjoy, so each morning we just rather routinely checked on the kayaks and paddleboats, ensuring that they were where they should be. Even the morning when one of the paddleboats was nowhere to be seen wasn't a cause for panic. We know this island and the people, so we knew it wasn't a matter of theft—we were certain the darn thing had just floated away. It was bound to be some place close by. So the search began up and down the shoreline, but to no avail. The next logical step was the "Cruisers Net."

"Cruisers Net, Cruisers Net, this is Guana Seaside Village. If anyone in the vicinity of Guana Cay sees a lonesome looking blue paddleboat, all by itself. just floating around in the sea out there, please let us know."

Within minutes in came the answer.

"Seaside Village, Seaside Village, I have your boat. However it wasn't anywhere near Guana Cay. I found it right outside Marsh Harbour. I pulled it behind a breakwater and have it secured."

Another instance when a thank you went out over the Net, which was helpful to all of us in so many ways. That thank you also included the gentleman who found and secured the boat for us. No big surprise, that's how things go here, and it sure is refreshing. Even though we were given the exact location to find our stray, it was three days before the sea was right for us to tow it back. I still am wondering how that darn thing got so far away without going ashore or crashing into a small island on the way. This probably isn't a real big story, but the fact that someone didn't just grab it, repaint it, and claim ownership certainly is. It's a story that points out how wonderful it is to be part of an environment where honesty, trust, and mutual respect are still cherished. Stories like this and many others also helped us explain to our guests why they really didn't need keys to lock up their rooms. Most were delighted, relaxed and could care less. But for the guests from New York, it takes a little longer—at least a day or two—to get used to the idea that this is a whole different world.

CHAPTER 6

Are We Running the In or Is It Running Us?

For the first time in three years we decided to close—not just for a couple of weeks, but for the last two weeks in September and all of October. Most places here, not only on Guana, but on the other out islands of th Abacos do the same. Some even close for a longer stretch because there just aren't any tourists. It also provided the resort owners time to address some real maintenance issues. And of course we at Seaside Village had a few, to say the least. I decided that the dining room needed a little sprucing up, as did the restrooms. Off I went to Marsh Harbour again to buy some lively colored paint. I would use it on the trim here and there, and Uncle Leonard had volunteered to paint all the walls. I rejoiced at that since it would mean he would be the one that had to skirt around our large mural and scoot in and out between our painted hibiscus borders.

I came back with some very bright red that I would splash on the banister that lead up to the dining room, and all over the walls in the Ladies' Room. I also brought back a pretty deep blue for the Men's

Room, but it to turn out more green than blue. It would work as long as folks didn't think I was trying to decorate the restrooms with a Christmas decor.

I started out in the Ladies' Room with a great deal of confidence, thinking that my past experience would be about all I needed. My intention was not to get any red on the white ceiling, but as luck would have it, 'things didn't work out that way. Now I needed a backup plan, something creative. I decided to stay as far away from the ceiling edges as possible. Just leave a wide strip unpainted and then slap on a wallpaper border to cover the bare spots. As a matter of fact I gleefully decided do the same with the Men's Room. After I finished both rooms, I invited Uncle Leonard in to see what a great job I had done.

"Well Mama, you left a bit undone," he chuckled.

"I know, and I did that on purpose!"

"What do you mean on purpose? Bet you want me to finish it up for you."

"No, not for a single minute. I'm going to Marsh Harbour and when I come back I'll be able to show you my creative plan."

"Okay Mama, I just hope it works better than those table covers with the fishing weights did."

I have no idea what I was thinking. I should have guessed that finding appropriate wallpaper borders in Marsh Harbour would be as successful as finding the right color green decorations for our St. Patrick's Day party. I would just have to wait until I got home to get my hands on some borders that pictured something besides pots and pans or teddy bears. I'd buy them at home—just tuck them in my suitcase and we'd be in business.

For the Men's Room I carried back a border with outhouses. It worked well because I also carried back a big picture of Bob to hang on the wall. It was a picture of him building a well house that looked just like an outhouse. He was wearing dungaree coveralls, and there was a lazy dog sleeping at his feet and a plaque that read "Our Fearless Leader." At one time it hung at the entrance of the factory we owned, but believe me it was the perfect touch for here. Everyone loved it.

The Ladies' Room—well now, that was just a different story. The border I carried back was a variety of very colorful plump ladies sitting in rather provocative poses with legs crossed. They were all wearing net stockings, some were wearing hats, and it was as vivid as could be. No one said they loved it—they just said, "OH MY GOD, HAVE YOU SEEN THE LADIES ROOM?" Wished I knew what they were really thinking.

So now I am sitting here in the sunshine with my feet in the sand and my face towards the calm green blue water of the Sea of Abaco. My back, however, is toward the Inn where things are tranquil if you happen to be a guest, but maybe not quite so tranquil if you happen to be the owner.

We knew nothing about running a resort, about the ups and downs, and certainly never dreamed it would be such a wonderful opportunity to make new friends, to bond, or to develop relationships that would last a lifetime. These were gifts given to us that made me truly believe "SOMEONE" had his hand on our shoulders, and in spite of all the hassles we were at least for the time being exactly where we should be. I really thought that once we got this place into shape, and the staff acquainted with the way we wanted things to operate, we would be almost free and clear, and have some down time to just relax and enjoy our piece of paradise. Oh silly me!

The first question we always asked when we returned from a visit to New Hampshire was, "Okay, what's not working?" Then we listened to the list. Amazing what salt water or salt-laden air can do to just about everything. Thank God I bought good mirrored stainless for table flatware. Nice dinner utensils. I thought I was truly blessed because only three of the knives and two of the forks rusted after a whole month had gone by. I also bought several Teflon-coated pans that worked well until staff scrubbed them with steel wool. After that, the only Teflon that showed was a little black ring around the top edges. Rather attractive if I do say so myself, but to keep things from sticking they put water in the bottom of the pans. Sometimes it was a little difficult to get nice sunny side up eggs with water in the bottom, and especially when they put a cover over the top.

In an effort to make grilling a little easier we brought in a well-advertised and highly recommended George Foreman Grill. It was a big one, an expensive one. After a short period of time, it only cooked on one side. Perhaps it wouldn't have been such a problem if it cooked only the top and not the bottom because you could always turn your burgers over. But this son of a gun cooked in a vertical pattern right down the middle, left side well done, the right side rare.

Most of the bread comes un-sliced here, so a simple plastic gadget to help get consistent slices is a handy tool—or could be—so I bought one. But it wasn't much help sitting on a top shelf in back of the kitchen along with the champagne flutes that we used only for weddings. I tried to give the staff bread-slicing lessons, but for some reason they didn't catch on. The complaint was that the bread came out too thin. "Well here's how it works. For thicker slices, go two slots back. For thinner slices, go one slot forward. I even made up a little song "one slot forward, two slots back," but that only caused confusion. What was necessary in this kind of situation was to simply set an example—show by doing. Needless to say, for quite sometime I was the Inn's expert at slicing bread.

"Let Miss Gerry," they would say. "She know how to do that."

I am glad to report that setting an example really worked. It only took a few weeks of my being called to active duty before everyone began to proudly use that damn, cheap, plastic guide for slicing bread. Of course they only used it when we were around. That was not nearly as troublesome as hearing an argument from the kitchen over the fact that we didn't even have any bread. Actually we had three loaves left, but the cook assigned the morning shift insisted that the cook for the dinner crowd NOT use that bread.

"No, you not be using that bread. People be wanting bread for breakfast," she insisted!

"Well, what about people that be wanting bread for dinner!" he shouted back.

I stepped in to play referee and mediator, a talent I had developed quite well to resolve home disputes when my kids were in junior high school. "Okay, I want you two to settle down."

"But Miss Gerry," she said, "let me say this..." and he chimed in right behind her, "Mudder, Mudder, listen to me." (Mudder is what he always called me. I thought it was some form of Mother and I didn't mind. I only hoped it was the complete title, and he wasn't secretly thinking the rest of the famous phrase.)

She was very short; he was very tall. So he was shouting over her shoulder, making it very difficult for me to look them both in the eyes at the same time, which I find an absolute necessity for an effective mediation. I wondered if "knock off the shit" would work, so I tried it. Not only did it work, but also to my surprise I learned a new mediation technique. "Why don't we just use dinner rolls tonight and save the bread for breakfast?" was my simple suggestion.

"We would," came the response, "but we only have two left."

My immediate thought was that if we were lucky maybe nobody would come for dinner. Now how's that for being an astute businesswoman? Thank the Good Lord that Bob can't read my mind, most of the time anyway. "Just warm the bread for dinner and I'll get some more before breakfast time." I think the blank looks I got were because I had forgotten where we were. You couldn't just walk down the street to the nearest Shaw's or Shop-and-Save and pick up a few loaves of bread, or anything else for that matter.

I don't recall just where we did get some extra loaves. Either the little Harbor Grocery Store opened early enough and had a couple of loaves on their shelves, or we borrowed some from a neighboring resort. But we did have bread!

We had a very small staff, which would lead you to believe that "teamwork" would be the Seaside Village motto. Instead, "it wasn't me" seemed to be the words staff lived by. Always the same, no matter how big or small a mistake might be, there was always the chorus of "It wasn't me."

I still can't believe that when I refused to serve an order of pancakes because they were really burned around the edges, Sandra, who had been with the Inn since the beginning, emphatically claimed that, "It wasn't me. It was the pan that did it!"

That I could handle, but every once in a while when one of those voices would add, "Maybe it was Miss Gerry," I really came close to losing it, probably because sometimes that accusation might have rung a little true.

It takes a bit of skill to really understand some of the Bahamians when they speak. At first I was really convinced Bahamians could clearly understand each other, but when staff ordered bacon bits from some fellow Bahamians and we got a large case of frozen Bagel Bites, I wasn't so sure. There are also expressions that sometimes still take me by surprise. *Karpunkeld-up* means "confused;" *Tarectly* means "soon" and your *bungy* is your "rear end." And no one pronounces the letter *V,* it is a *W* instead. You don't take *vitamins,* you take *witamins.* They never give anyone a ride anywhere they *carry them.* They don't wait for someone to arrive, they wait for them to *reach.* And no matter how old they are, they still all call their mother *Mummy*.

Sandra's word for serious is *ceris*. "This be *ceris,* Miss Gerry, really very *ceris.*"

It was *ceris* when she told me the story about this very nice necklace she had gotten from the Avon catalogue and someone had *thieved it*. I later learned that someone had also *thieved* the tarpaper off the roof of her home in Snake Cay. When she used the expression *the only thing*, it always came out, *the onlyest thing*. And when I asked about a certain task she'd respond, "Don't worry, Miss Gerry. I already done do that." Sandra didn't wait for the toast to pop up; she waited for the *bread to jump*. And whenever I was looking for something in the refrigerator, she always told me to look right behind the *thing-um*. You won't believe how many *thing-ums* I had in that refrigerator.

A few speak very clearly, like the young girl Shawna, who was for short time an assistant chef at the Inn. She was very understandable and except for grammatical errors, which Bob constantly corrected, was as good as it gets. When she said, "Where he be at?" Bob with some force would say, "Shawna, it is 'where is he?'"

Or when she said, "Where he go?" Bob instructed her to add the "did" to the middle of the phrase.

If Shawna said, "Where you are at," it prompted Bob to scream, "God damn, Shawna, say 'WHERE ARE YOU!' "

And it was never "Who is it?" but always "Who that be?"

She was young and didn't mind his corrections. In fact she seemed to think it was funny, learned quickly, and loved the attention. The sentence structure and phrases were not unique to Shawna—it's just the way some Bahamians express themselves. Not all of them, that's certain. Friends that we made in the Settlement, some in business, some just local homeowners, were very articulate, and we had absolutely no trouble communicating. There were others we had to struggle to understand, especially in the beginning. They were guests who came to the restaurant, sat at the bar or sat around the courtyard, and unfortunately some were staff members. They spoke rapidly, seeming to mumble at a fast pace. I sincerely hoped it was not contagious, but every once in a while I caught myself saying, something like, "What you did say?" or "Who that be?"

Perhaps the picture will really become clear if I explain how my five-year-old grandson Charlie handled a situation. Talking to a young

Bahamian his age, he stopped the conversation in the middle by declaring, "Excuse me, please. Sorry, I don't speak Spanish."

Shawna worked with us for less than a year and her departure had nothing to do with the grammar lessons. She claimed she had some sort of health problem, and after several days of not being able to do any work, or not coming in to even try, she decided to give it up all together. However, the reports I got back claimed she couldn't work with one of the other ""staff members, the one called Renee. Renee acted as a supervisor of sorts. She was actually in charge of the housekeeping but, as I will describe later, she often put herself in charge of everything else.

I helped in the kitchen and really thought I was an almost professional chef. But there was a time when Sandra had to go for a doctor's visit and when she reported back I got a little different picture.

"How did your visit go, Sandra?

"Okay Miss Gerry, but the doctor was wanting me to hurry up and stop giving her so many complaints."

"Why, did you have a lot of them?"

"Yes, Miss Gerry, and when she told me she already had a page full and enough was enough, I told her I had one more thing. You see, I said, sometimes when my boss be in the kitchen and I be watching her, I start to laugh. I try for her not to see me but I be laughing and laughing so much I get these pains right here in my stomach."

"And just what did she say?" I asked.

"She told me to not watch what you were trying to do, if I couldn't do that, then I should try not to laugh, and if that didn't work I should tell you to get out of the kitchen." "How can I tell you not to come in the kitchen, Miss Gerry? You be the boss."

Interesting that she recognized my status at least in this one instance. Even though I was causing her laughing pains, I had no intention of staying out of the kitchen. Besides I was curious to see if she'd find a way to follow her doctor's orders.

"Are we all ready for breakfast?" I asked.

"Oh Miss Gerry, you don't need to ask do we be ready."

"But the eggs are in the laundry room, the bacon's is in the freezer, the oranges aren't cut up, and the bread isn't sliced for toast."

"Don't worry, Miss Gerry, we do dat. I be *ceris* we do dat. YOU JUST TAKE A BREAK!"

There it was, YOU JUST TAKE A BREAK—translated it really meant, "Get the hell out of my kitchen!"

Even though I was sure the staff could handle breakfast, I just couldn't seem to help myself. So I went for the eggs, sliced the bread, cut some oranges, dug out the bacon, hunted desperately for sausage (which of course was all gone), and just had to ask about making the coffee.

"How many scoops of coffee do you use for this one pot of water?"

When the answer came back, "You put in four scoops, Miss Gerry… unless we have extra guests, then we put in six."

For the same pot of water we put in the number of coffee scoops according to the number of guests. I just wasn't up to try figure up the reasoning so I got out of the kitchen, knowing full well that I'd be right back there the next morning with "watch the coffee making" added to my "are we ready" list.

When we were really busy, I took orders, did some serving, made the salads and did the set ups in the kitchen. If we weren't too busy, I just checked up on little things. For example I wanted to make sure that guests had their silverware and napkins before the food was served. That only presented a problem at breakfast or lunch because the dining room tables were always fully set for dinner. However, it was more than a little disconcerting to see guests looking at their bacon and eggs with no utensils. So I'd run for the silver then be told by staff that I shouldn't have worried because someone was just going to do that.

Many times I said do it first PLEASE, do it first, make sure they are properly set up before you serve the food PLEASE. I really think my please helped because for a little while I had to run for silver only half as often. I heard someone mumble that I should be forgiven for being so demanding. After all, getting the silverware there first was probably just an American thing.

Shortly after we began running the Inn, Bob and I had lunch at one of Marsh Harbour's nicest restaurants and we sat there staring at our food and waited and waited for the utensils to finally show up. I couldn't help but think about the mumbling I had heard. Maybe they were right thinking that having something to eat with when your food arrived was an American thing. Either that or not having them was some kind of Bahamian tradition.

CHAPTER 7

We Don't Know What We Have, Why We Have It, or Where It Is

One of the most confusing things was keeping track of the inventory. For a short period of time, Glenn, the manager who had also been at the Inn since the beginning, had been in charge of all the ordering. There were times when he overlooked things, like having the most popular beer called Kalick on hand when we expected a big weekend, or being out of pigeon peas for the Peas and Rice, a favorite Bahamian dish. Peas and Rice is such a staple that you couldn't just grin and say to the guests, "Sorry, we haven't any."

There was one occasion when I searched all the possible hiding places for, if not a case of pigeon peas then at least a can or two, but found none. What I discovered instead were cans and cans of corn beef. We never served canned corned beef or used it for any of the dishes we made. I didn't eat it, Bob didn't eat it, and the guests didn't eat it—but somebody surely did. I guess Glenn was feeling a little guilty about that ordering mix-ups, because when I mentioned we were low on eggs and should go to the small grocery store and pick up two or three dozen to get us through the weekend, he had thirty-one dozen put on the very next ferry.

"Oh well," I thought, "maybe we could come up with a lot of 'egg specials.'"

Speaking of eggs, they do not travel well on the ferry or on the bumpy dirt road out to the Inn. Bob knows that as well as I do, but that didn't stop him from calling the supplier to let him know that in that thirty-one dozen, we had ten broken eggs. He actually asked what the supplier was going to do about it. "NOTHING!" was the answer. Bob just hung up and said with a sheepish grin, "Well, you can't blame a guy for trying!"

I must say, however, that the fault for not being properly stocked was not always ours. Supplies came on freight boats to Marsh Harbour a couple of times a week and went to wholesale markets. We tried to call early to place our order before everything was depleted. Sometimes I guess we just weren't fast enough to get what we wanted. Regardless of the order, whatever they decided to send us was shipped over to Guana Cay on a smaller freighter. Sometimes when they didn't have what you asked for, they just sent substitutes. Instead of small bottles of ketchup they sent a case of large cans, hardly appropriate for table use. Instead of small tea bags for individual cups of tea they sent over a carton of the large ones, the kind that makes a gallon of tea at a time. Because they had no sausage patties or links they sent a carton of sausage and cheese biscuit sandwiches. We requested three-gallon jugs of Joy and they sent thirty small bottles, which cost us an extra $80. We specifically stated we wanted liquid detergent for the dishwasher but they sent the powder kind instead. It wouldn't work well in our dishwasher, so that meant that someone (guess who—along with others) had to spend a lot of time rewashing dishes. Oh well, I guess I shouldn't have complained about substitutes—sometimes they didn't even send anything at all.

There was one time when we were engaged in a running debate with one of our suppliers. They were insisting they had sent us a crate of cabbages, yet they were nowhere to be seen. They were clearly listed on the invoice but sure weren't in any of the crates we unloaded. The debate and the mystery of the missing cabbages might have gone on for days if it weren't for our friend Leonard. He just came to the back of the Inn with a grin on his face and his golf cart full of cabbages. "Looking for these?" he asked.

"We sure are!"

"Well I guess the crate fell off the truck because all these cabbages were just rolling around the road and in the bushes. I figured they must be yours, so I collected them all, and here you go."

Unloading the freight was a real thrill; it was like opening grab bags—you waited with anticipation to see just what it was you'd gotten. I did wish, however, that they'd at least put our order on the right boat. We always firmly requested that they use Guana Freight. The young couple that operates that line are wonderful, and they always trucked our supplies from the dock right to the back of the Inn. And except for the time they lost the cabbages, they had always been dependable. We thought it was clearly understood that we wanted all our shipments to come by Guana Freight, but every once in a while we would get hailed on VHF 16.

"Guana Seaside Village, this is Carib Freight. We have a load of stuff for you piled down here on the dock."

Even Bob (who is not known for his patience) was learning. He'd simply shrug his shoulders, and mutter, "Oh damn, they did it again." Then he'd head for the van. He would have to make a few trips back and forth to haul home all our "goodies." He knew that perhaps in a month or two our suppliers would finally catch on to just who we wanted to use to freight our "whatevers" over to Guana. And he was right. After a few months it finally became clear.

There is a delightful small store in the Settlement called Guana Harbor Groceries that really bailed us out on a number of occasions. However, there were times when they just couldn't be helpful no matter how much they would like to have been. They depended on the freight boats just as we did. A friend of ours who was visiting for the first time went to the store on Monday morning to get milk for her little one. She was told that milk might be available at four o'clock. When she asked where the sour cream was, she was simply told that it might be there Thursday. She thought that was the funniest thing in the world, but then she was only visiting.

Sometimes I was concerned that we were eating up their inventory, but they were most gracious and cooperative. I heard rumors to the effect that they were thinking about enlarging and I wondered if we had anything to do with those thoughts. I suppose it makes sense for them to want to have something left on their shelves to offer other folks after they have bailed us out. When they couldn't bail us out, we borrowed.

At first, borrowing from our competition was a hard pill for me to swallow. We borrowed fresh fish, we borrowed horseradish, we borrowed bread, we borrowed plastic soufflé cups, and even shampoo for the rooms, just to mention a few things.

"Holy Smokes," I thought, "they are going to think we don't even know how to run a resort." WELL, DUH!

My bruised ego was quickly healed, however, when staff informed me that the borrowing went both ways. The list of what they owed us was nearly as long as what we owed them. It was not so much about competition as it was about cooperation, and quite frankly also about survival. On Guana Cay there is an attitude that what is good for one will benefit all. This attitude doesn't exist simply in those who are doing business here, but in the local folks as well.

Thinking about acceptance—and I should add respect and mutual caring—brings me back to our staff. Although some of what I have reflected on may make it seem like they were not cared about or valued, nothing could be further from the truth. The stories I have shared and will continue to share are only meant to give you a little flavor of the overall atmosphere.

The Original Staff

CHAPTER 8

ぐ⌒

Bartender, Politician and Lover

Glenn was our general manager. He was aboard in that position a long time before we arrived on the scene, and had a list of managerial responsibilities that had little to do with his actual talents and areas of expertise. We recognized that, yet did nothing to reduce or modify his role. Bob decided to take him in hand and show him step by step what needed to be done. He walked him through how to develop reports in a timely fashion, how to follow up with our suppliers when bill statements weren't coming through, explained why it was critical that the government tax be paid on time and how easy it was to keep track of the amount due, and other things that had to do with paperwork of any kind. And above all, why he could not continue to overdraw the payroll account.

Bob is not the most patient man in the world—ask the kids and they'll certainly verify that. However, he amazed me with his constant efforts with Glenn. That was at first, but it wasn't long before he became completely frustrated, and unfortunately so did Glenn. There were times when we were under the impression that Glenn followed Bob's instructions quite well, but as soon as we were gone for a week or two, it was back to business as usual. All of this managing business, including supervising staff, was certainly not up his alley. To compound the problem, he had been elected as the Island Council Representative.

Each island in the Abacos elects someone to represent them on what they call the Island Council. Their job is to attend to any needs that might arise: getting dock or building permits, attempting to find out why the government-run power company has once again left everyone in the dark, and just how long the blackout would last. Glenn fielded questions on why folks weren't getting any TV reception, why the road wasn't fixed, or where the powers that be plan to put a dump. It was an endless task and of the fifteen or so phone calls he got each day, perhaps two or three were related to the affairs of the Inn. The rest were either political in nature or were from his numerous women. And, believe me they were numerous.

I found these non-business-related calls quite troublesome, especially since I was the one who usually answered the phone, and if it was a political call I felt obligated to track him down. When it came time for his re-election I was feeling quite ambivalent about it. I wasn't so sure that it was a good thing as far as Inn business was concerned, but I certainly wasn't going to stand in his way. When he showed up all excited with a bundle of t-shirts in hand, I couldn't help but get on his bandwagon.

We didn't actually do any active campaigning for him. We just covered for him while he was out and around shaking hands. We did, however, constantly wear one of his t-shirts. On the front was a big picture of a smiling Glenn and on the back was a picture of a hat with an X beside it. It seems that in the Bahamas each candidate is given a symbol of some sort. I found it curious at first and then decided that it was perhaps to help people with limited reading skills to decide who to vote for. We all got a kick out of Glenn's symbol being a hat because none of us had ever seen him wear one. However, on election day you better believe he had on a hat.

The election for Guana was held in the small schoolhouse, and all day long Glenn was there with a hat on. He told me he wore it until the power went out and they lost the air conditioning. Then it got so hot he just had to take it off. It didn't seem to matter much because he received 98% of the vote. He invited Bob and me to go to the inauguration and was both surprised and pleased when we agreed.

The ceremony was to be held in Marsh Harbour and it would mean a regular ferry over, and a chartered ferry to get us back. All of this Glenn or the government would take care of.

We met his father and the lady he calls Mom, even though she isn't his mother. Both were just as delightful and friendly as anyone could be. "Mom" was a simple, pleasant lady, his father a really handsome charming man. He was impeccably dressed, and was sporting a jaunty pork pie hat. They shared a lot of stories, and both Bob and I got a lot of laughs. "Mom" told us that her husband had bought her a beautiful new automobile for Valentines Day.

She asked, "How come you bought me a new car when you know I can't drive?"

"Don't you worry about it dear," he responded. "No matter where you want to go I'll be sure you have a driver."

"And just who might that be?"

And his simple answer was, "It be ME!"

The entire ceremony was held at the government house high on a hill overlooking Marsh Harbour. It was a beautiful house and a perfect setting. There were speeches one right after the other—many, many, many, of them. Actually a "God awful" lot of them, but only one can I clearly remember.

A lady councilor representing Marsh Harbour really lambasted her fellow councilors. She spoke about all the people who had traveled far and wide to attend the affair. She said she was ashamed of the rest of the Marsh Harbour councilors who were too lazy to even walk up the hill and join the rest of us, a group which included many dignitaries. She then went on to name each one of them. Then said it didn't matter because the only ones that really counted were there, she and the other lady councilor standing right next to her.

"Don't worry," she told the crowd, "the two of us will take care of everything."

And I suspect she will. After an elaborate buffet we headed back to the Inn, really pleased that we had attended.

Glenn was a great politician and apparently a great lover, but the same couldn't be said of his management skills. I watched him struggle, understood, and was even a little empathic with his efforts to be effective. At least that was the case when Bob was there and losing his cool. But when Bob was gone and it was me-myself-and-I, my empathy wasn't so salient. Talking about effective managing, the ball really ended in our court.

What the hell were we thinking? Not sure if we thought that reducing his workload, or reassigning his tasks would hurt his feelings or what, but we sure took a long time to make some necessary changes—changes that would ease the level of frustration for all of us. We needed to free him up to do what he did best, and perhaps the sooner the better.

Glenn was a super ambassador for the Inn. He was wonderful with the guests, greeting them, getting them settled in, making sure they had all they needed. As bartender he was slow—really slow—but always laughing, and had concocted some prize-winning drinks, including one called A Jolly Bob. He'd spend endless hours behind the bar working late, sometimes when there were only one or two guests still hanging out, and even if they weren't some of our "favorites."

Families on this little Cay are a close-knit group—warm, friendly, and helpful, not just to one another but to outsiders like yours truly. Recently there had been a death in one of the most prominent families—an accidental drowning that saddened all who live here. Actually Glenn found the body.

"Oh my gosh, Glenn, you found the body?"

"Uh huh."

"How did that happen?"

"Well, I went down to a dock to bring him a can of gas and when I got there I saw some jeans floating in the water. I thought that maybe there might be someone in them."

"So did you try and find out for sure? Did you try and pull them out?"

"No, I just called the rescue squad and let them take care of it."

The Guana Rescue Squad at the time consisted of two men with a pickup truck. But they did come and do what had to be done. Because it was an accidental death there had to be a routine autopsy, so they made the arrangements to have the body shipped to Nassau. Once the autopsy was complete, Nassau would ship the body back to the family.

"Dear Lord," I thought, "don't let the authorities in Nassau take as long with this as they take with everything else." But lo and behold, they completed this unpleasant task in record time.

Now staff, especially Glenn, and the neighbors were all dressed up in their very best and just about to leave for the funeral when a call came to the Inn. There would be no funeral that day because Nassau HAD SENT BACK THE WRONG BODY. "They sent back the WRONG BODY." I kept mumbling to myself.

"Oh my God, Ma, they sent back the WRONG BODY," P.J. kept repeating.

We were in a state of disbelief, and so of course was the family because they had not only sent back the wrong body, it wasn't even the right color.

That's a story that is sad enough, however, there is one other that may top even that one. An American man married a delightful Bahamian lady and spent his life here with her. He lived here and certainly wanted to be buried here. Because he was an American there was a lot of red tape before the government would allow his final resting place to be on Bahamian soil. This family had the right body but it would be days before it could be buried.

This is not the right climate to have a body just hanging around. Some friends and family members got together to determine just what could be done. They decided that there was only one obvious place to store the body. They would take it over to the neighboring island, go to the only large grocery store anywhere around, and put it in the walk-in freezer. Everyone agreed that this was pretty clever thinking. Over they went to put the poor gent in the very back of the walk-in freezer. Now they had only to wait for permission from the government before they could proceed with the burial. Unfortunately there was one more hurdle they had to overcome.

Either because of lack of space or lack of forethought, they had put the body in the freezer in a sitting position. Now they had to thaw him out before they could fit him back in the coffin. Of course, I was learning that all you are told may or may not be one hundred percent accurate, but this story was known by enough people, even some very reliable ones, to have the ring of truth. So I believe this, I honestly do.

Today was a funeral for another family member. This time there were no mistakes made in Nassau. The deceased was safely home. Bob and I waited in the small dock area outside the church along with the minister, friends, and family members. Every family on the island was represented. We waited quietly for the funeral to begin There was not a lot of conversation, just a little reminiscing. The day was extremely hot, dry, and dusty, and the walk to the cemetery not too long for the procession, but quite lengthy for those who would serve as pallbearers. The decision to place the coffin in the back of a pickup truck to carry it at least part of the way was a wise one indeed. It would carry this lady up the small main street until it reached the dirt path that leads up the hill to the burial site. Then the pallbearers would take over.

The truck traveled slowly and all in attendance marched behind. There were numerous flowers but not the kind we find at home. Not the kind that fills our funeral parlors. Not the kind that drape the casket. Not the sprays, bouquets, baskets, or large arrangements displayed on pedestals. Not the kind that all seem somewhat similar, smelling the same, cost hundreds of dollars and will for the most part be shortly discarded unless someone has enough initiative to cart them off to a nursing home somewhere. There were flowers, a lot of flowers, but certainly different in nature.

The remembrance wreaths all started with similar bases—Styrofoam circles, hearts, or triangles but of different sizes. Attached to these bases were beautiful artificial flowers of every color and shape imaginable and arranged in attractive ways. Across the openings of each was a ribbon displaying a word like mother, sister, aunt, or friend. Very few florists involved; these for the most part were individually handmade and carried by almost everyone. These won't be discarded; they will be placed on the burial site as a remembrance and will remain there for months to come.

There was hardly ever an e-mail or a thank you note that didn't include Glenn. As a matter of fact, the guests loved our entire staff, at least the ones who had a consistent presence. There were a few who came and went and were not praised, nor should they have been. But Glenn, Renee (our assistant manager), and Sandra were the long-timers, and all had their own unique way to make our guests feel welcomed and special. For this we were extremely grateful. Without their brand of caring, the Inn would surely have lost its charm.

As for Glenn, he was still considered general manager even after we finally decided to wise up and let him be free to do what he did best: being a guest greeter, social host and first-class bartender. Most of the paperwork and supervision then fell to Renee.

CHAPTER 9

Girls on the Staff, Voodoo and Immigartion

It is a little difficult to describe Renee. Perhaps if there were such a thing as a "girl friday," she could have fallen under that description. She was ready and willing to do any new or differently-assigned tasks. The difficulty was in her refusal to let go of any other old assignments. She was a perfectionist who truly believed no other staff member would be able to do the job as well as she did. In some respects she might have been right.

When she took over supervising housekeeping staff, the hardest thing for her to learn was how to delegate. I honestly think that's something she would never quite be able to grasp no matter what role she was playing. Perhaps the only way this problem might be solved was be to find someone as capable and hard working as she was. It would sure save me a lot of saying, "Renee, why are you doing that? Renee, give that job to the housekeeper! Renee, put down that damn mop. You have someone to do the mopping! Delegate, delegate, show them how, then let them do it." The show-them-how part came easily, but the let-them-do-it most times didn't work.

They would do it and she would do it over, even if it wasn't really needed. Other times she'd add a little extra touch by doing something she envisioned should be done and wasn't, like washing the pillows. I made a valiant effort to explain why we didn't need to wash the pillows and dry them on the hottest heat setting possible every time someone checked out. I tried to explain in a calm, reasonable manner that this was why those wonderful smooth, nice new big soft pillows I had just recently purchased ended up as the little pile of shrunken dumpy, bumpy things I was crying over. Well, not exactly crying, but pretty close to it.

"Why, Renee. Why do you think it necessary to wash those pillows and dry them on the highest heat possible?" I asked.

"You do that because people use them." Being a perfectionist and having a real paranoia about germs seemed to justify her answer. Drying them on the highest heat possible killed the germs, but also killed the pillows!

I told her rather emphatically that we would no longer be washing and drying the pillows every time someone checked out. We would instead give them a light spray with a germ killer and use double cases. We both agreed with this so-called compromise. But I had a suspicion that pillows were still washed every time I was out of sight because that pile of shrunken, dumpy, bumpy things just kept growing and growing.

I suppose all the extra that she did—being everywhere, picking up the slack (and of course there was some), trying to address all the needs assuming they were her sole responsibility, would be admirable if she hadn't been killing herself and yours truly in the process. Clearly she needed a competent co-worker, and we sure needed to find one.

Not only was Renee a hard worker and fast learner, but her sarcastic wit amused most who encountered her. There were a few who found her sarcasm troublesome, but most accepted it, gave it back, and liked her. When she was on out on sick leave, the phone calls, e-mails and questions about her were numerous. It seemed everyone wanted to know how she was doing. Many said they missed her.

No one can begin to guess how much I missed her because for the two months she was out on sick leave, I picked up the slack. I did her job and suddenly was the one who did the lousy job of delegating. It wasn't that I didn't try—I honestly did.

We brought in a day worker who had a difficult time speaking English. She also had a name that was difficult to pronounce. It was difficult enough that Sandra just gave up.

"No way, Miss Gerry, can I say that name. I be ceris, I just be calling her 'Mary.'"

From that day on we all knew her as Mary.

About the only clear thing that Mary could say in English was "show me," so I showed her and you can imagine how that went. After I finished showing her how the job should be done the task was finished. No wonder that she came to me day after day with a smile on her face saying, "Show me."

I guess it was the day when she asked me over and over for Pine Sol and I brought her a pencil instead that I recognized the futility of the situation. I stopped trying for any meaningful communication and simply picked up my own bucket and mop. I stopped working for her and instead quietly worked with her. That was progress of some kind. But the real progress came after just a couple of weeks of those silent efforts when she really kicked in. She began to do an excellent job without any more "show me" requests and was working all on her own. Now at least all the housekeeping responsibilities were being covered. It was a great and comfortable feeling that lasted until the immigration officers deported her along with several others back to Haiti.

There are Haitian workers everywhere, but no one told us that some of them were "straight" and allowed to stay here, and others were "not." Mary was unfortunately one of the "not" ones. It was a lesson well learned so we made certain that the next housekeeper we hired was a Bahamian. She certainly had the housekeeping skills we needed, but we had a few little concerns about her personality. She really could have been a little more pleasant and friendly, but the rooms were being cleaned, the laundry was being done, and we knew there wouldn't be any immigration officers deporting her.

It was almost a year later when Mary returned, smiling, waving some papers, trying to explain that she was now one of the "straight" ones. Her timing couldn't have been better. A week before that was one of those rare occasions when both Bob and I were in New Hampshire together. Glenn called and in a panic because trouble was brewing, which wasn't rare at all! "We have a problem!" he wailed.

"So what else is new?" I asked.

"This is very serious," he responded.

"Can it wait until we get back or is it urgent?"

"Well, it is really urgent!"

Then he went on to explain that the current housekeeper was really causing a lot of grief. She walked around wearing headphones and completely ignored all the guests. If they spoke to her asking for extra towels or extra anything, she just frowned and kept on walking. In fact she more than frowned—she glared at them. No matter what arguments Glenn used or what kind of friendly advice Sandra tried to give her, she balked. The atmosphere was gloomy and the guests were uneasy. Over the phone, Bob explained to Glenn how to write her a warning letter, but when Glenn presented it to her she just laughed and tore it up. I told him to let her know that he had talked to us and we wanted her to follow his lead. After all, he was still in the manager's position. If that didn't work, then he should give her the opportunity to resign or face being fired.

She refused to resign even though Glenn had offered her a letter of recommendation. He also offered to pay her the vacation pay that really wouldn't be due for another three months. Nothing seemed to move her. We had numerous phone calls back and forth trying to stall things until we returned, but she made it abundantly clear that if we wanted to get rid of her Glenn would have to fire her. That was the stand she took and took firmly, so Glenn had no choice. He fired her and told her to go right then and there. He was really concerned that she would cause all kinds of trouble if he let her hang around.

Glenn said that as she was leaving she wasn't frowning, but grinning broadly as she went about casting a spell over Glenn and the Inn. She uttered some voodoo phrases and claimed that now we were cursed. Glenn was extremely concerned, so we tried to convince him to relax. We told him we did not believe in voodoo curses, black witches or any kind of so-called spells. We convinced him that it was all nonsense. After a while he finally relaxed and dismissed the whole episode. However, every once in a while when things seemed to be falling apart, I did give all those possibilities a little bit of thought.

CHAPTER 10

Two Very Different Management Styles

Bob has a tendency to do a lot of shouting, and usually it starts out with "God damn it." Guess that is why the staff thought Glenn should have called his award-winning drink a *God Damn It Bob* instead of a *Jolly Bob*. He really was not demanding anything out of the ordinary or what should not be expected, but the way he presented it often caused a chain reaction. When he shouted at Glenn, he would then shout at Sandra, then she would shout at somebody else—usually me.

I suppose you are wondering why I would tolerate that from Sandra—after all, we owned this place. But just think about it. If finding a simple housekeeper who can speak English, has the right to work, and isn't prone to casting voodoo spells is a difficult task, try finding a cook!

On the other hand I was probably a worse influence. I didn't shout. I consoled and tried to protect. Guess it was somewhat similar to the behavior of a mother in a dysfunctional family. The more the father demands and the stricter he is, the more permissive the mother becomes. That doesn't work well in the family setting, and it sure as hell didn't work well when trying to run an Inn.

Thankfully most of the time we were there together to offer each other support and provide the balance needed. I could say " Hey, Dad, idle your engine, cool it a bit, take a deep breath." He in turn could point out things that weren't really as they should be and encourage me to quit the enabling behavior. "That's not right, honey. God damn it, you have to quit defending and hand-holding," he'd say. But of course he said it in a much quieter way when he was speaking to me. About 90% of the time that worked. As for the other 10% . . . well hey, old habits die hard, but we kept trying.

It took Bob and me a long time to settle into a reasonable routine. Sometimes he was here on Guana and I was home in New Hampshire. Other times it was just the opposite. I can say one thing: regardless of our shortcomings, the Inn for the most part certainly ran better when we were (what we fondly referred to as) "on the reservation." But there was always so much going on at home in New Hampshire with the kids and the sixteen grandchildren that I knew I must be missing something! "One of these days," I thought, "I should really decide where my real home is, or better yet, what my life is supposed to be."

I returned to "paradise" after spending about eight weeks in New Hampshire. I had been at the Inn from the end of December until late April—the longest stretch ever. And for me it was a stretch because I had yet to cut the apron strings and get over missing my crew at home. I left for home in April after attempting to fill in for Renee from the end of January until she returned the first of the month. I didn't feel I should leave her the minute she came back, so I hung around for a while to help or hinder in any way I could. Only then did I think it fair to do a bold retreat. I guess it was a blessing that those months were the busiest ever, especially the end of February, all of March and April. It was also a blessing that most of the family came for a vacation in March because it really charged my battery. However, I hope no one in the Bahamian government ever finds out exactly what they did while they were there.

They took orders, waited tables, helped clean rooms, provided Sandra with much needed assisted in the kitchen; and the older ones tended bar and provided what some considered "entertainment." Working without work permits would most certainly have gotten us all deported. We owned the place, the kids were family and received no wages, but nonetheless we were in some kind of violation I am sure. Everyone who isn't a Bahamian needs a work permit before allowed to do anything!

There are a lot of different rules in this country and we sure were violating one of them. If someone had decided to turn us in, decided we belonged on that "hit" list, we would have been in deep "doo-doo."

Janet and Lisa Tending Guests

I don't mean to suggest that all the family did was work. They had plenty of time to play in between being called into service. They packed picnic lunches, took walks to a delightful cove, spent time snorkeling and just catching the rays. They played games in the pool, card games at night, and some even attempted to take kickboxing lessons from Lisa.

Grandson Charlie and Best Friend Kev

Granddaughters Hilary and Ali Watch the Sunset

Grandson Chris Surfcasting

They have wonderful memories of things they are still laughing about, like the Sunday they spent at Nippers. We encouraged all our guests to go to Nippers for the Sunday Pig Roast, especially if they had never been before. Well the kids had been at least a couple of times, but it certainly didn't dampen their excitement. Off they went with the van full and a full golf cart following behind. I thought they would stay for two or three hours but didn't imagine how long they would really hang out. They called to see if they were needed back at the Inn and when assured we were fine they just stayed and stayed. In fact they stayed all day. They danced to the live music, swam in the ocean, and watched what they described as a rather unruly crowd. After they returned, I gathered that they not only watched but were perhaps even a little part of that crowd they were describing.

Janet, Lisa, Ford and Hil at Nippers

Ford lost his wallet on the beach, Hilary lost her glasses in the ocean, Gigi lost a camera, David lost his jacket, Lisa lost her prescription sunglasses, someone lost their shoes; and to top it all off, they lost the golf cart. Assuming that Bob had taken the cart back to the Inn, they all piled into the van. Back here they discovered that Bob had not brought the cart back. So now there was a real problem.

I tried to be reassuring by telling them that on a real lively Pig Roast Sunday, golf carts often come up missing. That didn't mean people *thieved* them, they just borrowed them to get where they wanted to go. Certainly no one could have taken it off the island—it had to be around somewhere. That prompted Lisa, her husband Doug and our young grandson David to go on a cart hunt. I probably should mention that the van or the cart never left the Inn without David aboard, no matter who was driving or where they were going.

Shortly after they left, it began to rain and even though the rain was heavy like it is sometimes here, real tropical in nature, they were not deterred. Over two hours went by before they were back, but without the cart. They had looked in all the places where they had been told missing carts were often hidden or even parked in plain sight. It wasn't until late the next morning that someone else found it and brought it back to the Inn.

As they talked about all the things that they had lost, our grandson Ford decided that probably the most important thing they'd lost was their dignity. I guess as a mother and grandmother I had a tendency to agree.

All of them, the kids and grandkids, had what they considered a marvelous vacation. They claimed the best part of it was that they were allowed to pitch in. They were delighted to have been needed and only worried about who would pick up the slack when they had gone and left poor Papa and me behind.

Actually we did okay. We worked hard and because it was physical labor, we perhaps did so harder than we had for years. I have waited on a lot of tables in my lifetime, about the only kind of work a kid could find, and always enjoyed it. But I soon found myself asking who in the hell was the dummy that put the dining room up on the second floor of the restaurant, miles from the kitchen (or so it seemed), with doors to open and numerous stairs to climb. Guests often suggested that we should have a dumb waiter. All they had to do was watch me struggle to know there already was one.

Even though I had all that helpful experience waiting tables in the past, I had never tended bar and it sure showed. Sometimes folks asked if we had a Happy Hour. Well, when I was behind the bar a Happy Hour wasn't necessary; they got two for one almost every time I poured. In fact our dear friend Leonard, who did more than find lost cabbages, tried to help me the best he could. There were a couple of times when he leaned over the railing on the walkway, watching me pour drinks, and simply shouted out "WHOA, MAMA, WHOA!"

Remembering his "Whoa, Mama, Whoa" was the one thing that helped keep me somewhat under control. But the truth was we still didn't need a Happy Hour when I was behind the bar. In fact some guest would come, hang around the bar, and wait to be served until I came on duty. "It's okay," they'd say, "We'll wait for Gerry. We like the way she pours a drink!" That "Whoa, Mama, Whoa" advice was not all Leonard offered over the months. He was very observant and picked up on many little things that might be helpful. He was very careful when making suggestions or recommendations and always started out with, "This may not be any of my business, MAMA, but…" and that's when

I listened.

I remembered another recommendation I was given just about a month after we bought the Inn. This time it given by a delightful, sincere lady named Bobbie. She was paddling around in the pool suggesting that I take some pictures for the Website—pictures that would show that even older folks loved it here. When she finished swimming we sat and chatted for the longest while. She was from Vermont and had first gone there as a young child to a summer camp. Her father had been so enthralled with the camp, the setting, and the natural beauty, that he bought it and turned it into a resort. She grew up in that setting and when her father passed away she took over running the place. She did this for many years, so she knew a lot about this business.

Thinking this would provide me with an ideal opportunity to pick the brain of someone who had been there, done that, I asked if she could give me some advice.

"I sure can!" she answered in a deep gravelly voice. "SELL THE GOD DAMN PLACE!"

This time I didn't listen, not like I listened to Leonard. It was not only his advice that was valued, but also his real interest in the Village, and his many other contributions. Whenever Bob and I escaped "the reservation" for a visit home, there was always a surprise when we returned. The porch had been painted, a new walkway had been laid out, the bar had been repaired, a bulletin board built to display complimentary letters or shelves erected. These were things that I had simply mentioned would possibly make a good addition. There were so many things on our to-do list, and Leonard just did them. We bought him a t-shirt with the printed words, "I came, I sawed, I fixed it," which kind of says it all.

CHAPTER 11

Leonard and Larry

Describing Leonard physically is not difficult—it's the rest of him that poses problems. He is probably about five-foot-eight, has beautiful blue eyes, and a full head of white hair that he keeps cut short. I suspect he does this so his curls won't get out of control. And because I respect him I won't say he has a beer-belly. I'll simply describe it as a "liquid grain storage facility." He was most always dressed in a t-shirt and shorts. Only three times did I see him dressed differently. Once when it was cool he wore a sweatshirt with a hood; the other time when it was actually cold he was sporting a woolen ski hat and flannel shirt. And even though he was still wearing the usual shorts, it was enough of a disguise that I barely recognized him. The last time I saw him in different attire was at his son's wedding. It wasn't exactly what the family wanted, but it was a far cry from shorts and a t-shirt.

His son was to be married in a few months and there was more than a little concern on the part of the family about getting Leonard into a tuxedo. I thought that maybe on a quiet evening I'd try to do a little convincing.

"You know what Leonard"?" I said "I have a lot of pictures of you in your t-shirts and shorts. I even have one in that silly woolen ski hat. But I would really love to have one of you in a tuxedo. I just bet you would look handsome!"

Grinning, he answered, "You know what, Mama? Your flattering bullshit ain't going to get you nowhere!"

So that was that.

He was a friendly guy when there were folks around that he felt were worth being friendly with, but he had no tolerance for braggers or those he honestly believed were "full of shit," to use his phrase.

Whenever some of those folks showed up to the bar, he simply and quietly left.

"Sorry, Mama," he'd whisper,."I gotta get out of here before my mouth gets me in trouble. See ya tomorrow—if God spares life."

When tomorrow came, so did Leonard.

He had grown children, a couple of dear granddaughters, and a wife who was as sweet as she could be. Cathy was quiet but friendly, unassuming and hard working. She managed a gift shop and finished work an hour or two after Leonard did. In the beginning, when he first began to join us, he'd be sitting and chatting when out of the clear blue sky his two big dogs would come racing through the courtyard and over to Leonard's stool at the bar.

"Shit!" he'd say. "She let the dogs out."

That's exactly what she did. If he wasn't there when she got home she would just open the door and say, "Go find Daddy," and find him they would, from over a mile and a half away. She didn't do that for too long. Either she became comfortable with where he was hanging out or she just decided it was easier to call his cell phone. And if he didn't answer, she'd hail him on the VHF. To tell you the truth, I liked the dog act better!

We have another friend, a valuable asset, an interesting guy named Larry. He originally came from New York and after spending four years living on a boat he landed here on Guana Cay. That was in 1996. He fell in love with the island, so he formed a partnership with some friends and together they built a house. It was a lovely, rather large place with both an attractive main living area on the top floor and an equally attractive apartment down below. Because it sat on a bluff overlooking the Sea of Abaco, they named it Ridge House. The apartment was built out of solid concrete and was considered one of the safest places on the island and could easily serve as an ideal shelter if there were a severe storm. When folks became concerned over reports about Hurricane Floyd heading their way, they gathered in the downstairs of this safe place. Everyone was feeling comfortable and reassured until the roof blew off. There were no personal injuries—just some wet, frightened, uncomfortable people and pieces of the roof scattered here and there, even as far as a mile and a half away.

I don't think it was the damage done by Floyd that dissolved the partnership. Although Larry doesn't talk about what really happened, other people do. It's like that on this little island. Half the people believe there were a number of serious disagreements between him and his partners as to what should be done to or with the property after Floyd. There are others who contend the differences were more personal in nature. That's understandable because after a traumatic event like a hurricane, people's nerves are a little frayed and misunderstandings easily arise. Regardless of which story really had merit and even if the truth was a little fuzzy, it was certainly clear that the better part of valor was to dissolve the partnership. The friendship however did remain intact.

There were constant maintenance issues at the Inn that cropped up out of nowhere at the most inauspicious of times. The well pump, the generator, the water maker, the moorings, ladders on the dock, air conditioners, the van, and the golf cart—always seeming to need someone's attention. Bob of course was the "main man" but constantly by his side, doing his share and then some, you'd find Larry, and many times Leonard as well. I made a solemn promise to jot down notes everyday, to keep a regular journal so things wouldn't be forgotten. Unfortunately that was a promise I was either too busy or too tired to keep. Now I am trying to resurrect some memories, the good, the bad, the unexpected and the somewhat unbelievable.

Now back to Larry. His partners bought him out and now he could find a piece of land and build all on his own. In the meantime he would come with us, be a helping hand, a man who would and could do most anything.

You will notice that I didn't say Larry worked for us. Heaven forbid. He couldn't do that—he didn't have a work permit. We had a sort of bartered arrangement. Food, beverage and lodging in exchange for whatever came up that he could help with. He was very good on the computer and did a number of things that were useful as well as just plain fun. He created a form that Bob could use for ordering supplies. This was to help assure that we got just the things we ordered. The staff was also expected to use this form as a way of tracking inventory. It was set up in alphabetical order so they could note when supplies were getting low, and write down the number of items needed. It was really a very simple and foolproof process, and yet staff still insisted on writing things on napkins or scraps of paper and tacking them up in the kitchen or elsewhere. We, of course, were supposed to guess not only what was on their lists, but also where to find them.

No matter how I presented it, even walking around with them with the form in hand, Sandra would still pass me a damn napkin or a piece of paper bag with scribbling on it. Some old habits just won't die. So I thought, "What the hell, there are other things to concentrate on and if the form works well for Bob and our suppliers, two out of three ain't bad."

Larry wasn't quite as willing to accept my philosophy. He worked too hard on that form and certainly felt a sense of ownership, so he mumbled and grumbled the loudest. He helped Glenn write important letters, and he developed first class menus, gift certificates, and welcoming posters for guests who were here for special occasions. He took excellent photographs, especially of the weddings. He would download them and make collages that we could put on the head table for the wedding dinner as a surprise gift for the bride and groom.

The last time our family was here, he devised a very clever treasure hunt for three of our youngest. He loaded a "treasure chest" and carried it far up the beach to bury. Then he drew a treasure map with all the signs they should look for and planted them along the way. First they should spot a red ball, then further up the beach a green conch, then they had to look for the blue coconut, and last but not least, the coconut lady who was standing guard over the treasure.

The coconut lady was simply a coconut with a painted face and long fake hair perched on top of a stick. Good enough to fool four-, five- and six-year olds. To add a little extra excitement he convinced the guy next door to dress like a pirate with eye patch and all. He was to hide in the bushes, jump out when the kids finally got to the coconut lady and shout, "LEAVE MY TREASURE ALONE!"

No one realized the pirate would also shoot off a cap gun. It startled the parents, who were keeping out of sight in the bushes just to watch the show, and even startled Larry. I guess it could go without saying that it made Julia, the littlest one, cry—and cry a lot. Nevertheless with the help of Larry, they grabbed up the treasure then ran as fast as their little legs and the deep sand would let them. Back at the Inn they were all excited as they counted out the gold covered chocolate coins and shared the beads, baubles and numerous other trinkets. When I asked if they had run into any problems, it was Julia who answered, "No, not a single one!"

It had taken a lot of time and a lot of planning on Larry's part, but it was really a fun-filled adventure. Bob thought that Larry should plan more treasure hunts as a special kids' activity for other guests, and I agreed. It had been an outstanding success; however, I thought perhaps next time the pirate shouldn't bring a cap gun.

CHAPTER 12

Beginning and Ending the A-Team and the Tequila Shootout

Perhaps this is a good time to introduce Polly. We first met Polly when she came for a couple of days to visit Sandra. In fact, Sandra explained that there was a time when she had really hoped Polly would be her daughter-in-law. That didn't work out, but they have remained dear friends.

Polly was experiencing some personal turmoil and decided to escape the trials and tribulations for just a brief time. She needed some rest and relaxation but instead kept busy doing things she saw needed to be done. She was a great help both in the kitchen and with the housekeeping tasks. She not only knew instinctively what needed to be done, how it should be done, but she voluntarily jumped in and did it. With Renee out on sick leave, it was no wonder I thought of her as some kind of Guardian Angel.

Before she left, she gave me a schedule of her days off and vacation days, suggesting she would be willing to come over at any of those times if we needed her. She was working as a bridal consultant and managing a couple of duty-free gift shops on one of the larger Cays. I assumed that asking her to come on full-time would be a little ludicrous. There was no way we could match her current salary or expect that she would be thrilled to give up her current positions to revert to housekeeping and kitchen help. I simply told her how much we enjoyed her and how I wished we were in a position to bring her aboard. Besides, I understood it would be a big step down.

She responded by saying, "Miss Gerry, if it is good honest work I would never consider it to be a step down."

There were a few things she had to straighten out, she said. And if all turned out okay, she would love to join us. By the time we came back after our last visit home she was aboard full-time. I found her and Renee, who was also back aboard, working together in the kitchen laughing and describing themselves as the "A Team."

How I hoped she would stay, and also firmly hoped that this "team" spirit would last. However, I soon detected a little rough sailing headed straight into the wind. I have found that some Bahamians, just like other folks, can be super-sensitive, emotional, and at times even show signs of a tiny bit of paranoia. Certainly that's not true of all Bahamians— only certain ones in certain circumstances. You might recognize some of those traits in my staff. You decide.

If I were talking and laughing with Sandra and Polly, Renee wouldn't join us because she felt she might be interfering. If I was talking to Renee, Sandra had a tendency to wander back and forth trying to catch a word or two, just to ensure we weren't talking about her or about problems in the kitchen.

Sometimes when one was trying to joke with the other, it was misinterpreted. It seems that I spent more time than I should have trying to explain what we were talking about to the one that was left out of the conversation, or what I thought the person making the joke was really trying to say. In this case the response I usually got was, "It is not what people say, it's how they say it, Miss Gerry!"

Glenn didn't get involved in any of this. He was just there, and although he may have been thinking a whole lot of different things, he never said what he was thinking. But that's just Glenn. He was almost completely devoid of visible signs of emotion when these little episodes erupted. He was present, but not necessarily accounted for.

By the way, if you ask Glenn what time it is, you get a very complicated response especially, if it is Daylight Savings Time. He never adjusts his watch to any time change and always has it running fifteen minutes ahead. During Daylight Savings you really have to be on your toes to remember that if he tells you it is 2:15, it is actually 3:00 o'clock.

Perhaps I get too concerned about this nebulous thing called teamwork. Regardless of what goes on between them, they are absolutely marvelous with the guests. They do all they possibly can to see that the guests' stay here is memorable, happy and unique. What else should an innkeeper ask for, unless of course it was something that was perhaps out of the realm of possibility like seeing them treat each other with the same kindness and warmth with which they treated our guests.

The break up of the "A Team" was gradual and subtle at first, but then became so blatant that it was painful to watch, and after a few months impossible to turn around. Meetings with the two of them got me nowhere. Each had so much of value to offer, and each seemed to resent that very fact.

Polly talked only about how a professional should conduct herself and how Renee's entertaining around the bar with the guests was "disgusting." I explained that Renee was pretty good at reading the crowd and knew when to dance and carry on and when not to. The guests loved it. I also explained that the flowers in the rooms and the little notes that Polly left for the guests were special and also loved, regardless of the comments Renee made about them being ridiculous.

When we were busy and both were called on to serve in the dining room, there was a real and constant tug of war. Polly was very formal, and Renee very casual, often hanging around to chat a little. That left Polly seething!

"That is not right, Miss Gerry. Guests have a right to eat in peace."

"Well, who knows?" I thought. "Maybe it would be better if Renee did tone down the dining room chatter a little bit. There might be some guests who would appreciate a quieter atmosphere. No harm in talking to Renee about that."

"Renee," I said, "We are going to try a little different approach with our dinner guests. I still want you to be your friendly fun self, but don't hang around too long. Why don't you just suggest that you'd love to see them at the bar after dinner for a good old chat?"

"I'm not the only one who does that. You do also so I guess you won't be talking to them during dinner either!"

"Well I think perhaps my case is a little different, Renee. All I ever do is check to make sure everything is fine and thank them for joining us. I do not do as you sometimes do, pull up a chair and join them, even when I'm invited to do so."

Well that sure worked like a charm. Polly walked around, silent but smiling; and Renee for some time just stopped talking altogether. She didn't talk to the guests, not to Polly, not to yours truly. No conversation in the dinning room and none at the bar either.

Each had her own talents to offer and each should let the other do their own thing.

"Just read the e-mails from the guests once they have returned home. You can clearly see how each of you are remembered and appreciated."

I really can't recall how many times or how many different approaches I used to try and get that message across, but a war of silence waged on. Part of the problem was really just who would be the QUEEN BEE! But there was also another factor in play.

That became evident just after Renee introduced us to her new friend, Steve. He really was a delightful guy and had two precious daughters. We were pleased that she had found someone who seemed perfectly suited. It took about a month before Polly took me aside to announce that this guy Steve was married.

It disturbed me, especially since there were the little girls to consider. However, I was soon to learn that Steve and his wife had been separated for some time, so that made it easier— "just like at home," I thought. But when I heard friends of Renee asking about her stepdaughters, it certainly took on a different slant. There are acceptable relationships in the Bahamas that are not just like at home.

Renee's situation was very different, but it led to a lot of pontificating on Polly's part. I not only continued to hear about what it takes to be a professional, but now I had to listen to the right or wrong of how each of us should live our lives. I was truly sorry that Polly took this on as a personal burden. I just wanted her to let it go, to stop sitting in judgment, to be happy. And I told her so.

"I am happy, Miss Gerry. Every morning when I leave my room I leave with a song in my heart!"

That so frustrated me that I just blurted out, "Then why in hell don't you sing that song to the rest of us?"

That helped. Now it wasn't just Renee that wasn't speaking to me. '

She left for her usual two days off with four suitcases. I'm not a brilliant person, but that gave me my first clue. I asked her if she were coming back and she insisted she was. And she did come back for about ten minutes—just long enough to tell me that she wasn't coming back.

The Inn was fully booked. We had a large party to plan for, so when Miss Polly quit without notice, all that talk about being a professional was somewhat negated. I thought honestly that there was some other turmoil going on in Miss Polly's life, and I shall share with you what I thought.

I mentioned before that Polly and Sandra were friends. The friendship started when Miss Polly was going to marry one of Sandra's sons. That didn't work out and they each married someone else. Polly had divorced, but Sandra's son had not. The friendship between Sandra and Polly had lasted and I think the feelings between the son and Polly had also lasted. He began calling and at first would ask to talk to his mother. Sandra got a lot of calls from her kids, usually for money or help of some kind, but as long as we had been there, the calls from this son had been few and far between. Now they were more than once a day—first to Sandra, then quickly passed on to Polly. If Polly wasn't right on the spot, Sandra would run to get her, into the laundry room, out back to Polly's room, upstairs to the dining room—it was as if she were on a mission. That frantic running around seemed hardly feasible to me if the calls were for simple chit-chat, and believe me most of the time they weren't. You really don't have to hear the exact words, sometimes the tone of a conversation, the urgency, can be quite revealing. After a few weeks of this, I decided on a ruse.

"Miss Sandra," I said, "Last night I had the craziest dream. I saw Miss Polly and your son just carrying on, back to where they were years ago. Isn't that the silliest thing?" (Of course I hadn't dreamed a thing, but throwing that out might be worth a try.)

"Oh no, Miss Gerry, my son be MARRIED. True, Miss Gerry, he be MARRIED!"

The phone calls had only raised my suspicions, but the flustered, troubled response from Sandra just about confirmed them.

All of this was of course speculation, but it certainly would explain a lot. Miss Polly who read her Bible everyday and went to church every

Sunday, looked on Renee with disdain for the situation she was in. She now found herself in a similar situation, and certainly couldn't be a happy camper. She 'couldn't like herself and so couldn't like anyone else very much either. Just like kids engaged in inappropriate behavior: they can't stand their parents, can't stand their siblings, and don't even like the dog.

As she was leaving the island she tracked down Uncle Leonard just to say goodbye. The only thing he would share with me was to say that she said she left because of Renee. He felt badly because he really liked Polly, and so did I. As a matter of fact, I still liked Miss Polly and thought of her often. I thought about her expertise, her willingness to pitch in when necessary, and her little thoughtful and creative gestures on behalf of our guests. I also hoped that wherever she was, she was happy and at peace with herself. It really was a damn shame that the "A Team" had fallen apart. Now it was time to find a replacement.

Finding a replacement isn't the easiest thing to do. We were a little isolated here in our corner of paradise, so we really needed to find someone who would be willing to live here If that 'weren't possible, then we'd have to recruit in Marsh Harbour. If we got someone from Marsh Harbour, it would mean she would have to come over on the early morning ferry and leave on the last one back. Often our busiest times are during the dinner hours, and by then she would already be on their way home. But if that's what we had to do, so be it. Somehow I'd have to be available to pick up the slack.

I felt we really had to find someone rather quickly. Not only was Polly gone, Renee had to leave for three days to attend her grandfather's funeral, and a scheduled Barefoot Man's concert meant that the Inn was fully booked.

This was the time when the guest in room one, who was quite the party girl, decided that everyone around the bar should join her in a round of "tequila shooters" and she'd pick up the tab. There was only one catch—she would pay as long as Bob and I joined in. There sat a bar full of guests staring at Bob and me, anxiously waiting for their free tequila. So of course we didn't refuse. She carefully gave instructions to those who were unfamiliar with the routine.

"First, you down the shot glass of tequila, suck on a piece of lime, then lick the salt off the back of your hand. On your mark, get set, go!"

After the first round, no one needed any further instructions. Everyone caught on quickly and simply waited for those magic words "On your mark, get set, go," for round after round. Both Bob and I dropped out after the first round and thankfully not a single person noticed.

I filled the little glasses and Bob took care of counting so he could add the costs to the tab. It was a great night for bar business, and okay for guests who could sleep all the next day if they so chose. But it sure was a good thing Bob and I stopped playing early in the game. After all, we needed to be fit for work when the sun came up.

Facing a full house with no help meant I was the one changing beds, doing laundry and dragging around that mop and bucket. Most of the guests, the ones who had pulled themselves out of bed, sat around the bar nursing Bloody Marys and expressing their deepest sympathies as they watched me struggle from room to room. They assumed that we had stuck with them from beginning to end and were feeling as badly as they were. One delightful, concerned guest offered to pitch in. Pat was really sincere in her offer, but for the life of me I just couldn't see a guest cleaning johns or changing sheets. I made it through that day and the next, then, lo and behold, up pops Miss Nora Mae.

Nora Mae would be more than willing to live here as soon as she made arrangements for her niece to watch her children. That took only a week, and she came aboard. All I can say about Nora Mae is that although she was young, she was a fast learner and a willing worker. .She didn't write notes or leave poems for the guests, but she never failed to see that a bright new flower was in their rooms as a welcoming gesture. If there was a rush in the kitchen, she would be there to lend a hand. And on evenings when the bar was really overcrowded, she would stand shoulder to shoulder with Glenn until nearly midnight.

She was friendly, talked freely, and laughed easily. Even after she had been here a few months I really hesitated to say too much for fear of putting a hex on the whole scene. So suffice it to say I simply thought, "So far so good." I was really glad that we had Nora Mae to take Polly's place, especially since Renee abruptly told us she was leaving.

Renee needed to do something different with her life and have more free time, which I did not at all find surprising, especially now that Steve and the girls were in the picture. She was right—picking up the slack, trying to do it all was certainly stressful. She worked long hours, sometimes because we needed her to, others because she had chosen to hang around after work to play and be the "entertainer."

What did surprise me, and caused me half a morning of grief, was the fact that she was going to work for our competition just a mile down the road—and this wasn't the first time she had left us and gone to them. I am not sure exactly how long she had worked for our competition that first time, but when she left, there were two stories, as usual. One she quit, the other she was fired.

She returned home and went to work for a place something like Burger King, at least that's what we were told. That was certainly a waste, and it wasn't long before she began to call us. She would talk to anyone who happened to answer the phone. She made it clear that she had been unhappy working for our competition. The management had driven her crazy, she gotten all stressed out, and clearly wanted to come back.

Bob, Larry, and our daughter Janet all thought it was wonderful. They knew what she could do. She knew the Inn as well as many of the returning guests, and would certainly be an asset. They were excited at the prospect of bringing her back. Interestingly, I was the only one who objected. Certainly I knew all she could do, just as they knew, but I also had the strong feeling that she would leave just as she had before. Perhaps I was still a little gun shy because of the prior experience.

The first time she left Seaside Village to do something different with her life she explained she was too young to be stuck on this island. She would like to go back to school, perhaps to become a teacher. I offered to help her reach that goal, even help with the tuition, and so did Bob. We thought she would make a wonderful teacher, and were excited about her, her dreams of a different future and her potential. That's the last we heard of her goal or our offer. Next thing we knew she was working a little over a mile away.

Probably I was just being a poor sport, but be that as it may, I was clearly outnumbered so we brought her back. This time she stayed for a little under one year then moved back to the same situation that had stressed her out, rejoining the same management that drove her crazy not too long ago. Interesting how often people who are struggling to find their place think that changing geographical locations can make it all better.

I worried a little about how she'd do, and so did others who knew her well, and I knew where she was going. But I didn't have time to dwell on it—it was time to hunt for a new girl friday. But the hunt was short because Nora Mae came back.

We learned that Sandra's son got a divorce.

"Ha, Ha," I thought. "Now all we need to do is wait for the announcement that he and Polly will be getting married." I was really feeling rather smug about my intuitive powers.

Polly got married all right, but she married a different guy. Oh well, I can't always be right.

Renee no longer works for our competition. She lasted about a year and as usual the stories varied. "Oh, she quit," said someone.

"But not really," someone else answered. "She said she was going to quit but came back for the next shift saying she wanted to stay. Then the manager told her no way and fired her on the spot."

Some said she couldn't get along with the other staff members. Others believed it was because her mood swings were so unpredictable. At time she would greet the guests like long-lost friends, then at other times she'd ignore them completely. And it was apparent from comments made by the management that they did not understand or appreciate her wit which at times smacked of sarcasm. Maybe some of that was true but there was something else going on. Her very special friend Steve began to date someone who had been hired as a temporary staff member at the very same establishment.

She had been very much in love with him, and also with his daughters—the ones she referred to as her "step daughters," and now she was about to lose it all. How in the world could she work side by side with his new "honey?" I felt really sad for Renee. She deserved better than that!

I understand that after a brief stay in her hometown she took a position at another resort on a different island–a first class place. I hope she likes it and they like her, but most of all I hope she comes to understand that different geographical locations won't solve problems. If you are plagued with inner turmoil, it follows you wherever you go. I guess what I really hope is that she can find herself and be comfortable with who she really is.

CHAPTER 13

How Many Kids Can You Have???

In this country there are such things as in-children and out-children. The "ins" are those born within the confines of a marriage. The outs are those, well, I guess you know who those are, and apparently it is no big deal. I have listened to some fascinating stories, not rumors, not gossip, but as you might say straight from the horse's mouth.

Jason was part of a road crew who was here to do some road repairs, whenever the equipment was working, which it often wasn't. That gave him and a number of the other crew members free time to lounge around and chat. I soon discovered that many of the crew were brothers, although they looked nothing alike and acted as if they hardly knew one another.

"The same father but different mothers," Jason explained.

In fact the crew boss and a couple of other workers were brothers he hadn't met until he went to work as part of this crew.

"Do you have sisters?" I asked.

"Oh yes, I have sisters, but not sure how many there are because my father is only proud of how many sons he has—the girls don't count. I do know I have 49 brothers. I even have one that lives in Eleuthera with the same name as me, Jason Roberts. I guess they run out of names."

"Forty-nine brothers! How in the world did that happen?"

"My Old Man was a whore," he answered. "He dropped babies wherever he went. Some I know, others I don't."

"Oh my God" I exclaimed. "Does he keep in touch with all his kids?"

"Oh, he knows where they be, but don't do nothing for them."

"And you, are you doing the same—just dropping babies?"

"Not me. I have a wife and three kids. All good kids—they work hard in school and have good manners, and I sure do miss them when I'm on the road. I'm different than my brothers. They laugh at me and think there is something wrong that I'm not dropping babies here and there because they are, but not me Miss Gerry, not me. I learned from my Old Man and won't be no whore! If he ain't no whore no more, it's only because he's about seventy-four years old."

Glenn was there, listening to the conversation, adding only a comment or a soft laugh every now and then. He also has several out-siblings–and his father is a minister. In fact Glenn proudly showed us this great printed program that was one of the highlights of his father's 70th birthday party. There were over eighty-five in attendance, including many of his out-siblings, with his nieces and nephews. It was all so matter of fact, so accepted and so real that I found myself almost speechless. All I could think of to say was how proud I was of him. From the things he shared about his family there was no question he was being a good husband and good parent.

"Jason," I said, "do you know how right and how great it is that you have made a commitment to stay with the 'in crowd?'"

I think that type of life style is slowly changing. It isn't actually as bad as it used to be, but it still does exist. In fact when the new government took over recently, they worked hard to see that a ballot question addressed the issue of fathers supporting their children, even the out-ones. Unfortunately it was defeated by a three-to-one margin, probably because it was part of an overall bill dealing with a number of other 'women's rights. I strongly encouraged Sandra, along with others, to get to the polls and vote "yes."

"Oh no, Miss Gerry. I not be voting for that!"

"My goodness, Sandra, why not? Look at what it would do to help all women in your country. You have hardly any rights at all. There are double standards everywhere. This would certainly be a good beginning!"

"Miss Gerry, I be *ceris*. I not be voting for that NO WAY! It was men that write that law and you can't trust men NO WAY!"

She wasn't the only woman that thought that way, so that was that. It was defeated overwhelmingly.

CHAPTER 14

Working in the Dark

July was and still is regatta time in the Abacos. Hundreds of boats sail into our waters and most tie up at marinas and tap into the electricity. That translates into working in the dark from one power outage after the other. There would be no power on Green Turtle Cay, no power on Treasure Cay, no power on Man of War, and of course no power on Guana. It had been nearly a year since we experienced a loss of power that lasted for any duration.

We lost our power about 5:00 p.m., but we can usually function fairly well with our generator. Well, usually we can. But today as soon we tried to start the damn thing, it blew up.

Several new parts would be needed—parts that would have to be purchased in Marsh Harbour but would not be available until tomorrow. And getting our hands on them tomorrow was an extremely optimistic conclusion.

Even if we had lucked out, we would still have had that night to face without lights, without air conditioning, without water to wash with or flush the johns. And to top it all off, we had twenty-six dinner reservations.

It was one of Sandra's days off, and quite frankly I was a little glad. Sandra isn't one who can deal calmly with unusual circumstances and this was certainly going to be unusual.

Emily is the fill-in chef when Sandra is out, so she obviously was the one I needed to consult.

"Well Miss Emily, what do you think? Should I start informing the guests that dinners might not be a possibility tonight?"

"Don't do that," she answered with a smile. "I'm sure we can handle this."

And right behind her was Nora Mae, chiming in, "Don't worry, Miss Gerry. 'We'll be fine!"

And fine they were. I still marvel at how they managed those twenty-six dinners cooking by candlelight, flashlights, and a makeshift tiny gas generator that allowed them to first use one side of the deep fryer, then the microwave. Then back to the fryer and back to the microwave.

The kitchen was so filled with smoke that I could hardly make out my "stars of the day."

As the dishes began to pile sky high, I asked Nora Mae to pass me the Cascade.

"We need to start the dishwasher," I announced. Both she and Emily broke out with gales of laughter.

"How do you expect to do that, Miss Gerry, with no power?"

Next Beth, Larry's long time and very special friend, came hurrying in dragging a big fan.

"Here ladies," she proudly announced, "this should help clear up some of the smoke."

"And just where do you plan to plug THAT in they asked?" Now we were all laughing.

Larry had very thoughtfully filled a big old bucket with water from the cistern we no longer used. He couldn't understand why we all refused to use that water simply because there were tadpoles swimming all around.

The food was cooked to perfection, and the presentation (as nearly as we could tell by candlelight and flashlight) was excellent. The fact that the guests were fed an hour-and-a-half later than their reservations called for was about the only thing that I considered a drawback. However, the guests didn't see it that way at all. They reminded ME that we were in the Bahamas.

One group spent their time at the bar singing old Frank Sinatra tunes. They sang tunes I had forgotten Old Blue Eyes had even recorded. They must have been true fans because they knew all the words to any song that anyone suggested. The longer they waited, they louder they sang and the happier they got. And those who weren't singing did the applauding and got happy right along with them. All in all, even though it felt like utter chaos, it was a great party—an evening I shall not forget. Nor do I expect that Emily and Nora Mae will forget it either.

After the guests left, we just surveyed the utter disaster in the kitchen and realized it would take hours and hours if not days to clean it up. However, there was nothing we could do until power was restored, so Nora Mae and Emily just jumped into the pool. Miss Emily said she felt like a smoked salmon. We would face it all in the morning. Surely by then we'd have power, so I just went to bed.

Early the next morning Larry headed in the boat across the Sea of Abaco in search of the parts for the generator.

After a rather hot and restless night, all of us were anxious to find out from BEC just what the problem was and when they expected to give us back some power. It is interesting how many folks call Bob to find out what he knows and who he has contacted. They look to him for leadership, thinking he is more apt to get things done than they would. I guess they know he swears more than they do—and shouts the loudest.

Bob started his round of endless calls to BEC. He didn't have a chance to shout or swear because all the lines were busy or probably more correctly, off the hook. He did have Peter's cell phone number and since he was part of the crew here last evening, and one of the BEC guys we have such faith in, he decided to give him a call.

"Peter will know what's going on," he said as he was dialing.

He waited and waited and finally got an answer.

"Hey Peter, this is Bob Sylvester, Guana Seaside Village. What's the problem, and when can we expect power?"

"I don't know," came a foggy answer. "I didn't bother to go to work this morning."

At this point I discounted Peter as a reliable source, but he certainly had a chance to redeem himself in the not too distance future.

The sailboat *Run Away* was tucked nicely on one of our moorings.

The Miessers were one of the applauding couple at our bar last evening. They had intended to pull up anchor early in the morning to start their sail north, but now there was a change of plans.

Norman Miesser came ashore to see if he could help get that generator going. Just as he climbed up on the dock, Larry came with numerous parts. Now it was time to get to work.

After a couple of hours I wandered out to check on the progress. Norman and Larry were inside the generator shack, covered with grease. Bob was also covered with grease, but he was outside sitting on the golf cart, head in hands just lying on the steering wheel.

"Incompetence!" he shouted. "Damned incompetence." He was speaking about BEC. "I can't stand incompetence. How in hell do people live like this?"

"Dad," I answered, "they are used to it. This is all they know. You have a whole different set of expectations."

No matter how it was explained, he was still upset and pretty discouraged. And the fact that the golf cart he was sitting on was no longer working either didn't help matters much.

After seven long, hot and frustrating hours, the generator was fixed. It kicked on to everyone's delight, and five minutes later so did the power from BEC.

Norman dragged himself down the dock, climbed into his dinghy and headed for *Run Away*. Finally time to sail away.

We were grateful not only for his expertise and willingness to help but also for his extremely patient wife.

When they return, and I am sure someday they will, they will be entitled to a free room if the weather gets rough, or at the least a couple of free dinners with the lights on.

It did in fact take us hours to clean up the kitchen, but only minutes to discover that the power nonsense had cost us our microwave, which was only three months old, and a brand new coffeemaker.

As Bob headed out to Marsh Harbour to buy the replacements, I timidly suggested he try and find someone to come over and fix the cooler at the bar, which also wasn't working anymore.

CHAPTER 15

Rib Night: Karaoke Fun, Frolics and Folly

Our Rib Night, which we held on occasion, was a great success. Guests began to ask if we were going to offer them on a regular basis. Up until that time, we had been doing them only a couple of times a month, but we now decided that there was more than enough interest to make them a weekly event. Every Saturday night became Rib Night, and we always enjoyed a full house.

Bob was the official rib chef and, using the recipe that Jim (a friend of ours from Kentucky had shared with us), he became an expert rib cooker. I kid you not when I tell you that he received rave reviews, even from those who ran restaurants or were cooks themselves.

It was Lisa who suggested that it might be fun to add karaoke to our Saturday night affairs. Bob wasn't so sure. He really didn't think that karaoke would have much appeal here on the island so we asked around and got some very enthusiastic responses.

The next time Bob went home, he proudly called me and told me he had found a complete karaoke set-up.

"That's just great, honey. Was it very expensive?"

"No, not at all," he answered. "It only costs a hundred dollars."

"Oh Bob, that's for kids. A toy for inside. 'That's not what we need for the bar."

Getting that piece of information, and because he half-believed me, he decided to check with Janet.

She searched the Internet and found a first-class karaoke system—one with all the bells and whistles—just the kind you would expect Janet to find. Of course it was a little more than a hundred dollars, as Bob was quick to point out, but he still reluctantly agreed to the purchase.

Janet, Lisa and I were ecstatic. "Hooray, hooray, we can have karaoke on Saturday nights!"

There would, however be an occasional Saturday night when we wondered if we should have been so gleeful.

One night, there was singer who didn't know a single word, and I assume was too nearsighted to read them off the screen. No matter who was singing, she'd grab the second mike and make some ungodly cat sounds. They were meowing sounds, but horrible ones. She made them throughout entire songs, and she stayed meowing for a long, long time.

There was another night when a guest came with her dog, and every time someone began to sing, her dog would howl loudly. Even though we requested she take that critter home, she was adamant in her refusal. She just kept him there to annoy the rest of us, I guess. When she realized she wasn't being entertaining, wasn't making any friends or wasn't the most popular person at the party, she finally left with her howler. This was followed by a great deal of hooting, hollering, cheers and laughter.

And there were many nights when folks objected if we decided to close things down. When it got to be 2:00 or 3:00 o'clock in the morning and we decided enough was enough, they wanted to keep singing. And needless to say most of those folks couldn't sing worth a damn.

Jolly Bob's Famous Ribs

A Fun Evening

One night when we did manage to close at a reasonable hour, Lisa decided to go check out Nippers. She only stayed a short while and then headed back to the Inn for an early night. When she left Nippers, a number of golf carts began to follow, all intent on going to Seaside.

"Don't follow me!" she shouted from the van. But still the caravan continued.

"Go home!" she shouted, "The Seaside Bar is closed."

But nobody listened.

"There is nothing there. The bar is closed and the music is shut down, so go away!"

But they didn't go away. They followed her all the way to Seaside Village to have a drink and sing a song or two. So of course Lisa felt obliged, but that sure ended her plan for an early night.

I was half asleep when I heard the singing begin and I could only wonder what had happened, since I thought the party was already over.

Those were some of the times when we questioned our sanity at being so gleeful about our great Saturday night karaoke addition.

However, most nights were great successes, not only for business but for fun, laughter and fellowship. We would not just have a full bar, the Inn would be overflowing. Thankfully, friends like Judy and others would jump behind the bar to help in any way they could. They saw that the song selections were taken in turn, the microphones were passed around so all could share, and helped to see that the drinks kept flowing. It really took them, along with Glenn, Janet and Lisa (when they were there) and Bob and me to keep things under control

Bob and I always managed to sing, "I Got You Babe." Guests loved to see us participate and found it amusing and entertaining, especially since neither one of us can sing worth a damn.

I always requested the song "Sweet Caroline," so that when the chorus came up everyone could shout "THIS SONG SUCKS." I'm not sure why the crowd always got into that, but they sure did.

Then someone would always request "American Pie," and both Bob and I would cringe. We actually learned to hate that song. We had heard it so many times and it was a full eight minutes long. There were times when we thought maybe we should just sneak in and take a quick nap until it was over.

Late Night Fun

The local folks most always joined us and arrived about noon. They had lunch, and hung around the bar laughing and joking. Some went for a swim and a couple sometimes napped in the sun.

No Fun At All

When we fired up the karaoke, a neat lady named Suzanne began to sing. Her family and friends hung around her, applauding and laughing.

After she sang a couple of delightful country and western tunes, they packed up their ribs and fixings into go-boxes and headed out. All except one. He arrived well before noon, 6:00 a.m. to be exact. He sat at the bar, waiting for breakfast, sat there waiting for lunch, and sat there waiting for the evening's festivities. In fact, he still sat there when everything was over.

It had been one of those late, late, nights—actually about 4:00 a.m. —while Lisa was still out there cleaning up what had to be cleaned, that he announced he thought he'd leave.

"Why go now?" she asked. "Two more hours and you will have been here for twenty-four, and that surely will be a record."

"I don't care about no record. I'm going home now."

So home he went, but we still called him the "marathon man."

There was one very young girl who was an excellent singer. We often wondered how Tasha would make out on *American Idol*. She really had a great voice and was also very pleasing to look at. However we all decided that it wouldn't be the place for her to make a name for herself. It might just be a little too rough—something else would have to come along.

People who owned second homes or were repeat tourists usually ended up at Seaside. Many of them loved to sing, and thank heavens some really knew how. One such person was a delightful young man named Jason. He not only could sing but he also wrote songs about the island. He wrote a song about Nippers, which was hilarious, and he also wrote a clever ditty about the Seaside Village, which we really enjoyed. You surely won't be able to fully appreciate it without his voice and his guitar and the guitar chorus between each verse, but nonetheless it went like this:

WELL FOLLOW ME DOWN THAT SANDY ROAD
SEE THAT RED ROOF GLEAMING, START TO LOSE CONTROL
WHEN I'M HERE IT FEELS LIKE HOME
IT'S A GUANA SEASIDE NIGHT.

THAT BAR DIDN'T FALTER, THAT BAR DIDN'T FALL
WHEN FRANCES AND JEANNE TRIED TO TAKE IT ALL
WE'RE ALL HERE AND WE'RE HAVING A BALL

ON A GUANA SEASIDE NIGHT

THERE IS LISA AND JANET, BOB AND GLENN
YAYA IS SIGNING HER BOOK AGAIN
IT'S WHERE I COME TO SEE MY FRIENDS
ARE YOU FEELING ALL RIGHT?

WELL I THINK I'LL HAVE ME A FLYING DOG
GONNA WASH IT DOWN WITH A JOLLY BOB
WISH I COULD STAY AND QUIT MY JOB
I THINK I'M FEELING ALL RIGHT

WELL SOMEDAY HILL WILL TURN EIGHTEEN
LISA WILL BE THERE WITH A BOTTLE OF JIM BEAM
WATCH YOUR HEADS IF YOU KNOW WHAT I MEAN
IT'LL BE A GUANA SEASIDE NIGHT

FIND IT BY MOTOR, FIND IT BY SAIL
DRIVE YOUR CART OR WALK THAT TRAIL
THE FINEST DRINKS AND THE COLDEST ALE
IT'S A GUANA SEASIDE NIGHT

WELL RAISE YOUR GLASSES ONE MORE TIME
LIFT YOUR BEER, LIFT YOUR WINE
THANK GERRY AND BOB FOR A REAL GOOD TIME
IT WAS A GUANA SEASIDE NIGHT !!!!!!!

Karaoke Stars Purdy and Chuck

Some folks learned the lyrics, sang along, and all thought it really captured the atmosphere, the fellowship and the fun times. However, there was one Saturday night that didn't end on a happy fun-loving note.

We had a group of thirty-five who had joined the many others who were there. They were great guests, having a great time, and all here for a Bahamian vacation paid for by their boss. That evening they provided us with numerous duets. They would pair up and sing their hearts out. Actually some were quite good, and a few others even better.

Four of this group decided not to wait for the others to leave and headed out to Nippers. Not long after they left, Lisa loaded up the van to transport other guests who needed rides to their lodgings. It was on her way back that she came upon the accident, and it was a serious one.

It seems that when these four folks arrived at Nippers, they stayed only a short while then decided to head back to Seaside Village to end the evening with the rest of their friends. As they came to the large downhill, the driver decided to put the golf cart in neutral, just to see how fast it would go. Down they went at a fast clip, got to the bottom and made the curve quite safely. Apparently it had been so much fun that he decided to try it again. Back up the hill they went and down again, only this time they weren't quite so lucky.

The golf cart crashed, and the women who were sitting in the back went flying. The fellows in the front had only minor injuries but that could not be said for the women. Lisa had arrived just a couple of minutes after it happened and immediately called the Guana Cay Rescue Squad.

One woman lay there with a bone sticking out of her ankle, the other just moaning and saying she couldn't breathe. Lisa said the rescue squad members, Laura Sands, Troy Albury, and Captain Nicky Otten, had arrived as quickly as could be expected (all coming from different locations), but for all of them the waiting seemed like an eternity.

The one woman who couldn't breathe and was in the most distress started to berate the rescue workers. She was screaming at them for taking so long. They in turn pointed out that they were simply volunteers, giving their time, energy and expertise to help those in need. That really didn't quiet her, but Lisa explained that she wasn't being angry, she was just horribly frightened, and rightfully so.

She was airlifted that very night to a hospital in the states. Her internal injuries were so massive that she remained in intensive care for three months. The gal with the mangled ankle stayed on Guana until the following morning and then left to get the necessary medical care at home. Anyone who is completely devoid of common sense and plays games with a golf cart is a jackass. I wondered how this jackass felt, or if he even cared.

CHAPTER 16

Friends, Rumors and Folks with Strange Behaviors

After only a short period of time, we had right here in this small Settlement many friends who I firmly believed would be ready to offer assistance whenever a need should arise. We loved not only the natural beauty of Great Guana, the blue green waters, the beautiful beaches, the warm sun and awesome sunsets, but most of the people as well. Notice I did say *most* of the people.

Because it is a small island, only seven miles long and maybe a mile wide at the widest part, there are a few bored folks with little to do who are prone to spreading rumors. Interestingly enough it is not so much the natives as the "transplants." Folks from America and other countries who had built second homes here seem to be the worst offenders. They have a slanted view of exactly who belongs on this island, or who this island really belongs to.

Rumors don't usually bother me, thanks to the thick skin I developed serving in political office. They came with the territory. But island rumor mongering as practiced by this handful of people perhaps should have concerned me. We learned that in the past stories about others had been underground, targeted, and presented to government officials as the gospel truth. Clearly those efforts were to get people in disfavor thrown off the island, if not out of the country. And believe it or not, those efforts worked occasionally. They could talk about us all they wanted, but I certainly didn't want to do anything that would land us on someone's "hit list."

The rumors held that we bought Seaside Village for a family retreat, but when we learned about the tax ramifications we had no choice but to operate it as an Inn. That's why we were working so hard and busting our *bungies* to make a go of it. Only the last part of that rumor holds any truth, and was so simple it didn't concern me at all.

There was another rumor that saddened more than concerned me, because it was from an American new-homeowner whom I had really tried hard to like. She began at the Settlement telling folks that the moment she left her cottage to go back to the states, I went in her house to steal, or as Sandra would say, *thieve,* meat from her freezer. Fortunately for me, she was telling this story to real friends of mine. My first instinct was to be angry and figure a unique way to confront her.

That didn't last long because first the accusations were so ridiculous that most found them laughable, and secondly I realized that what she really needed was a little sympathy. She was the type of person who constantly struggled to be front-and-center. She was someone who wanted to be Queen for a Day, someone who walked into a room and said as loudly as possible, "Okay, here I am." She used the f-word constantly in an attempt to be amusing, never stopping to think it might offend someone.

If I were the vengeful type, I could really have enjoyed joining in when island folks talked about her and her many indiscretions, perhaps even list them here in alphabetical order. But I made a calculated decision to keep many juicy stories out of this journal. Not all of them, mind you, just a tidbit or two here and there—enough to give you an overall flavor of the island. To add more would be tantamount to turning Guana Cay into a mini-Peyton Place (and that would not be hard to do).

In the beginning we became aware that the prior owners had not really welcomed the local folks to the resort. We heard story after story, example after example, that clearly showed they wanted Seaside Village to be an exclusive resort of some kind. Apparently the only people who were treated in a friendly manner were those who were actually guests at the resort. I am not faulting their vision, but it sure was different than the one we had. We truly wanted to be part of the community and knew it had to begin with us. Acceptance, respect and a real caring were the only ways to show how grateful we were that these folks were willing to share with us their little corner of paradise. It didn't take too long before most of those burnt bridges had been repaired and we were welcomed.

The people of Guana are most accepting. All they expect in return is common courtesy, a respect for their culture, and non-invasion of their privacy. Second home owners who come ashore, build their houses, attempt to dominate the environment and act as if the island belonged to them were apt to find themselves in no great favor. One such callous gentleman comes immediately to mind.

Perhaps he was not the best example of what one might consider an outcast. Just because he didn't have the brains that God gave a biscuit, some really thought he might be crazy. Although he was a close neighbor I wasn't too concerned at first. I knew he completely lacked common sense, found him somewhat annoying—a little off base—but also thought he was probably harmless.

"Ma, what is it with that man?" a couple of my visiting kids asked.

"Oh, don't pay any attention to him," I responded. "He's just a little bit different!"

"Okay," they answered. "We guess because you think he is just a little bit different, you'll accept the fact that he was standing on our laundry room roof at 5:30 this morning without any concern."

"HE WAS WHAT?"

"Never mind, Ma. Guess you don't have to worry since you think there is nothing really wrong with him—he's just different. We sure don't agree, so I guess we are the ones that will do the worrying."

They certainly had a way of getting a message across. I still didn't do a lot of worrying, probably because I didn't have the time; but I certainly began to pay a little closer attention. The only problem he posed at the Inn was hanging around occasionally and annoying the guests. That is when Bob would step in and send him away. He would stay away for a while then back he'd come. Bob would repeat the firm request and he'd once again leave, only then he'd sit right on the edge of the property and watch what was going on. Often when he sat there he'd have a pad of paper, a couple of pencils and would take notes. He told us he was writing a book.

There were times when he wasn't asked to stay away. If we were having an open house, a potluck or some other kind of general affair, we never excluded him, his wife or his son. Usually he showed up empty-handed, but there was one time when he came carrying a beautiful platter. It had a glass dome lid that was etched and quite lovely. All around the platter were mounds of great looking purple grapes and in the center was a piece of cheese. I say piece instead of block because it was just that—a piece, a tiny little piece, a piece about big enough for two small crackers. We all thought, "So what? Those grapes would surely make up for that tiny piece of cheese, and perhaps they would have if they hadn't been plastic."

We received a startling report from one couple. They said that when they got up one morning, there he was sitting in their kitchen.

"What in God's name are you doing here?" they asked.

"I was just waiting for you to get up so you could give me a cup of coffee."

There were other reports from guests who were renting the cottages adjacent to the Inn. They said that often as they sat on their decks or porches late at night, they would see him creeping around. They would watch silently as he crept up on other porches, looked in windows, or checked out parked golf carts. They would give him some time then shout out, "Hey, what are you doing?"

"Nothing," he'd answer. "I'm just out for my evening walk."

These guests were life-long friends and ones who vacationed together. They returned year after year, always renting the same cottages. Now they were discussing the possibility of trying to jointly buy this man's property, hoping to get him out of the way. Of course he abruptly proclaimed that his property wasn't for sale, neither now nor in the future! Of course things change, and we all know that there can come a time when anything or everything is for sale.

As the days went by, all kinds of stories began to surface. The main one was that he was picking peoples' garbage. I really discounted most of them, but so many folks reported actually seeing him pick out leftover food from Nippers garbage on a Pig Roast Sunday that I assumed there must be some truth to all of it. However, garbage picking didn't concern us as much as the treatment of his son did.

One hot day, Lisa was driving to the Settlement and saw his son walking the road. She stopped and asked if he wanted a ride, but he refused. Three more times as she went back and forth she saw him either coming or going, and again she stopped.

"You have been walking for a long time, so hop in."

"I can't," he said. "I am not allowed to take a ride!"

"Why? Tell me what's going on."

"I was late for the ferry this morning so my punishment is to walk to the Settlement and back four times. I would really be in trouble if I let you help me!"

Well, walking to the Settlement and back amounted to walking over five miles, and to have to do that four times on an extremely hot, dry, dusty day was certainly extreme punishment. It seemed to us that this kid was already in as much trouble as any kid could possibly get. There were other things as well. We didn't believe he was physically beaten, but we often wondered how well-fed he was and what other kinds of sanctions they were imposing on him. We do know that at one time the Bahamian Social Services did an investigation, but nothing came of it.

Eventually this neighbor did put his property up for sale. At first, the price was much more than was warranted, so there were no takers. Next the price came down to within reasons. There were quite a few prospective buyers, but none willing to make a firm commitment. Most of them expressed a concern that they just couldn't deal with a crazy person. Interestingly enough, it wasn't him they were talking about, but his wife. She followed them around the property, giving orders about what they could and could not do if they purchased it. "Hell," they thought, "if we owned it we should be able to do whatever we want." Not so, according to her. There would be numerous stipulations in the sales agreement and she listed a number of them. They were so unreasonable that these folks just backed away.

Eventually the property did sell and they left the island, only to return a few months later. They were looking for other property on Guana and either couldn't find anything to their liking or couldn't find anyone willing to sell to them. It was apparent that they just weren't accepted.

"That's just fine," she declared as they boarded the ferry. "There are beaches all over the world, so we certainly don't have to be here!"

CHAPTER 17

Hurricane Floyd: The Damage and the Elusive Truth

There is a Hurricane Floyd story that might be worth telling. Or perhaps I should say a couple of competing stories. There was once a great resort here on Guana. In fact it was about the only really nice one around. It had housekeeping cottages, a motel-like structure, a pool, dock, a lovely restaurant, and community room and gift shop. It was owned by a couple of brothers and had been for sale for some time. Then along came Floyd. It didn't actually total the place but it did considerable damage. The brothers flew over to do a visual assessment and three days later the resort caught fire. It was started, or so it was claimed, when a generator blew up. That was somewhat of a mystery since there was no power anywhere on the island. Some folks, at least, believed that when the brothers realized it wasn't a total loss, they might have taken things into their own hands. The theory was bolstered when it was realized that many things of value, including beautiful Japanese glass fishing floats, had been removed the day before the fire.

Regardless of the origin, there was one story filled with praise for the locals who risked their lives fighting to put out the blaze. They were, it seemed, determined to save the rest of the resort for the owners. The other story states that the brothers were so disliked the locals set the fire.

Finally the resort was once again put up for sale. This time a professional auction company was hired to handle the transaction. And it wasn't to be an easy task. All the property was divided into the numerous remaining pieces. The motel-like structure, the dock, the piece of land where the restaurant, gift shop and community room once stood, the few cottages, a lot adjacent to the pool, a small beach bar and a couple of other now-vacant pieces were all put on the auction block as separate items. It was to be a set auction but it sure didn't turn out that way. When one of the owners didn't get the amount of money he wanted, he reneged. The last I knew, the high bidders were suing the auction company, and the auction company was suing the owners. The battle of who really owns the dock still rages.

There were only a couple of parcels that survived this auction fiasco. One parcel contained the small beach bar, two-thirds of the swimming pool, and the housekeeping cottages. The other parcel was about an acre of mostly flat dirt that was adjacent to the housekeeping cottages and the small bar. That parcel also included the remaining one-third of the swimming pool, if you can imagine such a thing. Those who were lucky enough to be able to finalize the deal on the parcel that included the bar and housekeeping cottages went to work right away. They expected it would probably be a little while before they actually got government approval, but were anxious to move ahead.

They started out by ordering custom-made furniture for each of the cottages, and each cottage room would reflect a special theme. If the cottage theme were turtles, then the bedposts had hand-carved turtles and the theme was carried out in numerous other ways: carved turtle pulls for the dresser drawers, turtle lamp bases, turtle murals and turtle throw rugs. If the theme were starfish or shells or whatever, the theme was carried out in each of the cottages in a comprehensive manner, including the carved bedposts. It took quite a while to get all that custom-made furniture finished, but there actually wasn't any hurry because it took even longer for the government to approve the purchase of the property. Months went by before they could open up and welcome guests. It was a much longer span of time than anyone imagined, and in the meantime all that beautiful carved mahogany furniture and accessories were just sitting in storage.

"What will I do if they don't rule in our favor?" the principal owner asked me. "I will probably have to sell all that beautiful furniture I had made."

I certainly was glad for her sake that it didn't come to that. As far as I could tell there wasn't a large market out there for turtle-themed carved bedposts or turtle-themed carvings of any sort.

Once all the red tape was out of the way, all the furniture moved in, and the renovations and decorations were complete, they left and rarely came back to visit their site. I suspect it was for that reason that they decided to lease out the small beach bar and have someone else in charge of renting the cottages. They also decided they would not continue to use the original name and renamed the place "Floyd's." It seemed like a terrible choice, unless they just wanted to pay tribute to the hurricane that had blown the rest of the place apart.

The first person to take over the bar was a great guy we knew as Captain Easy. I never did learn what his real name was but Captain Easy sure did fit this fellow. He was hard-working, laid back and always smiling. Rumor had it that he was part of the new ownership and perhaps he was, but if so he was the only new owner doing any work. He began a great fun potluck affair on Wednesday nights, which brought tourists and locals together. He also decided to rename the bar "The Sunset Beach Bar and Grill." That was a simple but pretty smart move. It got rid of the hurricane memories and described one of the best spots around to watch the sunset—probably only second best to Seaside Village. But then of course that's just my opinion.

After the next two hurricanes, Francis and Jeannie, he really got tired of busting his *bungy*, and he decided to give it up and just enjoy some quiet time on his boat. That is when Chorene, a lifelong resident of Guana Cay, and Jerry, her newlywed American husband, decided to take on this effort. They both worked diligently at least six days a week, adding some delightful Bahamian decorating touches. They ran specials, promoted the drink named the Guana Grabber and continued to call the bar the Sunset Beach Bar and Grill. They encouraged everyone to come enjoy it and get "grabbed." They also strongly promoted the Wednesday night potluck affairs. They got the locals to join the tourists, the second home owners and the boaters. The only thing more diversified than the folks who gathered was the home-cooked dishes they brought to share. You never knew for certain what would be on that big long table, but you could be sure that everything was mighty tasty and there would always be more than enough.

At the Inn, I would always cook enough food and then some to cover the number of guests we had. We would not only drag the food down to the potluck, but we would make as many trips as necessary to transport our guests. We wanted them to enjoy the food, to hopefully buy a "Grabber" or two, but even more than that, we wanted them to meet new people and enjoy the fellowship. There was always a good crowd, 45 or 50 people, and on a couple of Wednesdays there were as many as 100. Because of that I didn't hesitate to suggest to the visiting preacher and his wife that they might want to drop by and make themselves known.

I didn't really think they would listen to my suggestion but when they did show up, there were only about twelve of us there. I hoped he didn't think I had been lying. Don't ask me what happened. Maybe the good Lord didn't think having the preacher visit if the usual crowd was around was such a great idea. Or maybe it had just been the pouring rain that kept everyone at home.

It was only rarely that the owners showed up. Then they did little more then strut around while this great, hardworking, caring couple busted their *bungies* in order to make enough profit to cover the cost of the lease. I guess it is too much to expect that somewhere along the line they'd get a break of some kind. If they didn't, then at least they'd be shown they were appreciated.

Guess it wasn't meant to be. Another group of new owners came aboard, renamed the place "Grabbers," and fired Chorene and then Jerry. I think the new people will do well—at least we all hope so, but I also hope that no one forgets that it was Captain Easy, Chorene and Jerry that helped rescue The Sunset Beach Bar and Grill from the pits and got lots of folks used to going there.

The second successful auction bidder wasn't very happy with the way things turned out. He objected to the fact that folks coming to the little beach bar and grill were using his flat acre of dirt as a parking lot. He had no immediate plans for it, but it was his and that's all there was to it. He wasn't around often enough to police the property, so he had bags of cement delivered to circle the area and prevent golf cart access.

That effort was successful, however, try as he may, he could not figure out a way to block off his one-third of the swimming pool. At first folks were a little angry at him, but they found another parking spot and only laughed at his effort to claim his share of the pool. The next time he paid a visit, they just ignored him as best they could.

He checked into one of the rooms, ordered from the bar and grill, and just sort of hung out. He didn't make any friends, so that might help explain why it took three days for it to dawn on someone that they hadn't seen him anywhere. They knew he hadn't checked out, so he probably was still in his room. They decided they should knock on his door, which they did, but to no avail.

"Maybe he left without telling anyone."

"No, that's not possible, someone would surely have seen him!"

"Maybe we should try knocking again."

And so they did, but again there was no answer. They decided to unlock the door and go on in. That's when they saw him dead in the bed.

How many days? No one knew for sure—but you can't help but wonder if he had made at least one friend, just one, somebody who wasn't mad at him, there might have been a different outcome. If it wasn't a sudden death, if he had had some warning signs, if he had believed there was someone he could call out to, would it have made a difference? Too late to speculate and certainly no longer room for anger.

Along with the sympathy there was utter chaos. Just imagine this scene in the states. There would be a medical examiner, a crime scene expert, pictures taken, the corpse being examined, a doctor to perform an autopsy quite quickly, and some answers sooner rather than later. Here we had a couple of policemen off the ferry to handle a body that everyone assumed was three days old. That the gentleman died of natural causes was also the assumption, but there was only limited staff to take care of the aftermath. The only thing left was for some to wonder what would happen with his acre of dirt and one-third of a swimming pool.

CHAPTER 18

Maybe We Shouldn't Be So Off the Beaten Path

There are other sagas to tell about that did not involve the everyday workplace. There was the saga of the GARBAGE DUMP, and the one about the ROAD REPAIRS. The Seaside Village motto "Off The Beaten Path" was for a very good reason. We were about two-and-one-half miles from the Settlement by land and a mile-and-a-half by water. We did have a dock, so folks could dinghy in and join us. We also had a few moorings that were free for larger boats as long as the folks aboard come ashore for either a drink or a meal. But the truth is that most came by golf cart over what could loosely be called a road, but was amusingly called the "Guana Cay Interstate."

Some people loved it. They thought it was like being on a mini safari or an exotic Disney Ride without the need to stand in line. They gladly accepted it as part of the overall adventure. There were others, however, who loved the Village, considered the food the best on the island, loved meeting the staff and contended they would return more often if it weren't for that "damn" road.

I really didn't blame them. Those were the ones that shared my sentiments exactly. Most of them probably had kidneys the same age as mine. I dreaded going to town or down to meet the ferry. There were deep ruts, big humps, and after a rain storm there were puddles deep enough that people were tempted to lift their feet as they traveled through. But if it hadn't rained for a while you ate dust. Often when golf carts met going in opposite directions one had to back up and find a space in the bushes to pull into so the other could pass. I expect you've gotten the picture.

There is a gentleman on Guana who owns much of the land from near the Settlement to about a mile from us. It is land that he inherited from his father, who in turn received it in a bartering arrangement his grandfather had with local families.

This was a poor island, with very few resources, leaving most families struggling to survive. His grandfather would come in with freighter-loads of scarce and much needed supplies and simply exchange those necessities for land. When this gentleman inherited the land, he decided to subdivide most of it into good-sized lots. He was granted the right to subdivide by promising to take care of all the necessary amenities, one of which was paved roads. Lots were sold, wonderful homes were built, but it seems the road part had been totally forgotten. I certainly didn't know anything about Bahamian politics, but I wondered if a subtle reminder to government officials might jog some memories.

I attempted to frame the letter as one of innocent inquiry, asking simple questions like: "When someone makes a bargain with the government, do they have to keep up their end?" "When the government grants certain rights to an individual but insists that certain criteria be met, does the individual have to meet the criteria or can they simply ignore it?" "Would government officials think that fourteen years was a reasonable time frame for someone to deliver on a promise they made?" Of course these "leading questions" were part of a longer epistle dealing directly with the road, or lack of one!

I am not certain that the letter got things moving, although the property owner certainly thought so. Much later, after the road was nearly completed, he came to meet with Bob and me, looking for some assistance in another road deal. He claimed that he was forced to do the current project because someone who would remain unnamed wrote a very nasty letter about him to the Prime Minister.

He didn't confront me directly, but had he done so, I would have, with tongue in cheek, fallen back on that favorite Bahamian saying, "It wasn't me." After all, who could believe that my nice letter was a nasty one?

The new road would certainly be welcomed, but there was one small problem. This gentleman would stop the road repairs—and rightfully so—right where his property ended. At the end of his property, and if you were headed our way, you would face one tremendous hill going up and another going down. They were known as "the hills from hell." Then there is also a small stretch where most of the puddles gather. It involved only about 710 feet, but that 710 feet was the road's worst challenge. At this point in time it was almost impassable.

Bob decided to take the lead and meet with the contractors. His knew that if that section of the road was ever going to be widened and paved, then the only time to tackle it was when all the heavy equipment was already on the island. Beyond those 710 feet is a small dirt lane that leads right to the Inn. We wanted that left just as it was, with the exception of perhaps a little fill here and there.

People seem to enjoy that part of the ride. It adds to the ambiance, and certainly supports the notion that we were "off the beaten path."

After many discussions about the major project, the contractor told Bob that $32,000 would be the price to do the section we were concerned with—$32,000 to do what needed to be done.

"Thirty Two Thousand Dollars! Where in the world will we get that amount?" I asked.

"Leave it to me," he answered. "It won't be easy, but I intend to raise at least half that amount from the home and property owners who will benefit, and we'll pick up the balance."

It was common thought that because we were the business at the end of the road, we would be the ones to reap the biggest benefit. We had absolutely no disagreement with that thinking. The balance would be raised from the adjacent owners, $600 apiece. At first there were three or four who expressed some concerns. A few years back, they had been asked by a certain individual to contribute $200 apiece for road improvements. There had been no improvements—in fact none had even been planned. Not a one of them had ever been able to get his money back.

Obviously it took a little persuasion for Bob to convince them that this was an entirely different situation. Once over that hurdle, he began in earnest to contact everyone who would be involved. Some of the owners were on the island, others were here, there and everywhere. Homeowners were a little bit easier to find than those who just owned property. But in either case, trying to locate and find contact numbers for anyone who wasn't hanging out just around the corner presented a definite challenge.

Bob was undaunted. He had a definite purpose and wouldn't allow himself to get discouraged. He just plugged away and plugged away. Finally, in his little road folder he had almost everyone lined up. Almost, that is. The gentleman who owns more property than any of our other neighbors, and who without a doubt was the wealthiest one among us, simply declared that he couldn't afford the $600. Shortly after that announcement, one other couple, close friends of his, also withdrew their support.

"Don't worry, honey," he assured me. "We can do it without them!"

He was quite comfortable with his progress and had only a couple of more calls to make. These he would do from the states, as we were preparing for another trip back to good old New Hampshire. The night before we were to leave, a different couple came to the bar. They began to spout off that Bob's idea was absolutely crazy. Nobody wanted to pay that contractor and go with the current plan. They claimed they had an alternative, and that they had talked to a lot of people who thought their idea was far superior and would cost less. They even named people they said they had contacted. Some Bob had spoken to, others he had not.

"Well, tell me about your alternative. I am willing to listen," he said.

"Simple," they said. "We will get some concrete, and we already know someone who has a mixer that they will let us use. All of us can pitch in, maybe hire one Haitian to help and do it ourselves."

Bob had already checked out numerous alternatives including using concrete. He explained it in detail; the cost of the concrete, the cost of freighting it over, the need to find a place to store it and the problem of getting it to the site. Those costs alone far exceeded what we were going to pay for the repairs and blacktop. I think they were surprised that he had already done that much background work, so now they had to come up with something different, or at least the wife did.

"No one is going to hurt those palm trees I just planted . . . or disturb my flowers along the road!" she wailed.

I had been quiet long enough but now couldn't resist.

"What the hell are you talking about? The road repairs stop long before the dirt lane where your palm trees are. Nothing is going to happen there. We want that left just the way it is!"

I know that is not the best way to win an argument or to keep friends, and I had thought they were our friends. However, I felt so badly for Bob I just couldn't help myself.

"I just can't stand the guy that is doing the big road project," she said. "I just hate him so much I don't want any road that comes anywhere near our little lane to look anything like his road!"

That argument was so ridiculous it didn't deserve a rebuttal of any kind. Besides, I had to remind myself that a while back this was the same lady who had put logs across that little dirt lane to act as speed bumps. Folks on golf carts had to stop their three miles an hour "speeding" down that little lane, hop out, and lug the logs aside. As soon as they removed them, out she would come again and put them right back. This went on until the authorities made her cease and desist. Even remembering those stories and realizing she was the fly in the ointment and did not necessarily have her husband's full support didn't cool me down. I simply knew it was time for me to go to my room. Inside, I wasn't sure if I should have a "hissy fit" or cry a little. "Poor Daddy," I was thinking. "Daddy" is what I call Bob when I'm loving him a lot. "Poor Daddy, they are deliberately trying to undermine his efforts," and that was tearing me apart.

Back home, he began the phone calls again. He talked to those he hadn't reached and reconfirmed with those who had already made a commitment. A couple of days had gone by when the "concrete suggestion guy" called. He was just checking, wanted to know how things were going. Bob told him just fine and threw back the names of those who were aboard. Interestingly, some of those folks were the very ones he had told us would never participate. He then sheepishly suggested that if this was the way we were really going, then he guessed he'd go along. I will bet you anything that his wife wasn't around when he made that call.

Once we returned to the Inn, he came by to say he was sorry for making me angry. I tried to explain that I was more disappointed than angry. Besides, all of that nonsense was behind us and I still thought of him as a friend. He came down quite often after that, but always alone.

The others, so many others, were not only 100% cooperative, but pleased to be part of the effort. They said it made them feel really a part of the neighborhood. The fellow who had previously collected those $200 fees even gave us his check for $600. I was really pleased and shared the information with Uncle Leonard. "See what I have," I said, showing him the check. "And you told me this guy would never give us one cent."

He just grinned and said, "Wait until you try to cash it!" Good old Uncle Leonard, he not only knows the island, he knows the people. Of course the check bounced. Even that really didn't dampen our spirits. We were on our way.

The contractor told Bob he could expect the road repairs completed the first week in December. By the end of May, they finally started. Perhaps it would be better described as started, stopped, started, stopped and then really stopped. —For how long, no one was able to tell us.

At first we had been really thrilled to see all the big equipment and the road crew here in force. In fact we had nine members of the crew staying with us at the Inn. We were delighted and viewed it as a great chance to measure their progress. The first Monday they left bright and early, worked right through lunch, and arrived back about 7:00 p.m. They were tired and hungry but we were as excited as could be. Perhaps it was really happening.

Tuesday they took a regular lunch break that lasted a couple of hours and were back here by 5:00.

Wednesday they worked only until lunchtime.

Thursday they played in the pool and took naps.

Friday they played cards around the bar and did a little fishing off the dock.

Saturday they all left for Marsh Harbour.

Only one piece of that equipment had been used, but it had nothing to do with repairing the road.

The big old pickup truck they traveled in was parked on our back lawn when the flat tire was discovered, the kind of flat where the rim was hanging out. They found a spare somewhere but now they had no jack. It was essential to fix that flat, if not to get them to work, then at least to get them to the ferry for Marsh Harbour.

As a substitute for the jack they drove a 982 Caterpillar great big front-end loader about 40 miles an hour down that little dirt lane, right across our back lawn, and used it to pick up the truck. Watching them I thought that it might have been a really good time to call the speed bump lady back into action. The tire was finally fixed and they were off to the ferry for Marsh Harbour, planning to return and really start work on Monday.

The first time when they hadn't worked was because some equipment had broken down, and everyone had to wait for a part to come from Nassau. Well, the part came but no one knew how to put it in the machine. Now they had to wait for someone who did know to show up. They returned on Monday. Now the equipment was ready to go, but the workers weren't.

They still were not going to work, but this time the problem was a little different—and for me at least a little more unsettling. On that Monday and Tuesday, as they were hanging around the bar, sitting by the pool, or pacing back and forth, there was a real air of discontent and frustration. They understood that they wouldn't be paid for the days they didn't work, but had expected to be paid for the time they had.

One of the reasons they had gone to Marsh Harbour was to collect their money the boss had promised them. However they couldn't find him. Now they were just waiting for him to get to Guana Cay. If he didn't show up by Tuesday, back pay in hand, they were out of here, off the island and headed back home.

The first ferry that Tuesday came in without the boss aboard, the second and third ferry, the same story. Now the fourth and final ferry, and thank the Good Lord the boss was aboard with money in his pocket. Tomorrow they would begin, and hopefully, with no more broken equipment or workers proposing a revolt, they would begin to work on a daily basis.

They actually started working full days on that Wednesday with their past pay in their pockets. Praise The Lord!!!!

We not only housed this crew, we fed them as well. Our instructions were to limit them to either a fish or chicken selection. Everyday it was fried fish or fried chicken .We were told that was what they wanted, and what they were used to. These were to be served with either peas and rice or French fries and served for both lunch and dinner. They didn't place individual orders, we were just told to mix it up. Just prepare so many chickens and so many fish and the same with the peas and rice or fries.

The fellow who placed the order was Frank, the second in command, and he had decided they could just sort out who ate what. The system worked fairly well. Only once did I hear a debate about some guy eating the other guy's French fries. I was really hoping that whoever grabbed a piece of fish for lunch would be fast enough to grab chicken for dinner. However, if we were really tired of serving the same thing, I reasoned that they surely must be tired of eating it.

The big boss wasn't around to discuss any alternative, but when I asked Frank what we could do for a little variety, he came up with a couple of suggestions. First was curried chicken with mounds of white rice, and the second possibility was Bahamian Pea Soup.

"Sandra, can you make Bahamian Pea Soup?" I asked.

"Sure I can, Miss Gerry. But these guys are from Nassau. I don't know if they like what I be doing. Can you find out what they be wanting in their soup?"

That was a reasonable request, so I went directly to Frank and posed the question and learned that Bahamian Pea Soup had the following ingredients:

Salt Beef
Ham

Chicken

Conch

Plantains or bananas or some of both

Pumpkin if you can find some, if not then use sweet potatoes

Dumplings

Peas, of course, and in this case Sandra would have to use Pigeon Peas, because that's all we had on hand and I knew we had PLENTY !

I had no idea of how much of any of the above goes in the pot, nor could I figure out how you make dumplings that come out in big long strips. I only know that Sandra busted her *bungy* getting that soup together and it was a major hit. She certainly was proud that she could match what a cook from Nassau could do. She was also pleased that they liked it so much they wanted it again the next night. With all those ingredients there is no such thing as a small pot of soup, so for two nights the road crew and the rest of us ate nothing but Bahamian Pea Soup.

There was now real progress on the road, even taking into account two days of rain. A little rain is good. I guess it settles down what has been graded and rolled. But a rain like we had at night and well into the morning really meant they had to redo much that had already been done. However, it didn't seem to concern the crew. They all headed out bright and early, ready to do whatever had to be done or done over. I could hardly believe it, but there it was, another encouraging sign.

The New Road

I am not quite certain who told us about the garbage dump. This outrageous plan would put the dump about 300 feet from the Inn. It wasn't Glenn who told us and since he was the Island Councilor you might think he would have brought us the news.

"A garbage dump, Glenn" What the hell is your government thinking?" screamed Bob.

"Don't worry, Mr. Bob. We will have some meetings to listen to everyone."

"You had better do something to stop the nonsense before we have any G-D meetings. Don't you understand that a garbage dump right next to this place will put us out of business!"

There is a vacant lot adjacent to the Inn. The government owns acres and acres, and supposedly it was to be offered to Bahamians in sort of a land grant deal so they could build their own homesteads. Apparently the Government had completely ignored that policy and commitment and just decided it would be a good place for a "sanitary landfill."

I could just envision our new Website saying, "Wouldn't you love to spend a quiet laid back vacation? Come to Guana Seaside Village. We have a lovely courtyard bar, a nice restaurant, clean and pretty rooms and a fresh water swimming pool. The Sea of Abaco is right at our front doorstep. If you walk 300 feet to the rear of the Inn you'll find the Atlantic Ocean with miles of beautiful deserted beaches. Walk the same distance to the left of us and you can visit the brand new garbage dump"!"

I had nightmares about flies, rodents, and feral cats. Bob was right—it would destroy us.

Then the meetings began.

These were meetings not to listen to everyone, but to listen to no one. When Bob attempted to speak, the administrator very rudely asked him just how long he'd been here! It was as if he didn't belong.

There was a lot Bob could have said. He could have answered that he'd been here long enough to add to the economy of the island, to contribute to every worthy cause when asked, and to keep Bahamian citizens employed. But he was right to just remain silent. They didn't even listen to the lifelong residents, so why would they listen to an "alien?" Their message was clear, simple and stated emphatically.

"We don't care what any of you think or what you have to say. We have decided the dump is going on that land."

We were then told we wouldn't have to worry. It would be a sanitary landfill, owned and operated by the government. You had only to think about the telephone company, the electric company and the airline that were owned and operated by the government to conclude that it was the worst possible news. Owned and operated by the government— God help us all !

Months went by, more meetings were held, but always with the same results. Then came election time.

Thankfully those in power lost and a whole new group came aboard. The administrator who was so arrogant and so determined was reassigned to some other remote area. We had a chance to start the battle anew.

Although the party Glenn supported and campaigned for was the one thrown out of office, it didn't affect any of the locally elected folks. He was still the Island Councilor. Now he decided he'd contact the new Prime Minister on behalf of his constituents, and organize yet another meeting.

This one was to be quite different, however. He arranged for just about anyone who would have any influence to come to Guana Cay. They wouldn't sit in the schoolhouse to do any browbeating. They would come directly here and look over the land in question. The Ministers of Public Health, Environment and Tourism were all present and not a single one of them could believe what was being proposed. That was it. There would be NO dump on that pristine land.

Glenn was both pleased and proud that he had been able to pull this off, and we were most grateful. I did wonder why he had not taken a firm, strong and active role before. Could it be that he found it easier to go to the new officials and put them on the hot seat than to buck the old administrator who was his buddy? He certainly had chosen not to go against those he supported and those who had supported him. That happens all the time in the world of politics—we see it everyday in our own government. Who knew? It was over and we were pleased. At least for the time being. But there would however be other concerns and battles in the future that would have to be addressed.

CHAPTER 19

Permit, Permit, How Much for Those Permits?

We had no idea what to expect when Fall rolled around, but September was really quiet. The whole island seemed deserted except for the local folks. Around the middle of August we watched boats either motor or sail by our dock in tremendous numbers. They were all headed for the states and no one, absolutely no one, was coming this way. Marsh Harbour was empty and Bakers Bay, which is about a mile-and-a-half from the Inn, may still have had one or two boats at anchor, when at the busy times you could count as many as forty or fifty.

Although weather experts will tell you that hurricane season is from July until the end of November, it seems that September causes the most anxiety. The first year we were here also held the memories of last September—9/11. They loomed large, were painful and still lingered with a rather numb kind of uncertainty. I was convinced this added substantially to the quiet time. People wanted to be close to home, close to their loved ones, and I could certainly understand that.

The Inn was half full until the first week in October. The guests were all wonderful, fun to be around, and made the most of every day. They loved the fact that they not only had a little private resort, but with hardly anyone else around they felt like they had their own private island.

They all checked out on the same day. The following day the staff left for four weeks. They would be on vacation and we would be closed to the public in order to do some necessary little things around the Inn. I found myself standing on the walkway, lonesome as all get-out, thinking, "What in God's name do I do now?"

Don't get me wrong—there was plenty to be done. But I couldn't seem to get motivated. I felt completely lost because there were no staff or guests who needed me.

Bob, however, was on a roll. He decided one of his first tasks would be to prune the hibiscus bushes and other trees in the courtyard. I am not sure if you ever watched anyone pruning with a chainsaw, but it sure is a frightening sight. He just went through like a man with a real mission, cutting this down, lopping that off—he spared nothing over a couple of feet tall. Watching him work in a frenzy with that menacing tool made me stop worrying about what was happening to my poor courtyard and start worrying about my husband. Before I stopped watching and escaped to our room, I had one question for our friend Leonard, who by the way is now known as Uncle Leonard to our family. I wanted to know which VHF channel the Guana Cay Rescue Squad monitored, just in case.

I was pleased when that little project was over, with the chainsaw back in the shed and Bob still in one piece. I wish I could say I was also pleased with the new austere look of our courtyard.

Watching him tackle some tasks and knowing I'd soon have to join him reminded me that we had not yet received our work permits. Most people believe that for owners like ourselves work permits should have been automatically transferred when we purchased the property. Maybe when they get around to giving us a deed, they might also give us work permits. In the meantime our new attorney advised us that we shouldn't be doing anything at all without permits in hand. If someone turned us in, then off the island we would go.

Naturally we decided to fill out the necessary applications, which was described as an easy process. All that was needed was a complete police background check, all our medical and financial records, numerous letters of recommendation, signed statements as to just what we intended to use these permits for—all of which had to be notarized by a Bahamian official.

After completing this so-called easy task, and with all the documentation in hand, Bob headed to Marsh Harbour to visit the official in charge of work permits and other things. The first shock came when he was told that it would cost $10,000 for each permit. Once Bob explained he wasn't in a position to pay out that kind of money and would forget the whole thing, the price magically came down to a mere $2,000 apiece. I didn't come to any hasty conclusion about where that extra $16,000 would have gone, but after we agreed that we would pay the new price I couldn't help but wonder what work permits really cost, especially since they have to be renewed on a yearly basis.

Several weeks went by before Bob called to try and determine when we could expect the permits and was told that the applications had not been filed because he hadn't paid the administrator the required $50 filing fees. This was something we knew nothing about. An unhappy Robert headed out on the ferry to Marsh Harbour to give the gentleman his filing fees. Unfortunately an even unhappier Robert returned fussing and fuming. The applications couldn't be filed without a cover letter stating why we wanted them and how we intended to use them. Of course all of that was already clearly explained in the notarized documents, but apparently that didn't matter.

As I typed out a cover letter I thought to myself, "I wish I had been there this last visit. I would have simply said, "'Give me a piece of paper and a pen and I'll write you that damn cover letter!'" Probably a good thing I wasn't there. Most officials don't take kindly to resistance, especially from a female.

Back on the ferry went poor Bob with letter in hand. Now he is assured the whole process was complete and will be forwarded to the appropriate authorities. Several months went by until we finally heard from some "government higher-ups" in Freeport. The price for each permit was now up to $7,500. Remembering that this was a yearly process with a yearly fee, we decided the only thing we could do was restate our case all over again, this time to a different set of officials.

Another long wait ensued before we got the message that we must send them the necessary dollars as soon as possible. We were not sure exactly what transpired, but the price was back down to $2,000. However we suspected that those permits would be issued from the date we first filed our applications. That would mean the year was just about gone, and it would be almost time to start the process all over again at God knows what price. We waited and waited for the longest time but were still without work permits.

The Health Department does an annual inspection. We usually passed with flying colors, without any reprimands and only a couple of simple suggestions. This year was an exception. They came right at lunchtime and began with the kitchen. Sandra was struggling to get a number of orders out, which certainly wasn't easy with them milling around and getting in her way. As soon as they left the kitchen and headed for the room inspections, I jumped in to give Sandra a hand. Dear God, I know the rules and should have known better.

"Excuse me," said the head of the team as she dallied right outside the door. "May I please see your health certificate"?"

"I don't have a health certificate," I mumbled, thoroughly intimidated.

"You are NOT allowed to work in the kitchen or even behind the bar without a health certificate!"

My first thought was to ask "Why in hell would I need a health certificate when I DON'T even have a work permit," but for once a calmer head prevailed.

Bob and I ventured over to the government clinic two days later to get our comprehensive examination. We waited for a couple of hours, had our pulse and blood pressure taken. And that was it. No blood work, no X-rays, no cultures, no nothing! I could have been another Typhoid Mary walking around and no one would have known! The only advice I was given was to NOT let my fingernails grow long. We walked out with our health certificates.

It sure was easy, but we have to go back to have those certificates renewed every six months. I don't have to worry about long fingernails because mine never grow anyway. I'll just have to try as hard as I can to keep my pulse steady and my blood pressure under control.

Listening to Cruiser's Net daily on VHF 68 you'll hear a segment named "Mail Call." Anyone who is leaving the Bahamas headed for the states volunteers to carry flat, stamped, unsealed mail for folks who need to mail something in a timely fashion. They give you their location—either it's a boat, a marina, a cottage, a ferry dock, or any number of places where they can be reached. They also give you a cut-off day and time. The response is tremendous.

Bob and I had often carried plastic bags with an assortment to drop in a mailbox as soon as we hit home turf. What it actually boils down to is folks receiving mail in two or three days time as compared to two or three weeks, or perhaps even longer.

CHAPTER 20

Pink Buildings and Red Tape

We had a post office box in Marsh Harbour and for the longest time it was the only way we could access our mail. Then the government built a neat tiny government building right here on Great Guana and painted it a bright pink. Half of the building was to serve as a post office. The other half would be a police station.

The mail was sent over from Marsh Harbour and we could retrieve it from our own little post office any Monday, Wednesday, or Friday from 11:45 a.m. until 12:30, or 1:00— whatever, provided the Postmistress decided to open up and Marsh Harbour had sent it over.

When a bit of important information reaches us late, we wonder how it would take a couple of weeks for a letter to come on the ferry across the Sea Of Abaco for seven short miles, especially when the ferry crosses four times a day. But that's how it was, at least at first.

Before long, we found ourselves facing another problem. The Postmistress quit and no one was appointed to take her place. However inside that neat little pink building there was mail in most of the slots, a large mailbag unopened in the middle of the floor, but no one to unlock the door so folks could retrieve what was rightfully theirs. I couldn't help but wonder what was in there or just what emergency epistle might belong to us.

Eventually the door was opened and folks gathered up their cards, letters, notices of late bills, threats of power or phone shut-offs and whatever else had been sent their way weeks before. Then the door was once again locked and stayed lock. That meant back to Marsh Harbour and another post office box.

The other half of that new little pink building, the police station, was also closed because we had no policeman. We had no policeman because we had almost no crime. If something should happen that needed police attention, they would send officers over from Marsh Harbour. The only time I was aware of just how that worked involved a fellow from a neighboring island.

Apparently he had been into some heavy drinking and decided to go into one of the rooms in a vacant resort. He probably would have done no damage, just stayed there to sleep it off. That would have worked if he had been alone, but when his hiding place was discovered unfortunately for him he had an under-aged female with him. There was no question that the 'girl's irate mother would immediately file an official complaint. This meant that police officers had to come on the very next ferry to interview witnesses, take statements and make an arrest if one was necessary.

It would have been a simple process if the ferry captain had not refused to let the policemen board the ferry. The government is responsible for paying ferry costs for officials, but this ferry captain decided they couldn't board because the government had really poor credit, and already owed the ferry company big bucks. Glenn solved the problem quite quickly by borrowing $60 from Uncle Leonard to cover all costs. Needless to say, the one to lose out on this deal was good old Uncle Leonard. It was an unusual situation and didn't point to any need for us to have a policeman on Guana Cay. Be that as it may, we still had a pretty little pink empty police station right next to a pretty little pink empty post office.

We didn't, however, have a medical clinic. We had one once that was opened two days a week for a couple of hours, for emergencies. If you were to have an emergency, I guess you had to plan it for either a Tuesday or a Thursday from 11:00 a.m. to 2:30 p.m.

Hurricane Floyd came through and destroyed the little building that housed the clinic, so that was that. I have no idea why someone 'didn't decide that the new little empty pink building could be used for a medical clinic. Even if it were only open as it was before, it sure as heck would be better than nothing. Perhaps because we had a good rescue squad with a pickup truck and a retired dentist on the island, they figured we were covered.

The Postal Service is not the only thing the government owns and operates—so is the telephone company—BATELCO, the electric company—BEC, and an airline—BAHAMASAIR.

BATELCO was up for sale to any private group that wanted to run it. Listening to the radio one day I heard a great statement from a government official. He was opposed to privatizing. He claimed that BATELCO was doing a wonderful job. After all, they were making a profit even, if they were OVERCHARGING THE CUSTOMERS. He thought they should be given another chance before turning it over to aliens! Well who knows, maybe "aliens" could make the real phones work on a regular basis and figure out why some cell phones worked and other didn't.

There was a disparity between cell phones of the same make. BATELCO had reprogrammed some of the phones for a hefty fee and they still didn't work. Oh well, too bad. It was the owners' fault, not the government entity's. Just another example of "it wasn't me," or I guess in this case, "it wasn't us."

Trying to get an itemized bill is something I guess must also be an unbelievably difficult task. Bob visited the Marsh Harbour office in an attempt to get one of those hot little items. The lady who was supposed to be helping him took a bathroom break and after a twenty minute wait Bob explained he had a ferry to catch. The response from one of her co-workers was, "Well, I guess you'll just have to come back tomorrow."

Now Bob is nobody's fool. He was smart enough not to return the next day but waited for almost a full week before trying it again. Still nothing was ready.

The next effort was a couple of weeks later, on our way to the airport for a brief visit home. Joe Knowles, our usual cab driver, and I very patiently waited outside in the cab for nearly an hour while a not-so-patient Bob waged war inside the office. Finally he returned with two months' of itemized bills, mumbling that he guessed two months out of five was at least a start.

He also returned $1,286 poorer. They couldn't provide any complete information on the calls that were placed, but they sure could figure out a bottom line. We had no idea how real those charges were, but knew that their threat to cut our service was as real as it gets, so you pay. There was no way we could risk having our phones disconnected—AGAIN.

It had happened twice already and both times it was for what they claimed was an unpaid bill of $26.75. Even though we had an escrow account of $400, they couldn't figure out just where it was or how to apply those funds. We also learned of many folks who also had their service disrupted twice just as we had, for an unpaid balance of—you guessed it—$26.75. What an amazing coincidence! They say misery loves company, but not in this case.

Almost as soon as we arrived home, even before unpacking, Bob began to review the two itemized bills, only to discover numerous errors. No big surprise there! The next day the phone calls to the manager began, three in fact. Each time the manager wasn't available but promised to call back. Of course he never did. Next he tried the e-mail route with a request for an answer, but of course there was no answer. His final try was a fax, and the only request was for an acknowledgment that it had been received. You guessed it—there was no acknowledgment. The only choice now was to wait until we returned to continue the battle.

A few months later when our daughter Lisa was visiting, she took a startling phone call from this efficient company. Again they were threatening to disconnect.

"What in the world is wrong now?" she asked.

"It's about your bill," was the reply.

"Look," she said, "My Dad went to your office three days ago and paid all four of the phone bills in full."

"I know but he paid us too much!"

"But if he paid you too much, why in the world would you shut off the service?" she asked.

"Because we don't know what to do with the extra money," was the reply!

"Paying you too much is not like he didn't pay you at all. You can't cut off the phones because of that."

Again the answer was that they didn't know what to do with the extra money.

In a very lengthy discussion, Lisa explained over and over how they could just credit our account with the extra dollars. "It's simple," she said, more than once. "Just subtract that amount from their next bill." They agreed and she honestly believed they "got it."

Oh, that poor innocent child of ours. She honestly believed that they would follow through on her reasonable suggestion. But I honestly believed those extra dollars would end up in the same place as our escrow account, wherever the hell that might be. But of course the good news was she managed to keep our phones on, at least until the next fiasco.

There isn't too much I can share about the government-run airline BAHAMASAIR, only to mention that sometimes they would fly and sometimes they wouldn't. If they did, they most often would not be on time. It might also be interesting to note that on at least a couple of occasions they had actually taken passengers to the wrong destination. Sort of a surprise flight I guess.

Taking passengers to a wrong destination is bad enough, but refusing to let them board could be even worse. In one situation it certainly was. A small family from the Midwest had been planning their Bahamian vacation for almost a year. Their phone calls were full of excitement and we made sure we would be ready for them, their four-year-old son and newly-adopted little daughter. Everything went smoothly on the trip to Florida. Then they attempted to board BAHAMASAIR for the last leg of their journey. They were turned away because their adoption certificate and a letter from a judge stating the documentation was good for travel anywhere in the world wasn't acceptable. There was nothing in Bahamian law that allowed for that. It clearly states a "BIRTH CERTIFICATE" not an "ADOPTION CERTIFICATE." And clearly they must have thought that this little one was a potential terrorist or a drug smuggler.

God knows there was no point in continuing on with their various arguments. There was no way they were going to be allowed to board, so back home went this little family.

There was nothing in the rules and regulations that I could find which would exclude an adoption certificate as valid documentation. I believed that it was a case of a ticket agent being too damn lazy to pick up the phone and check with someone. The family had turned around and gone home, so there was nothing we could do to change the situation. Perhaps the best we could hope for was to make sure it didn't happen again.

I immediately sent an e-mail to the then Chairman of the Board of BAHAMASAIR to register a complaint and voice my concerns. If adoption certificates were not valid, then they certainly should let folks know—put it in writing along with all the other rules, regulations and instructions for what is needed to enter the country. I also suggested that perhaps they should check their staff, find out which ones were too busy chatting on the phone or gabbing with boyfriends or polishing their nails to pay attention to passengers' needs.

He responded in a positive manner, thanked me for pointing out the problem, and assured me he would see that it didn't happen again. It was only after I had contacted him that folks informed me some of his own children had been adopted. Apparently that was helpful in getting this problem solved. Since there seemed to be fewer complaints about this airline as time went on, perhaps they had improved their service. I just can't say for sure, but by suggesting that, I might avoid getting sued!

Now it's time for me to write a disclaimer of sorts. I do recognize that even at home in the good old USA, privately-run companies and services for the most part do a much better job than those that are government-owned and -operated. In the private sector there isn't the needless red tape and hoops to jump through that are an integral part of any bureaucracy. However if you think it is all *kerpunkled up* at home, you ain't seen nothing.

Unfortunately, here it is not just government services that get bogged down, ignore you, or make unfilled promises—it's the norm.

I realize that nearly two-thirds of these reminiscences are already about power failures. This is yet just another one, only this time we couldn't blame BEC. I suppose I could have pointed a finger at the phone company, BATELCO, but they really didn't cause the problem—they just put the wheels in motion.

All the phone equipment was housed in a shed out back. Not just the lines for the Inn, but also the lines for almost all of our neighbors. There were times when the lines were so full of static that it was impossible to carry on a conversation if you were lucky enough to make a connection. Both Bob and Larry were certain that replacing one of the existing circuit boards would solve the problem, but BATELCO disagreed

Out the workers would come, pull on a few wires, jiggle this or jiggle that, and decide everything was now okay. There would be a little improvement, but even that would last only a few days. Back they would come and go through the same exercise. Replacing that circuit board would really have been a simple job, but they sure weren't about to tackle it. They just liked to jiggle around, I guess. Because Bob could not get the workers to listen, he decided his best bet was to go to the "higher ups."

He went over to Marsh Harbour, spoke to the managers, and made a good solid case for the circuit board replacement, but it got him absolutely nowhere. They now insisted we needed a whole new cable, and if we didn't follow through there was nothing they could do. We would just have to live with the connection the way it was, meaning I guess that they wouldn't even send the "jigglers" over anymore.

Bob purchased the 275 feet of phone cable and hired the best man on the island to come and dig the trench. There were no maps, no schematics, no plot plans to show where everything was buried, so it really wasn't the fault of the guy on the backhoe when he cut our power lines in half. Both power lines were cut right in half, the one from BEC as well as the one from our own generator. We were in big trouble—*ceris* trouble—and the only one we could think of was Peter. Maybe Peter could lend us a hand.

Thankfully Bob was able to contact him and went on his way to Marsh Harbour to pick him up. Peter was willing to come on over, stay overnight and was also quite confident that he would have all the necessary repairs done by early the next afternoon. I guess that was before he discovered the illegal wiring.

"Bob, I am really concerned about the big Country and Western Rib Night we have planned."

"Don't panic," he answered. "If Peter says he can be done by three in the afternoon, he can."

"But even if he can, we will be trying to prepare all the food in a dark kitchen. It is a rather big undertaking, in case you haven't noticed. And what if he CAN'T? Just suppose he CAN'T, then what?"

"I think I'll change the date. Call those who have reserved and announce over the VHF that our Rib Night will not be this Saturday. 'We'll hold it on Tuesday."

"Change it to Tuesday and I bet you won't get anybody!"

"Bet I will!"

"Bet you won't!"

Peter, along with Bob and Larry were on the job by 7:00 a.m. At 11:00 p.m. they decided to call it quits. Not only did the challenge involve repairing lines, but a total rewiring of the Inn was absolutely necessary. Peter just couldn't understand what in hell the prior owner was thinking. The way the place had been wired, he was surprised someone hadn't been electrocuted or the place hadn't gone up in flames.

Bob's first task in the morning was to head back to Marsh Harbour. Now we needed 275 feet of electric cables, new panels, and a bunch of other electrical stuff. Just about a new everything was necessary for the job to get done correctly. Peter stayed with us for another couple of days until he got us back in good shape. He mentioned he'd like to come back tomorrow, which was Tuesday, shut everything down to recheck, and double check it all.

"Are you sure we are now safe?" I asked.

"You sure are," he answered.

"Then please don't come back until Wednesday," I pleaded. "I changed our Rib Night for tomorrow and we are already fully booked. I don't want to take any chances of being without power for even an hour or two."

My only regret at this point in time was that I had not bet Mr. Bob real money on just how many would attend the affair on a Tuesday. We actually had to turn folks away. After two days of darkness and almost $3,000, BATELCO informed us that a new cable probably hadn't been necessary after all. They then declared that if that one circuit board had been replaced, it probably would have been good enough. Ask me if Bob was smiling?

On the other hand, I decided, in my somewhat simple mind, that we had been deliberately pushed into this fiasco so that the wiring problem could be brought to our attention and corrected, keeping us safe. You know the old Pollyanna attitude, "Everything happens for the best"." Well, I believed this was one of those things!

CHAPTER 21

Left in the Dark

BEC had a couple of really dedicated workers, Lenny and Peter, who were usually assigned to this island. An occasional blackout is accepted and understood, but when they are frequent and prolonged it's these two guys who take the brunt of the screaming and yelling.

There was a time when we had power outages five days out of seven. Thank God the Inn had a generator. As long as it didn't leak oil, run out of fuel, overheat, and kept chugging along, our guests at the Inn would be comfortable.

The guests in the cottages weren't quite so lucky. Only one of the six adjacent cottages had its own generator. The others did not. However, they were all tied into our water supply, so they could at least wash their faces, brush their teeth, and flush the toilet. Not true of the seventh cottage, the one called "The Big Yellow Ocean House." There was no separate generator, and it was just a little too far to be tied into our water system.

During the day most guests were off exploring, enjoying any number of things, so as long as there was sunshine, nobody cared. Once the sun set, it was a little different story. The first day of this off-again on-again power the guests in the Yellow Ocean House became most inventive. They cooked on the grills by flashlight or candlelight, the kids played hide and seek in the dark and told stories, even spooky ones. It was considered quite the adventure. However, the next night wasn't quite so much fun. They began to feel like enough was enough.

Those that had battery-operated radios were all over the VHF asking the expected questions—checking to see just who had power and who didn't. In this case, all of Guana Cay was in the dark.

"Has anyone seen BEC?"

"Have they sent anyone over from Marsh Harbour?"

"What's the problem, how long is this going to last?"

"Are Lenny or Peter on the island?"

We could recognize just who was checking in by their call signs. There was "Young Lovers," "Ocean View," "Blueberry Hill," "Baharini," "November Rain," "Coco Paradise," "Nippers," "Aquarian," "Dolphin Beach," "Longview," and "Wind Chimes." There was also "Captain's Point," "Twin Beaches," "Ridge House," "Bay View," "Poor Boy," "Flying Dogs," "Pirates Crossing," "Nut House" and many others, with "Guana Seaside Village" right in the middle of it all.

We were not only all over the VHF but Bob was all over the phones, calling every BEC manager he had a number for. He repeatedly called not only Marsh Harbour but Nassau as well. Unfortunately, but not unexpectedly, not a single higher-up answered the phone.

Nothing we could do but wait for the workers—wait for poor Lenny and Peter. All of us had great respect for these two. We understood how hard they worked, how hard they tried, and we also understood they had little at their disposal to work with. The necessary equipment was either outdated or nonexistent. There were times when they had to borrow tools or even a simple thing like a ladder. That probably explains why they, along with other workers, raised hell when all the BEC managers were given new cars to cruise around in. But then I digress, back to the guests.

We asked the guests at the Inn, including my cousins Laurie and Sonny, if we could borrow the cushions off their pull-out sleepers, providing of course they weren't using them. Everyone was more than willing and pleased to pitch in. They helped drag those cushions to the only vacant room available and even helped spread them out on the floor here and there and everywhere. We then invited the guests from the Big Yellow House down for a sleep over. A little crowded we all had to admit, but at least they had an air conditioner that worked, could take a shower, brush their teeth and even flush the toilet.

The kids loved it—thought it was just one more part of an exciting adventure, and the adults were stoic about this turn of events. "After all," they said, "what's one more night?"

The power came on during the day and the cheering sounded loud and clear over that old VHF. But then nightfall came, and we were back in the dark.

By the fourth night, our guests were a little tired of dragging down their pillows, pajamas and toothbrushes, and we were damn tired of dragging cushions back and forth.

It was interesting, but when power was finally restored no one could identify what the problem had been. Even Lenny and Peter couldn't figure out what happened, so they didn't really fix anything. But for some mysterious reason we had power! Now our job was to pray that it stayed on.

This wasn't a usual happening. Power may go off for a few minutes, a few hours or perhaps the better part of a single day, but this was the first time that we had to struggle for days. Now when there is an expected power failure, BEC announces over the VHF how long they think it will be off and the reasons why. Interesting, but they start those warnings by saying, "The power will be out at Seaside Village and other parts of the island." Nice to be given special recognition and I suspect it was the result of Bob's constant calls. Bob's calls didn't stop when the power came on. They continued until he got folks in Marsh Harbour and Nassau to answer their "god damn" phones.

Even after the apparent hardships for the guests in the Big Yellow House, they said they still enjoyed their visit. They were grateful for the extra efforts we had made and said they would certainly return. They also stated that they were going to write a scathing letter to BEC, so we gladly gave them the address as well as the address for the Minister of Tourism. After all, we reasoned, two letters might be better than one. I didn't have the heart to tell them that BEC would probably read those letters with the same frame of mind as they answer their phone calls.

CHAPTER 22

Meet the Families

There are only about five prominent families that make up the native population of Guana Cay. There are the Pinders, the Roberts, the Sands, the Alburys and the Bethels, all life-long residents of the island

Ted and Todd, of the Sands family tree, are twin brothers who were among those native to the island. There are several different branches of Sands and after six years I am still unable to distinguish who was who. I think they are all related somehow but have never been sure just who was an uncle, who was a father, who was a mother, who were the cousins, or who the brothers and sisters were. But both Bob and I enjoyed them all for different reasons and in different ways.

Ted and Todd were most always together and whenever I see them they greet me with a big smile, a wave and a loud, "Hello Sweetie." I always answer with "Hello TEDTODD" because I 'can't tell them apart.

There is Earl who always smiles but never says a thing unless prompted. There is Raymond—I went to his wedding, met his wife there, but have never seen her ever again.

There is Suzanne, Jeffery, Clint, Mitchell. Joshua, Brandon, Baby

Summer, Shawna, Steve, Jimmy, Blake. And I am sure some others that all fit on that part of the family tree. There is Junior, Tressa, Henry, Rita, Tasha, Ricky, Alton, his wife Laura and their daughter Ami Lee—all on a different branch, I think.

Donna Sands has the golf cart concession and also leads and is involved in most community projects. Even though Glenn is the duly-elected Island Councilor, folks often turn to Donna when they want something accomplished. Her husband Charles is the major contractor for this island and others. Donna's sister Jackie is married to Charles' brother Andy and when Donna fully retires her niece Mindy takes over running the golf cart business. They are on a Sands tree, but I've no idea which branch to hang them on. I guess it would be safe to say I could hang the men on a quiet branch because neither Charles nor Andy talks very much. In fact they hardly talk at all—they just leave what needs to be said up to Donna and Jackie.

Then of course there is our dear and loyal friend Uncle Leonard—he's a Sands as well. So then are his wife, his twin sons Christopher and Craig, and his daughters Tiffany and Gina. Craig's wife Tammy was a Bethel before she married and her parents Robert and Madge also live here on Guana. Every place you go it seems like a family reunion. Uncle Leonard also has grandkids who are on Guana. There is Cloe, Aidrian ,Shannon, and Shania.

I think somehow all of the above belong on Uncle Leonard's branch. But since Gina married Ronald, who is a Roberts, and her sister Tiffany also married a Roberts, perhaps I have some of them up the wrong tree.

I suppose I could start to list all those on the Roberts tree, but quite frankly I am confused enough as it is. In fact I am wondering even now if I haven't already made a mistake. Maybe my friend, good old silent Earl, isn't a Sands after all; maybe he is a Roberts, but now that I really think about, it he might even be a Bethel. It really doesn't matter—he is a friend!

Johnny is the heart and soul of Nippers, the world famous beach bar and grill. It is no longer surprising to see someone sporting a Nippers t-shirt in numerous airports or on many city streets. There is even now a Nippers replica at the Hooters resort in Las Vegas. That kind of success doesn't just happen. It is the result of not only Johnny's efforts but the hard work of his family.

His father was usually on hand just to make sure things were going right. Bob would often tease him and claim he was only there to count the money. His mother Jackie, sister Christine, and brother Anthony were also around to lend a hand when needed. However, it didn't end with just his immediate family. His wife Jenesse was clearly his right hand "man" and his in-laws Bill and Annette were also doing all they could to be helpful and supportive.

Friday night was Chicken in the Bag Night at Nippers. It really was just fried chicken and French fries wrapped in foil. They would add whatever you liked—hot sauce, ketchup, whatever—or keep it plain. Simple enough but always tasty, and that along with plenty of music managed to draw a Friday night crowd. However the crowd was a small one compared with Pig Roast Sunday.

Pig Roast Sunday was always a madhouse. Local folks, tourists, second home owners, along with hundreds of people who came over on ferries all converged on Nippers to enjoy the menu and the loud and lively band.

At the Inn we always encouraged our guests to get up there to check things out and even provided them with transportation. And on Sunday mornings when I made my usual VHF announcement, I also encouraged those listening not to miss it. However, I did conclude by saying that if any of those listening had already been there and done that and were looking for a quiet peaceful alternative, Seaside Village was the place to be.

That worked well. Not only those who weren't feeling up to repeating the Nippers experience (mostly people my age), but those who were at Nippers for a while and wanted a quiet place to recuperate joined us. Although there weren't hundreds of folks, those who came our way kept our courtyard, pool and bar full. I felt good about supporting our "competition" and at the same time subtly taking care of our own business.

The only time there weren't hundreds of folks for Nippers to tend to was during a Barefoot Man concert, when there would be 2,000 plus. And on Easter Sunday for their famous Easter Egg Hunt there would be easily 1,000. People came from everywhere and who could blame them?

The beach was sectioned off in age-appropriate blocks with signs designating which children should hunt where. Johnny would use a loud speaker to give the start time and also encourage parents to let the little ones find their own eggs. It was great fun to watch hundreds of little kids scrambling all over the beach. Many were ignoring the boundaries and just as many parents not heeding the plea to let the kids find their own eggs.

Those ages nine to eleven hunted for the eggs on the water's edge. Older than that, they swam out to the reef with snorkeling gear to look for treasures. These hunters not only included young kids but adults as well.

Each egg had a number written inside with indelible ink and there were charts developed to identify just what those numbers stood for. It took several pages with an assortment of letters and numbers to cross off as prizes were claimed. It also took several days for members of the Roberts family to mark the eggs and coordinate the pages.

Prizes included kites, beach toys, decks of cards, free sodas, hats, t-shirts, games, beach balls, snorkeling gear, kites, flags, large and extra large Easter Baskets and many other types of goodies. Most thought that the best eggs of all were the money eggs. Some eggs were $20 eggs, others $50 and still others were worth $100.

Starting out, two people would attempt to open the eggs, read the number, find it on the charts and pass out the prizes. When the lines got just a little too long, a third person would jump in. The actual egg hunt started at noon and went until 5:00 p.m. That made for a long day, but just imagine how many long days and some nights went into the preparation for this grand affair. And grand it always was year after year!

There were also some interesting and somewhat amusing cases of what might be called Bahamian "Pioneer Justice."

A young couple was building two rental homes adjacent to Nippers. During the entire process, Nippers was there to meet their needs and help in anyway they could. The couple had free phone privileges, were allowed to have supplies delivered there, were given road access across land owned by Nippers, and when the projects were completed they used, free of charge, Nippers' credit card machine.

This was not at all unlike the folks at Nippers. They always did whatever they could do to be of help to any on the island who needed it.

One day a fellow named Aubrey with his old rickety pickup truck, without a muffler, was collecting garbage from Nippers to take to the dock containers. The gal who had built next door apparently found the whole thing unacceptable. Instead of raising the issue with the folks at Nippers, who had been so good to her, she decided to go to Marsh Harbour and register a formal complaint. She went to the authorities and complained about air pollution, noise pollution and I guess a number of other things. The authorities contacted Nippers and made them aware of what had come to their attention.

Shortly after that there was a backhoe digging a hole and piling up the large mounds of dirt to completely shut off the access road that was on Nippers' land. Not even a golf cart could reach those two new houses. And Michael, one of the owners and Johnny's father, just stood by that backhoe with a grin a mile wide. When anyone asked Michael what happened he responded simply "I dug a hole, I dug a big hole."

It took a great deal of time and effort before that couple could finally develop a new way in and out to their properties. No big arguments—nothing, it just happened. Like I said, I called it Bahamian Pioneer Justice. Bob just commented that anyone should know better than to get in a fight with a 4,000-pound gorilla.

I suspect that a common sense approach to justice is passed down from one generation to the next. Can't believe that there are any genetics involved, but it is there nonetheless. Johnny took his turn at executing a little of that Justice and the target was one of his employees.

Nardise was a Haitian who had legally worked for Johnny a number of years. He was one of those called "straight" ones. Out of compassion Johnny had built him a small house to live in. Often Nardise would ask to borrow Johnny's golf cart, and of course the request was granted. However, one night Nardise just grabbed the cart, took off and was gone for a mighty long time. So long in fact that when Johnny closed the bar and was ready to go home, he had no way to get there. He waited and waited. And while he waited, he decided to go to the small house he had built for Nardise, take off the door, remove a couple of windows and throw Nardise's belongings outside.

The next morning Nardise was wailing and crying: "Mr. Johnny he broke my house. Mr. Johnny he broke my house!"

Johnny's only response was, "You're lucky. If I had the truck here I would have taken down the whole damn thing!"

Needless to say, Johnny helped repair the damage, and needless to say, Nardise also learned a lesson—a lesson he's not apt to forget. Don't ever take something that doesn't belong to you without permission. How difficult can that be?

I have already shared the sagas of Michael Roberts and his son Johnny and their brand of Guana Pioneer Justice. However there is much more to share about that branch of the Roberts family tree.

There is one other real Roberts I want to tell you about. His name is Mickey and everyone knows him. He is a bartender at Nippers and always has a joke or a story. Sometimes the jokes are the kind you could repeat to your kids or your elderly aunts, and there is the other kind! He really is a good bartender most of the time, but when he is either tired or cranky he just shuts everything down. The lights go out, the music stops and the crowd is invited to go on their merry way.

At one time Mickey worked with his Dad, Tommy. They owned a nice place called Coco Paradise. Coco Paradise rented neat cottages, had a beach bar, a beautiful view of the Atlantic Ocean and a great span of pristine beach. The beach was still there but the view became obstructed when Tommy re-married and his new wife wanted to build a pavilion-like structure. It was massive with long picnic tables, benches, a kitchen, a wraparound railing, and an inside bar. The view from the pavilion was just fine, but nothing except this massive structure could be viewed from the cottages.

I heard it stated that the whole goal of this expansion was to give Nippers a run for its money. Not everyone involved thought that was an admirable goal or even a reasonable idea. Mickey didn't think you should try to sabotage relatives and after all, his Dad and Nipper's' Michael were brothers, making him and Johnny' cousins. In one of his weak moments, Mickey explained to me how he had warned his Dad, even begged him not to marry "that woman." It was obvious from the very beginning that they were not going to have a warm loving stepson-stepmother relationship.

The cottages weren't renting as well as they had in the past, and with everything else that was going on, upkeep didn't seem to be a priority. The scheme to put Johnny, Michael, and Nippers out of business was a horrible blunder and a failing. To compound things, a chef was hired to run the new kitchen. He was supposed to be a first-class chef. He could cook okay, but he could steal even better. Every time Mickey pointed out that he was robbing them blind, he was completely ignored.

Things went from bad to worse. A divorce was now in the mix, the "stepmother" left the country and Tommy returned to Nassau to resume some former business activities. Mickey along with Aubrey tried for a while to keep things up and running, but the bar was the only thing left that amounted too much. Finally Coco Paradise was sold. The pavilion with all its "amenities" was demolished. The cottages were completely renovated and the new owners named it "Flip Flops on the Beach." I'm not sure the name is a great one, but the new look is.

Mickey is living in a delightful home on Captain's Point. The home is owned by a great American couple named Patricia and Captain Bob who live on the island year round. He seems content working with his Uncle Michael and his cousin Johnny, but I wonder if he ever thinks about what was or what could have been.

There is one thing I am quite certain of. If the romance between our granddaughter Kristen and Blake, who really is a Sands, leads to something permanent, then things could get really confused. If the Sands Clan and the Sylvester Clan are somehow joined together, there would not be a person in the world who could sort out who is who.

The Pinders are also well known on the island. Cheri Pinder taught in Guana's one-room schoolhouse for years. She is now in Florida for health reasons, and Guana has to rely on different teachers from different places. They do an excellent job, but are not long-timers so it doesn't seem quite the same. Cheri really was the heart and soul of the little school.

Every place you look you'll see a Pinder real estate sign. It doesn't matter if it is a house for sale or a lot for sale. It also doesn't seem to matter if there are already other real estate signs posted. Ed Pinder just sticks up one of his own. He figures that since he is right there on the island and he spots a potential buyer, he has the right to jump right in and try to make the sale. Not to worry, he'll straighten out the commission details later.

They have a son who was the chef at the Blue Water Grill, a daughter who is a Wedding Planner and two baby grandsons. However, the most famous Pinder of all is a legend by the name of Milo. There is hardly a tourist, second-home owner, or visiting boater who does not know Milo. He has a fruit and vegetable stand in the heart of town. And since he grows a variety of vegetables in raised beds, they are always fresh and usually plentiful. He also sells fresh fish when his realtor brother Ed has time to catch a few. If you go for fish and he hasn't any, he won't let you leave until he has talked you into a lobster or two. The price for the lobsters might be a little high but at least he won't let you walk away empty-handed. He also makes shell jewelry, coconut figures and sells t-shirts and paintings.

One day, coming back from the local grocery store I spotted Milo sitting patiently behind his little booth. I hadn't purchased anything in the last couple of days and was feeling a little guilty.

"Stop," I told the girls. "I have to buy at least something from Milo."

I picked out a small handful of cherry tomatoes and asked what they would cost.

"Nothing, Miss Gerry, you and Mr. Bob are good people. Besides, he brings me a lot of seeds for my garden. Nothing, nothing, you don't owe me nothing, I like you good people."

"Come on now, Milo. I'm glad you like us, but you're in business so how much for these tomatoes?"

Without batting an eye he answered $7.

I gulped twice then passed him a $10 bill.

"For that," he said, "I'll give you something extra." And then he smiled and threw a papaya in the bag. No change, just a papaya, and a pretty old one at that.

When I got back in the van, the girls were doubled over with fits of laughter.

"You sure drive a hard bargain, Ma," was their only comment.

"You just don't bargain in a situation like that. I would feel really cheap if I had stood there and dickered with Milo about the price of a few little cherry tomatoes!"

I would not only highly recommend Great Guana for a vacation spot or a neat place to buy a second home, I would also suggest that if you ever get that way to make sure and introduce yourself to one Mr. Milo Pinder. He really is a Guana fixture and a delightful gentleman.

Although there are also many members of the Bethel family, like Johnny, Marlene, their children, Brianna and John John, there are two special ones you should get to know.

Miss Emily is warm, friendly and always smiling. She makes everyone she meets feel as if they are right at home and is the 'island's creative cake maker. She makes wedding cakes, shower cakes, birthday cakes and anniversary masterpieces. She'd make whatever you'd like—just describe it and she'll decorate it to your liking. And then there is her other half, Sylvon.

Since Sylvon owns and operates the Corner Harbor Grocery Store that provides all the staples for the island, you would be hard pressed not to meet him. But in addition to his role as grocer, he also plays a key role for the little church. He is responsible for the Sunday services and along with Miss Emily he arranges for the evening meetings. He makes arrangements for the visiting reverends that come from far and wide, and he acts as sort of a host and a master of ceremony. He made sure new visitors were introduced and repeat ones from past years were welcomed back. He would lead us in prayers for those that needed our special attention and made sure we sang Happy Birthday for anyone who had celebrated one in the week past. He led us in other songs as well, and even on occasion paid attention to special requests.

"We will now sing hymn number 91," he announced when a little voice in the back of the church shouted, "Sing 'Jesus Lubs Me.'"

"Did I hear a request from the back?" he asked.

"SING 'JESUS LUBS ME!'" came back even louder the three year-old named Chloe.

There was no question that we were all to close our song books and sing "Jesus Lubs Me" loud and clear.

I am hoping that sharing just that one story will give you a picture of the value placed on the children. They are recognized, listened to and included. There are many more examples, but that one sort of sums it up.

Even the smallest children attend most of the service and are amazingly well behaved. If the babies fuss a bit, or those a tiny bit older talk out loud, no one scorns them or even scowls. And when it comes time for them, even those in kindergarten or first grade, to read their favorite Bible verse, everyone sits quietly and listens patiently.

Usually their verse is written out by their parents in block letters on small pieces of paper. They not only read their verse but they also identify the chapter and verse that it comes from. It takes a little time for them to get the words out, but they are always pleased with their accomplishments. Over the years I watched those little ones grow past the need to hold on to their little pieces of paper. They just opened up their Bibles and read. Somehow I most always found their readings more meaningful than those of the adults. There is Sunday School of course, and when they all parade out before the sermon begins, dressed as if every Sunday was Easter Sunday, everyone is smiling.

Every Easter there is a sunrise service. I don't care how much hell you raised the night before—if you really wanted your battery charged, your feet to be firmly planted, or a trip back to what is real, then the sunrise service is a must do. It is held at a place on the southern end of the island called High Rocks. High Rock had been for years a favorite spot for the locals, tourists, and second-home owners. Everyone went to High Rocks to sit on the beach, have a picnic, or snorkel. That was before the Orchid Bay Marina and Resort developed. Then things began to change.

As lots were sold and expensive homes began to crop up here and there, the owners of Orchid Bay decided to put up a big iron gate and hire gatekeepers. Now for a simple swim, a family picnic, or even to visit one of the homeowners that might be a friend of yours, it is necessary to go to the office, declare your intent, and hope to be given a pass. That pass had to be shown to whoever was on duty. There was at least one gatekeeper you usually had to wake up so you could show him your pass. Then and only then would he open up the damn gate and let you in.

But Easter Sunday is a different story. Jimmy, who manages the resort, opens everything up so anyone who wants to enjoy the sunrise service can just go right on through, just like the old times. He also provides coffee, juices, and an assortment of breakfast pastries for everyone to enjoy. The rest of the morning affair is arranged by Sylvon with the help of church volunteers, and as he would surely say with the help of the Lord.

He brings a portable keyboard for Lynn who always provides the piano music for the regular church services. He brings along the visiting minister and printed song sheets. A large wooden cross is placed on the top of those magnificent high rocks and everyone waits for the sun to come up. Trying to tell you what it really is like would be like trying to describe the song of the nightingale by writing down the sharps and the flats.

As the sun slowly makes its way over the horizon, it bathes the cross with a beautiful and stunning light. Regardless of what you might believe or not believe, it is an awesome, inspirational and moving tableau. No matter how many folks are crowded around, during those first few moments there is always complete silence. You can hear those around you taking deep breaths, relax a little, then grab the song sheets and try to sing.

"It is really a good thing that those two people over there know how to sing. It helps the rest of us we can just follow their lead," This was a casual comment I over heard.

"They ought to know what they are doing—after all they, are part of the church choir," someone responded.

I knew they were referring to Ruth and Henry Sands and couldn't help but put in my two-cents worth.

"They aren't just part of the church choir, they ARE the church choir."

That was for the most part absolutely true. There would be times in church when Sylvon would announce that we would now listen to the quartet and three people would step forward. Or he might announce that we would now have the pleasure of listening to a trio and two people would make their way up to the microphones.

This didn't happen very often, but no matter what number was called, or if a singer were missing, there was always Ruth and Henry up front for us to count on, and they were most often joined by Miss Emily.

If you come to Guana Cay and would like to do some deep-sea fishing, you should look up Henry Sands. He is the best captain and guide around. Just don't expect him to be available on a Sunday, because he will be busy singing in the chapel.

Once in a great while, when no visiting reverend, minister or preacher—whatever name we called them—wasn't available, Sylvon would simply play a video and the service would go along as usual.

And only once in a great while did we wish we had a video to watch rather than listen to the preacher addressing us.

On one such occasion, some people were struggling to follow along in their Bibles the passages the preacher was quoting. They sat there frantically flipping the pages, but to no avail. Others fell asleep, and at least one man named Bob sat grumbling and getting more depressed by the minute. As we left the chapel this preacher was telling us to make a promise to God.

"Make a promise to God," he kept insisting.

Once outside, Lisa turned to me and said, "Mom, I have already made my promise to God."

"You have Lisa? And what might that be?"

"I promised God I would never come here again!"

Of course that wasn't true. She was there the following Sunday morning and whenever she was on the island and we both could get free from the Inn, we went to church.

Bob didn't go back immediately; for a few weeks he made up excuses. Finally he got back on track. But before he loaded himself in the golf cart to head for the chapel, he would have already checked with several regular church-going friends to find out what they knew or thought about that week's visiting preacher. When they told him he would really enjoy this one, then he'd gladly go. When the answer was that he'd better stay away this week because they were afraid he might once again get depressed, he just as gladly stayed away.

I enjoyed the service whenever I had the chance to attend. I found it uplifting and usually left with a message that served as gentle reminder about the necessity of caring, sharing, being kind and nonjudgmental. I left feeling happy, not just because of the service and the message but also because it gave me a chance to sit with my young friend Shannon.

CHAPTER 23

My Buddy

It wasn't long after we took over the Inn that I met Shannon, a 15 year old student at the Every Child Counts School in Marsh Harbour. Part of the program included learning some work skills and Shannon was to work with us at the Inn for a couple of hours a day, two or three days a week. We folded napkins, polished silver, set up the tables and did other assorted chores. Her favorite day was when the freight arrived. She was always very curious about what was in the boxes and crates. She loved to stack those dozens of eggs in neat rows in the refrigerator, and if we had a shipment of oranges she insisted we grab a couple and go out on the lawn to play catch.

The first day she was with us she "worked" for about an hour.

"What do you think I owe you, Shannon?" I asked.

"Thirty dollars," was her very rapid response, but she settled for three.

We settled into a fairly simple routine. The first half of the time we did chores, the last half she worked on her homework. That wasn't always what she really wanted to do, so often homework time started out with excuses.

"I can't do homework today because I have to leave early. So call my Mummy to come and get me!"

"And just why to you have to leave early?" I would ask. The answers would vary but not a one held an ounce of truth.

Perhaps a good example was the time she told me she had to leave because she was going to be in the Christmas play at Church and they were practicing that night. That was hard for me to swallow since it was in the middle of April. There were a few more excuses about as far-fetched as that one, but once she realized I might be a little hard to fool she settled down nicely.

There were times when she didn't come to "work," she just came to play. The pool was there for her to splash around in all the time shouting "Watch me, Miss Gerry! Watch me!" At times there were sea grapes she wanted to pick for her grandmother. Often she would wander out on the dock to lift up the trap door at the end of so she could feed the fish. One day when the barracuda that hung around splashed up close to the trap door opening, scaring us both to death, she spent the next several hours sitting there with a makeshift pole in hand in a vain attempt to catch him. Whenever she was here and no matter what she was up to, I enjoyed her. We were really friends and that friendship was clearly evident in church.

Each Sunday we managed to sit side by side. If I arrived first, she'd find me; and if she got there before I did, I'd find her. At first she needed some help in finding the right page in the hymnal, but as time went by she not only could find the right place but began to reach over and show me just which page I should be on. That may seem trivial but it wasn't not for Shannon. It pointed out the progress she was making—progress that I found heartwarming. We sang together, bowed our heads in prayer together, and perhaps I shouldn't mention this but we also laughed together.

The laughter wasn't the out-loud kind. We would just look at each other see the facial expressions, the raised eyebrows, the mouths closed tightly so no sounds could escape, and with our heads bent slightly we both knew exactly what we were sharing. There was never anything really spectacular, just little happenings; a small child climbing all over a bigger sibling, another one leaning over the pew trying to play peek-a-boo with someone sitting behind her and the parent struggling to get her to turn front and center.

There were talkers also, children who would every once in a while babble something out loud. No one would pay attention, unless of course it was Shannon and I. We did our silent laughter when a lady lost her hat, when we saw someone sleeping, when Bob was to read a short biblical verse and went on and on reading a whole lengthy chapter, and, sadly, whenever he sang loudly. If I explain that when Bob was a little kid in school and everyone got to sing, he was made a designated listener, then perhaps you'll understand.

Shannon graduated from the Every Child Counts program. She was one of three students in the first graduation of the school's twelve-year history.

She is tall, quite stately, pretty, and looked very proud in her cap and gown. She now works as an apprentice in another school setting in Marsh Harbour, working with younger kids. Needless to say I am quite proud of her, my friend, my buddy. Shannon is on her way.

CHAPTER 24

They Come from Far and Near

Each Spring, Nippers hosts a concert featuring the Barefoot Man. He actually lives in the Cayman Islands, but since he was originally from the Abacos everyone considers him their local celebrity, their hometown hero, their real live "Jimmy Buffet." Special ferries run all day long so that literally thousands can enjoy his performances.

The Barefoot Man

Nippers

The day before the scheduled concert he was riding a regular ferry along with two of our guests—Abe and Myra Sternberg, a delightful older couple from Connecticut. They were paying their first visit to the Abacos and headed for our Inn. When they reached the Settlement dock, Abe turned to the Barefoot Man and said, "Here boy, take care of my bags."

The Barefoot man obliged, picked up the bags and threw them up on the dock. That, after all, is how bags from the ferry are usually taken care of.

"No, no, not like that!" shouted Abe, "Carry them up to the end of the dock."

The Barefoot Man, being the sport that he is, once more obliged, and Abe out of gratitude tipped him $1. The next day Myra decided they should go to the concert. They wouldn't stay long, just long enough to get a glimpse of this oh-so-famous artist. So off they went to Nippers. They saw the crowds, listened to the cheering and yelling, and watched people push forward to get an autograph. When it finally dawned on Myra just who was the center of attention, she said, "Oh my gosh, Abe, isn't that the man you asked to carry our bags?"

"Oh, you are right Myra. That certainly is."

They stayed for only a short while, returned to the Inn, and retired to their room.

Following the concert, the Barefoot Man and his entourage came over to sit at the bar and relax a little. This was something he usually did and it delighted us. After a short while, out came the Sternbergs to join all the others, and of course they were immediately recognized.

"Hey," said our celebrity, looking directly at Abe, "weren't you the cheap bastard that tipped me a buck?" However, he laughed when he said it, which surely set the tone for the rest of us. Everyone including Myra and Abe laughed over and over again as the story was told and retold. We grabbed the digital camera, got a terrific picture of the three of them, printed it out, and passed it on for a cherished autograph. It was signed, "To Myra and Abe, my dear friends, thanks for the dollar. The BAREFOOT MAN." They couldn't wait to get back to Connecticut to tell the story and show the picture to their "kids."

They told us about another small inn they had visited years ago. It was on a different island but reminded them of the Seaside Village. It also had been off the beaten path at the end of a small dusty little dirt road. The lady who owned the inn had greeted them with a nice big cold rum drink and a native flower. I was thinking what a wonderful idea and was pondering how I could get away with doing something like that myself. Then they continued to tell us other things about this marvelous little place.

One of the things they remembered with a genuine affection was being served dinner by the owners' daughters. They were actually too young to read menus or write down orders, so they merely recited what the dinner offerings were and remembered what the guests had chosen. There were three of them, all blond and beautiful and always dressed alike. One of the favorite outfits Myra and Abe described were little white and red polka dot dresses.

"We often wonder what ever happened to those little girls," Abe mused.

"Well, one of them is sitting here right next to you," came a response.

And sure enough there was one of those "little girls," all grown up of course, but still blond and still beautiful. Needless to say, their afternoon was spent chatting and remembering.

Myra and Abe had been delightful guests, fun and easy going, but when they first arrived I had a surprise from the kitchen.

"Miss Gerry," asked Sandra, "do these guests want some ham or bacon with their breakfast order?"

"I'll ask, but since they are Jewish I really don't thinks so."

"Oh no Miss Gerry. You be *ceris*, that true, Miss Gerry? They be Jewish, that be true?"

"Yes Sandra."

"Where they be staying Miss Gerry. What room they be in?"

"They are in room four, but why do you ask?"

"OH Miss Gerry, you show them to me when they come out because I never did see a Jewish!"

I saw her sneak a peek at the guests from room four, then walked back to her kitchen shaking her head and talking to herself.

"Sandra," I said, "are you surprised that they are just like everyone else?"

"I didn't know, Miss Gerry. I told you I never did see a Jewish before."

CHAPTER 25

Famous or Infamous

I know I promised I would not picture Guana Cay as a mini-Peyton Place, but some things have too much intrigue or are a little too funny or perhaps even a little too sad not to mention.

There was one lady who owned a lot of property and spent a great deal of time on Guana. I felt certain that she was the kind of person who would do just about anything for anyone when she was sober, but then she hardly ever was. Except for a handful of folks who understood her problem and wanted to help, most others just stayed away from her as far as possible. When she was under the influence, she did crazy things.

She always called whoever was speaking to her as her "very, very, very, very, very best friend." And if she was introducing you to someone she'd say, "I want you to meet my dearest, dearest, dearest friend." Then she'd look at them and ask, "What's your name?"

There was a time when she was bringing over some provisions from Marsh Harbour and somehow lost a precious leg of lamb. She really went on a tirade, accusing everyone she knew of stealing her leg of lamb. Friends helped her look. They searched her cupboards, her freezer, even her oven, thinking she might have already cooked it. It was all to no avail.

She continued badgering folks, almost everyone she saw, and even got on the VHF telling the world about her stolen leg of lamb. Then lo and behold, she finally found it sitting in her boat, just where she left it. In fact it had been sitting there in the sun for almost a week, but that did not deter her.

The next thing you knew, she was inviting, in person and over the VHF, just about everyone to come to her house because she would be having a dinner party and proudly announced she would be serving a great leg of lamb

One day she stood by the side of the road and begged anyone who passed by to call 911, but of course there is no such thing as 911 on the island. She was really upset, claiming she was being stalked. The man she thought was stalking her was actually the real estate agent she had asked to come over and evaluate some of the property she might want to sell.

On another occasion she told everyone who would listen about one of her workers who had gotten stuck in her cistern. She had no choice but to hang over the side, breast down, so she could help pull him out. She pressed down so hard that it had caused her breasts to go flat.

At the Inn, I received a call from a friend of hers in Marsh Harbour pleading with me to go and rescue her. She explained that this gal had called a mutual friend of theirs in the states and was hysterically claiming that she had been beaten and raped. She wanted the friend in the states to call 911 and since that wouldn't work, this friend relayed the message to another friend in Marsh Harbour, who then turned to us. It wasn't the first time we heard her make these type of claims, which were false, but damn, who knew? Maybe this time it was real. We decided that Bob should go but certainly not alone, so Janet agreed to go along.

Because it was an interruption of a busy time, Janet commented that if it was another cry wolf, if she really hadn't been beaten, then she'd like to beat her herself. When they arrived, they found the only problem was that she was dead drunk.

I am sure there was a time when she wasn't looked on with disfavor—a time when her reputation was good and solid and people didn't mind being in her company, or didn't shy away. Like anyone who lets the booze take over and does crazy things one after the other, the past really doesn't count. The positive reputation she might have built over her lifetime, all the good she might have done or the good person she might have been, was shot to hell.

There was an exile living on Guana who had been there for some time. It is safer if I don't mention the country he came from because he fears that "they" are still after him. In his own country he had been an attorney, but when turmoil broke out and he found himself in the midst of it, he had no choice but to flee.

Recognizing his voice on the VHF was never difficult because his accent was clearly recognizable. He was friendly, would always call out a greeting loud and clear, and when our grandson Charlie was on the island, he would respond to that greeting with, "Hello, my little friend," in an accent that was pretty close to the real thing. At least close enough for a little kid to imitate.

Here on the island he obviously wasn't practicing law but was doing just about everything else imaginable. He fixed broken-down equipment, helped owners complete projects, like finishing woodwork or laying tile. And occasionally he was the pilot on the freight boat. He also took delight in salvaging old boats and getting them back in working order. He also spent what little free time he had windsurfing. Most of the projects he was involved with turned out just fine, but there was one that didn't quite make it. That was the infamous submarine.

I can't remember just how long it took him to build this thing. Understandably it was quite a while. After all, building a submarine from scratch can be time consuming. I can remember, however, that most everyone was watching this project with interest. Finally here it was—a small bright yellow submarine ready for launching.

There was a great deal of excitement as folks gathered around to watch the big event, but something was wrong. Here was a submarine that wouldn't submerge!

Back to the drawing board he went to make some adjustments. Before too long it was time for the second launching, and again folks gathered around. This time down she went underwater as smooth and as sweet as could be. And people cheered clapped, and just thought it was great. But there was another problem. As clever and as innovative as this fellow is, he had made an unbelievable mistake. He had placed the escape hatch on the bottom, not the top.

That was it for the submarine. It is now just sitting on the beach at one of the coves, not bothering anyone except perhaps for me. For the longest time when I went by that cove, spotted that bright yellow contraption, the song "We all live in a yellow submarine" rented a space in my head and I sang it over and over. Now I am no longer singing that tune. In fact I am just quietly watching and waiting to see what will happen when he finishes building his helicopter!

The Submarine

CHAPTER 26

Guests from Heaven, Guests from Hell

As I mentioned before, guests were coming back again and again, which was delightful. Most of these guests—about 98%—we welcome with open arms. It's almost like a family reunion. Then there is the other 2%.

Most all of our guests were just plain wonderful, relaxed, glad to be here and easy to please. They came back again and again, often making reservations for their next visit even before they left. Once in a great while we encountered one or two that we could describe as high maintenance. We had just such a guest on an evening when Glenn was not on duty. She came back to the resort after a field trip with Abaco Outback and inquired about a drink called a *Coconut Blast*. She had heard a lot about it, in fact some folks ordered one at the end of the adventure, but she of course hadn't bothered. A *Coconut Blast* is really just coconut milk with lots of booze added, and it packs quite a wallop if I understand correctly. But it's a drink we didn't happen to serve.

"I'd like a *Coconut Blast*," she announced, as I practiced my new bartending skills.

"I'm sorry, we don't make them," I politely answered.

"Well, why don't you? You have plenty of coconuts right up there in the trees. I should think you could at least get one down to make me a drink."

"We have no way of getting them down," I again answered politely.

Then she pointed to the very small white lights we had wrapped around the trees to add a little atmosphere.

"Why can't someone just use those lights as footholds and go up and get one?"

"Because those little Christmas lights wouldn't hold up anybody," I answered still politely but getting weary.

"Well, the branches look good and strong. Get a rope, throw it over a branch and have someone shimmy up."

The bar was very busy, I was very busy, and thought to myself, "Won't this ever end?" Besides, if we got a damn coconut I didn't think there was anyone around who could open it, so I sent her to one of the locals who often joined us.

"You know what, perhaps that fellow over there can help you out. If he gets one down and opens it up, we'll gladly make your drink." Mind you, I am still stiffly smiling although my thoughts were, "Just go away. 'Won't you please just go away"?"

The local gentleman offered no help. He just suggested, in no uncertain terms, that she forget it and have something else to drink. She did, at least for the evening. However, she hadn't completely forgotten about that *Coconut Blast*. The next day it was still on her mind and she was still asking. I sure was glad that Glenn was back on duty, because I simply turned her over to him.

I still don't know how he managed to get a coconut out of that tree, or perhaps he just faked it and used some canned coconut milk, but either way she got her *Coconut Blast*. In fact she got it before lunch no less. I'm not certain what she did with the rest of the day because I didn't see her again until nearly dinnertime. Maybe there is a reason why they call that concoction a *BLAST!*

She e-mailed us to say what a wonderful time she had, and how great everyone had been. However, most of her message was praising Glenn and thanking him for his extra efforts on her behalf. Amazing that she could remember.

There were a couple of routine guests who did give me a little concern. One morning, well before noon, two women came to the bar. One ordered a Diet Coke, the other a Bloody Mary. I could tell that this Bloody Mary was not the first drink of the day for that gal.

"Gerry," she said. "Everyday you share a thought over the Net, and some are inspirational. Tell me something that would make my life better!"

I mumbled something like, "The shadows in your life are caused when you stand in your own sunshine." Stupid, I knew, because it didn't mean a thing to her, and I wasn't even sure what it meant for me to tell her that.

A little while later she went into the restroom and passed Sandra, who was on a break.

"Sandra" she said, "Tell me what can I do to make my life better?"

Sandra's answer was, "Don't get drunk quite so often."

I was proud of Sandra. She had the courage to call it as she saw it—just some simple Bahamian logic.

Shortly after we took over the Inn, we had our first large family group. They took most of the rooms and one cottage and had a great time, or at least it seemed that way. They swam, went snorkeling, fished, hunted for shells, and played in the ocean and in the pool. The young ones were in constant motion and the mothers often sat on the porch in front of the Seaside Rooms, laughing and joking as they looked on. It was a good feeling to see so many really enjoying their stay. A feeling that lasted until the day before they were to leave, then two of the gentlemen asked to meet with me.

"Geraldine, we have to talk to you. This isn't at all what we expected!"

"I don't understand. You were certainly given a clear picture of what we had to offer, what we were all about," I responded.

"Yes, we know, but it still wasn't what we wanted or expected!"

"Were you misled in anyway?"

"No, we weren't, but we are still not happy and need you to make some adjustments."

"Like what?"

"Well we think you should at least reduce our total bill by 30%!"

After I caught my breath I was able to answer.

"There is no way I can do that. I watched your family all week long and they had a blast."

"Well, if you can't do that, then at least you could pay for our transportation in the morning. We have an early flight and the only way we can make it is to charter a private ferry. At least you should be willing to pick up those costs."

I refused to do that also.

A couple of nights before, two gentlemen from this illustrious group had chartered a ferry to Marsh Harbour then chartered a private plane to fly to Nassau and back, just to do a little gambling. If they could afford that, they sure could afford to get their family over to Marsh Harbour in the morning.

"Geraldine, we are not trying to badger you."

"But you certainly are. You are the first large group we have had the pleasure of entertaining and what you are telling me certainly doesn't reflect what I have been watching all week."

After continued lengthy discussions I made an offer I really shouldn't have made. I told them that their last dinner would be on the house. Man what a mistake that was!

After the offer was made, Glenn and Bob told me that these were the people who ordered a hamburger for their kids off the 'children's menu, then helped them eat it. Since this was to be a free meal, the bets were that they would order the most expensive things on the menu. That's exactly what they did—lobster and steaks, even for the kids, who clearly just wanted a hamburger—a whole one of their own!

The tab came to over $600, which I promptly presented, causing some brief but extreme consternation. I explained that they weren't expected to pay, but I wanted them to see the total so they could figure out the gratuity they were expected to leave for the staff who had so faithfully served them. They did leave 15%, but I doubt that would have been done without my somewhat aggressive intervention. Face it, just because I do dumb things doesn't mean my staff should suffer.

The next morning they thanked us, smiled, and while they waved goodbye told us they would be back in two years. I smiled, waved back, and thought to myself, "You'll be back only if I forget who the hell you are!"

I also had a little bit of perverted secret pleasure when I learned that on the chartered flight back from Nassau the gamblers had to share the plane with that body, the *right* body I told you about, that was finally being shipped to the family here on Guana. Now the long awaited funeral could take place and the transportation of the loved one was at least in part paid for by these cheap bastards.

Another example of that "two percent" that comes to mind was a group of eight adults. They booked a two-bedroom suite and a seaside room. They decided that six of them would stay in the suite, which is really accommodating for two couples or a family, but a little crowded for six.

Then for a little private time (and you can imagine what else), the couples would take turns sleeping in the seaside room. It was like a musical bedrooms sort of thing. Of course that meant housekeeping felt obligated to treat the seaside room as a check-out every single day. These guests also brought along coolers filled with food and somehow managed to get their meals together by using the small in-room microwave and a small hibachi they had tucked in their luggage.

They set up for meals on one of the courtyard tables using the paper products they had also dragged along. At least they didn't put their booze on the table—they just kept going back to the room for refills. We of course received the money for renting the rooms and an additional $89.75 for other purchases. For the life of me, I can't remember what those purchases were—probably ice for their coolers.

They did have a wonderful time; they described this vacation as the best they had ever had. That was pleasing to hear, even though we played a totally irrelevant role. They could have pitched a big tent somewhere with much the same results.

They said they can't wait to come back, but before they do I think we should have a few policies in place, especially one that covers "musical bedrooms" at our Inn.

There have been other guests who started out a little rocky, causing me to give sideways glances to staff members who signaled, "Oops, here we go—just be polite, but hang on tight."

There were two families—four adults and five kids—traveling together, and there was also one small dog. They arrived by boat on a really hot day. As they unloaded the boat, I loaded their gear on our one and only, sometimes goes sometimes doesn't golf cart to carry it all up to their rented cottages.

I was tugging at big bags and little bags when I heard someone say, "Oh, it's so hot. Look at the poor little dog—put him in the pool to cool off."

There is a sign by the pool that says "No Diving." I just never thought to add "No Dogs."

Next came the issue of a golf cart.

"We really need a golf cart today," is how the conversation began.

"We had called Donna's Cart Rental and were told none would be available until after the wedding."

They also had called us a couple of times and were told the exact same thing. I reminded them of those calls and answers, but apparently that wasn't acceptable.

"Oh for heaven's sakes, just call again and tell her we really need one now, and tell her we'll pay extra—however much it takes."

"Sorry. Donna doesn't work that way. She is a pretty fair lady and not one who would readily accept a bribe. If she had a cart, she would gladly rent it to you, but she just DOESN'T have one!"

I think I might have been a little snappy with my answer because I had just barely missed running over one little stupid wet dog who was yapping as it ran back and forth in front of the golf cart. I was trying to drive, keeping my eye on the baggage that was overflowing, and on kids who were determined to hang off the side.

Next, there was a little concern from one of the guests about the differences in the cottages, although both are basically the same.

"I want a different cottage."

"What's wrong?" I asked.

"Well my friend has a TV in her cottage and we don't!"

"That TV is just for watching videos," I responded. "We can bring you a unit from the hotel and you can borrow all kinds of videos from the Inn."

"Well, what about regular TV? Won't they be able to watch regular TV and we won't?"

"No, there just isn't any reception."

"What about cable? Don't you have cable?"

"What we have is a satellite, with a dish, and a receiver with a card that sometimes works and sometimes doesn't. If we are lucky and the weather is right, we can sometimes get regular TV in the dining room. If you are interested in watching whatever comes in, please feel free to come and join us."

To myself I'm thinking that maybe an alternative like swimming, snorkeling, playing in the pool, sitting in the sun, exploring different spots in that nifty boat they had, or reading a good book might just suffice.

After everything was unloaded and I was about to escape from the cottage scene, I heard yelling from one of the kids standing on the porch.

"Hey, hey, don't go yet. My mother said one of the closets in our cottage is locked!"

I explained that the closet held the personal belongings of the folks who owned the cottage. When they weren't there themselves, they used one closet for storage. I asked that he please go explain that to his Mother. I honestly thought that would be that. Oh, silly me!

"Hey, hey, stay here. I told my Mom what you said and she still wants the key. She thinks it might be fun for one of us kids to sleep in that closet."

There were two bedrooms and a pullout sleeper, so there was plenty of sleeping room without the closet.

"THERE IS NO KEY, AND THERE WILL BE NO KID IN A CLOSET!"

I learned a little later that both families had playhouses for their kids. Both playhouses had a microwave, refrigerator, sofa, table and chairs, and one even had cable TV and wall–to–wall carpeting. The kids also told me they hardly ever played in their playhouses, so maybe the closet would have been a lot of fun, a real down-to-earth adventure.

All I wanted at this point was to make it those 200 or so feet back to the Inn to catch my breath or hide in my room or something like that. But I wasn't free quite yet.

"We need to go to the store, and since we don't have a golf cart you have to take us," was the cry from one cottage.

"No we don't," was the response from the other. "We have everything we need."

The debate raged back and forth—what they had, what they needed, what they could do without at least until tomorrow. It was quite clear that nothing was necessary for survival.

But the lady who almost fainted when she found out there was no TV, and also thought she could buy her way to a non-existent golf cart, was determined as hell that she was going to the store.

Great, now I have a way out. I simply will turn this one over to Bob. It can clearly be his turn. That's what I did, and he took her, not gladly, but took her nonetheless to the store as fast as he could over that old bumpy dirt road.

It is interesting to note that when they finally got their rented golf cart they hardly ever used it to go anywhere, including to the store.

They were staying for ten days and I couldn't help but wonder how they would make out, not only with us but also with each other. As far as I could see there was already friction between the ladies. It was amazing how they had reached the conclusion that they would like to spend a ten-day vacation together.

The men were happy as could be and really got along well, doing their own thing. Since they appeared to be good friends, I guessed that this togetherness was probably their idea.

The families spent a lot of time on their boat, at the Inn, at the courtyard bar and in the pool. The only complaint any of the staff had was that they usually waited until an hour-and-a-half after the kitchen closed before deciding to order lunch. At least for one of the families this was a common occurrence.

Sandra would already be in her room resting. The little kids would be sitting on the barstools saying how hungry they were, and one of the mothers would find a way to solve the problem. Not by going back to the cottage to fix a lunch, but just by telling them, "Well, if you just ask Grandma Gerry to fix you something to eat, I bet she will."

Of course I would, and did. Those little kids were great little kids, every single one of them. It didn't take too much energy or any culinary skills to throw together some peanut butter and jelly sandwiches, a few chicken fingers or a grilled cheese or two. Any "grandma" could do that.

I am not certain, but I think it was the kids that made the difference. As the days went by, their polite demeanor, their friendly and lovable greetings (usually with a big hug), and their laughter certainly brightened the atmosphere and adjusted my attitude. Getting to know and enjoy them was the first step to getting to know and enjoy their parents. The last few nights I spent a lot of time with the mother who wanted a golf cart immediately, who wanted to unlock that closet, who insisted on going to the store even if it wasn't really necessary.

We sat together talked and she shared a lot. Once I gave myself a chance to really know her, I found the reason for that tough veneer, and underneath it all I found an absolutely delightful person. She apologized for being what she called a "bitch" when she first arrived and thanked me for giving her a second chance.

As they were leaving, the kids asked if I would come and visit them. They all had big houses with lots of room, and one little guy suggested I would really like staying in his playhouse. His was the one, he stressed, that had cable TV.

Suffice it to say that all's well that ends well. They are welcome back any time.

"Do you remember me?" asked a gentleman checking in with two other people.

"I should, you look very familiar and I know you have been a guest here before."

"I was here last year with my son and a friend of his. We stayed in Seaside Room number one."

"Oh my God," I thought, "how could I forget!"

This trio had stayed three nights. Each morning they were up early to go fishing. Each evening they cooked what they caught on the walkway right outside their room and went inside to fix their drinks with their own liquor.

The fourth morning, Nora Mae told me they were gone.

"Sure," I said, "they have gone fishing just like they usually do."

"Oh no," she answered. "They are gone, just plain gone!"

She was absolutely right. They were gone—just disappeared, and I might add, without paying their bill.

"They didn't even bother to say goodbye," Nora Mae whined. She had the habit of making friends with everyone, regardless of the circumstances. She was almost as upset that they had ignored her as I was that they had "stiffed" us. Bob of course had the answer.

He got on the VHF and announced to the world that we had a problem. He described the trio, gave out the name of the boat, and asked anyone who spotted them to gently remind them that they had forgotten to pay their Seaside room bill.

I was amazed. I thought that Bob would have made a different kind of announcement, something like "If you see these cheapskates tell them to get their asses back and pay us what they owe us."

It worked. Of course it worked. It wasn't fun for them to be reminded by fellow fishermen, other cruisers, or dock masters that there was a bill they should settle. I guess they felt a little pressured because a couple of days later they came back. There was no hello, goodbye, explanation, or apology—nothing. They just paid the bill and left.

I guess it didn't matter because as soon as Bob had cash in hand he once again got on the VHF. He thanked everyone for their help, said the situation had been resolved and perhaps these guys need no longer be looked on in disfavor. That was the last we heard from them until the very moment the gentleman named Fritz stood in front of me explaining that the three of them were back and he would like to book the very same room as last year.

That room wasn't available, so he settled for a two-room suite at the very rear of the Inn. "Good," I thought, "this way we can keep a closer eye on him."

As it turned out, that wasn't necessary. There was a complete transformation. Either he had hit the lottery, the leopard had changed his spots, or perhaps, just perhaps, the episode last year had been a simple mistake. I only wished he had explained.

They still went out fishing early in the morning, but this year they asked Sandra to cook their catch. They ordered salads and sides from the kitchen and each day gave her a substantial tip for her trouble. In the evenings Fritz joined us at the bar. He and Bob seemed to hit it off and I found him to be interesting and entertaining.

Sometimes we encounter problems even with guests who aren't actually staying at the Inn.

We always offered transportation for guests who would like to come for dinner. They made the reservation and we would *carry* them both ways. We received a call on the VHF from a couple of guests who wanted to be picked up at 6:30 for dinner at 7:00.

Beth was with us and once again volunteered to help. She would be the taxi driver. She left in plenty of time but wasn't back in time for that 7:00 dinner reservation. When she still hadn't returned by 7:30, we hailed her on the mobile radio. She had been waiting on the dock where the guests had taken a slip, and could see them still on their boat.

She said she had called to them several times, hailed them on the VHF, but had gotten no response to either effort. Just as we were suggesting that she forget about it and come on back to the Inn, they came out of the boat and staggered to the van.

The 7:00 clock dinner wasn't served until close to 9:00, because (as they explained) they needed to relax and have a drink before dinner. I thought, "One more drink and they wouldn't be able to tell what was on their plate or if they even had one." Guess we wouldn't have to worry if it were overdone, not done well enough, or even done at all. They wouldn't be able to affect our reputation one way or the other.

We were being patient while we waited for them to finish their dinner so we could *carry* them back. *Carry* was probably a most fitting description in this case. When they finally decided to leave, they informed us they would be back tomorrow night for another wonderful dinner. Tomorrow was the lady's birthday and they wouldn't dream of celebrating it anywhere else. They wanted to make the same dinner arrangements and same pick-up time.

"Okay, fine," I said, "but please be there when we come for you."

"Oh, don't worry, we will be. After all, it will be her birthday and we'll want plenty of time to celebrate!"

The next night it was the same scenario all over again. It was after 8:00 o'clock when we finally got them rounded up and out to the Inn for their 7:00 o'clock birthday dinner.

"You were late picking us up," she complained.

"Oh no we weren't," answered Bob. "That van was there and waited for you for over an hour."

"We saw the van but didn't see any driver!"

"She was walking around looking for you. What did you think, the van just got there by itself?"

"I don't care what you say, you spoiled my fucking birthday."

"OOPS!" I thought, "here we go!"

"We didn't spoil anything—you did that yourself."

"Maybe you don't know this, you fucking idiot, but the island is full of my relatives and not a one of them will ever come here again and neither will I—and I am leaving!"

"Go ahead and go, who cares!"

"You have to give me a ride back!"

"No, I do not!"

"Then I am going to call the police."

If it weren't such an explosive situation, that suggestion would have had me laughing out loud. I had no idea what police she thought she could call.

"My husband is out back and if he hears what you are doing he'll come out here and beat the fucking shit out of you!"

"Bob," I said "GO TO YOUR ROOM!"

He stood there with his ears a-blazing red, which is clearly a warning sign, and asked me, "What did you just say?"

I said, "GO TO YOUR ROOM. GO TO YOUR ROOM RIGHT NOW!"

He went to his room and I went out back to talk to the husband.

I said in a very sad voice (or so I wanted it to appear) that losing them as customers was one thing, but I couldn't stand the thought of losing them as friends."

Would you believe that he told me that was the nicest thing anyone ever said to him?

Back they came to the dining room, which was completely empty by now, and had a very late dinner for a really screwed up birthday.

Since I was the one who so cleverly enticed them to stay, I was the one chosen to tend out to them. I did just that until after 11:00 p.m.

During that time I learned so much gossip that I couldn't sleep a wink. In the morning I decided just to tuck it all away and tuck it away for good. The better part of valor was not to share any of it with Bob—especially the part about Glenn having a wife. I knew he'd have a hundred questions, asking me how Glenn could have a wife and fiancé at the same time. Worse yet, he'd expect me to have the answers.

I have no idea how it happened, but we had a full house coming up and two families with the same last name booked into the same two-room suite. We had all the information necessary for the Eliot Miller family but could find no paperwork for Charles Miller and his party. All we could determine from the charts was that the check-in and check-out dates varied by a day as did the number of expected guests, so we knew we were dealing with two separate parties. I back-tracked e-mails and responses and went through all the reservations month by month, but to no avail. Then Glenn had what he thought was a brilliant suggestion.

"You have Elliot Miller's phone number, so why don't you call him?"

"And do what?" I responded.

"Just ask him what his name is."

"OH I see, just call and say 'Hello Elliot, is your name really Charles?' I don't think so Glenn!"

So the search continued and finally, in some year-old records that for some unknown mysterious reason were stored in Glenn's room, we discovered what we needed for Charles Miller.

He had booked the year before, couldn't make arrangements at the last minute and requested that we save him the same room and the same dates for this upcoming year. No one bothered to check—just added his name to the reservation chart. Now at least I had a phone number for the real Charles Miller and when contacted, he once again asked us to hold his deposit. He couldn't make it for those dates either, but would try to join us soon.

They say that if you smile when you are on the phone the person on the other end will sense it. I wonder if poor Mr. Miller—Mr. Charles Miller—could sense my real glee. I hope not, because if he could have guessed how happy I was', he may never decide to join us.

How do I share with you the stories of some of the greatest little people we have had there without leaving out so many? If I were to go family by family. it would be a whole new journal pages long. I can, however, say that most all the kids we got to know were really good kids. I can't vouch for how they behaved at home, but at least while on vacation they were superb. Quite honestly, we did experience the antics of a couple that one might call "spoiled," and both were teenagers.

Since we had been there, done that, it was easy for us to just take them in stride, knowing full well that when they returned next year, they would have grown some and changed for the best.

Usually we had perhaps two or three families at a time. We were only inundated when our own Sylvester crew moved in all together or at Easter time when the Ottens, and Riches, and the Kiss family with their sons invaded, and in Fall when the Tropeanos, their family and friends took over. We not only enjoyed our own little guests, but also the children from other nearby homes or rentals who came for lunch, to frolic in the pool, play games and make new friends.

Right now I am thinking about Noah, perhaps because he sent me a disk full of wonderful pictures. There were pictures of beautiful colored fish his Dad had taken with an underwater camera, pictures taken from the plane flying over, pictures of the Inn, and of course a lot of pictures of Noah. There was Noah snorkeling with his Dad in the Sea of Abaco, sitting on his 'Father's lap learning to handle a kayak, and feeding the fish at the end of the dock. There were many more, but my favorite was Noah standing by our dusty van, wearing a safari hat, sun glasses, and holding his fingers up to show "I love you" in sign language. Perhaps he also sticks in my mind because of a little bit of flattery he sent my way.

When they were talking about the boat they were going to buy when they returned to the states, he declared that he thought the best name possible for the boat should be "Miss Gerry." Believe me when I say it doesn't get any better than that. Actually they named the boat "Intuition" explaining that they were dipping "into Noah's college tuition" to pay for it.

There is always something to learn from children. The young gentleman from England, Master Butler, shared with me on a daily basis all the wonderful things he had observed. If I remember correctly, he was about seven years old. The day he told me he had watched lizards mating, I raised my eyebrows just a little.

"It's true, Miss Gerry. I saw them having sex."

I glanced at his Dad, who gave a small nod of confirmation.

I couldn't believe that I was learning about the mating habits of curly tail lizards from a seven year old. I then got a comprehensive lesson on how to tell a male curly tail lizard from a female. I still can't tell the difference unless they are side by side and I can notice that one is bigger than the other. I certainly have no intention of picking them up to see what else I might see.

The Butler family were unique and very special guests. Because of the distance they had to travel, plus the fact that they were quite intent on giving their young son and even younger daughter a variety of experiences, I suspect they will not be repeat guests. They did however express the feelings that this vacation was one of the very best they had ever taken. Can't ask for much else!

Then of course there is Antonio, Sandra's ten-year-old granddaughter. She taught me a lot about fish. We usually feed the fish that hang out under our dock day-old rolls, breads and leftovers. But she insisted we make sure they had some green beans because it was good for their kidneys, and some corn because that would keep them from getting liver cancer. Since she could name all the fishes we watched swimming around and I couldn't, it was difficult to contradict her wisdom. When we fed the fishes together, I made sure we had some green beans and at least a little corn.

Bob sometimes comes off a bit scary to little kids. Twin girls who were about four years old certainly didn't mind his gruff look.

"Miss Renee, where is Mr. Bob?"

"In the office," was the reply.

A few minutes later, back came a couple of sad little faces with one of the twins saying, "Miss Renee, he just isn't in there!"

Renee using her loud voice of authority declared, "NOW JUST WHY DO YOU WANT MR.BOB?"

The quivering response was, "We just want to tell him we love him." And love him they did.

They were his shadows for the whole week—following him, watching what he was doing, asking the kind of questions only four year olds ask.

Whenever he sat at the courtyard bar, there was always one little girl on each side sitting close and smiling at him. He in return would smile back and chat in a gentle way. He really was tickled pink and I found it absolutely amazing as well as delightful.

When they were ready to leave, they were insisting that Mr. Bob come to their house as soon as he could. I didn't get invited nor did anyone else, just Mr. Bob—over and over and over. It was and still is hard to figure out just how an attachment of that sort develops. Perhaps he reminded them of someone at home or maybe even someone from a different time and place.

And then there was little Miss Natalie. She was absolutely adorable and very much in love. In between swimming, playing in the courtyard, or walking the beach with her parents, she spent time drawing and coloring pictures for Mr. Bob. Although she was only two-and-a-half years old, she managed to sign those pictures with "I love you."

Her conversations always involved Bob and not necessarily me, except for the time she had something she wanted to report.

"Miss Gerry, we saw snake tracks on the dirt road!"

"Are you sure?" I asked. "Because in all the time we have been on this island, I have never seen a snake!"

"Well, there is one here because we really saw his tracks!"

"Oh my gosh," I answered. "I wonder where he was going?"

"He was coming right here, right here to your Inn!"

"Oh no, don't tell me that. Why would he be coming here?"

"I guess because he needed a drink!!!"

The next day I checked the dirt road looking for what I thought would probably be bicycle tracks. There were some of those but also, hard for me to believe, some honest to goodness snake tracks headed in the direction of the Inn. I never saw him or her, but believe me I really didn't go looking.

Natalie had an uncanny sense of knowing when Bob was around. We went to Blue Water Grill for dinner and were seated way in the back of the dining room, when we spotted her and her family who were also coming for dinner. We saw them but they hadn't seen us. Natalie's mother told us that as soon as they were seated Natalie began to tell them that Mr. Bob was there somewhere.

"He is here, Mommy. I *know* he is here."

I don't think so, Natalie—, and if he and Miss Gerry are here, they just probably want to have a nice quiet dinner."

"No, no, he is here and he will want to see me. Maybe he's in the kitchen. OH NO, maybe he's in the MEN'S ROOM, but I know he is here somewhere."

About this time Bob and I stepped out to the porch, and when we did she saw us. She bolted from the table, ran to the porch, threw her little arms around his legs, hugged him hard, and said simply, "I knew it, I knew it!"

Neither one of her parents could explain the attachment. In fact they stated that she had never done anything like this before. Never taken to anyone the way she had taken to whom she now called HER MR. BOB!

There were a lot of females who stayed at the Inn, but as far as I know it was only the youngsters who crowded around him at the bar or grabbed his legs in a big hug. But like I said, "as far as I know."

I am certain that every single guest who was here when little Shawn stayed with us will never forget him. He provided daily entertainment— same time, same place—and most of us just waited patiently for it.

Right after lunch his Dad and big brother would take off on an adventure of their own and Shawn and his mother would retire for their afternoon nap. No more then ten minutes after they went to their room, we would see the door quietly open and out would come Shawn.

He was a rugged little guy, not quite two years old, with a big grin and a mop of curly hair. Everyday he would wear great big sunglasses, a hat, and absolutely nothing else. Around the walkway and the pool he'd parade, marching in time with the music from the bar.

"Where is your mother, Shawn?" someone would ask. And the reply was always the same.

"Shh! Shh! Mama's seeping."

However, his escape was usually short-lived. Soon his Mother would burst out of the room to recapture the little guy. This was the last act of the great show for today. All we could do was wait for the repeat performance tomorrow.

There are so many to remember—those who first came, still young enough to be by their parent's' sides, and three years later definitely more independent. It was as if they had magically crossed over from childhood to being young adults.

A little guy, Demy, the grandson of our helpful retired dentist and his wife Kitty, who was one year a silent one year old, and the next year a two year old, chattering constantly, amazing everyone. Each time I walked by or came into sight, his little voice would shout out, "Hey Lady!" He never failed to thank me for letting him swim in my pool or tell me how good his grilled cheese was.

The last thing I heard him say to Glenn was, "You want me to bust your chops? You want a piece of me?"

You can't help but wonder how all this happened seemingly overnight.

Those children who came back time and again had a belief that this was their place. In fact when Josh arrived for his third visit, he was quite concerned because there were strangers swimming in HIS pool. I could go on and on with kid stories or simply tell you about adults who, when they found themselves in this laid back, out-of-the-way bit of paradise, away from all the social norms and imposed societal restrictions, became kids again. They proved the point that growing older doesn't necessarily mean you have to grow up.

The one group that surely proved that point consisted of four sisters who had never vacationed together since childhood. They were all very different in nature and had all gone their own ways, so this was an experiment, a test. And, I will say, a test they passed with flying colors.

They all had cowboy hats, specially designed t-shirts, bandannas, and games to play around the pool. They not only entertained all of us here at the Inn, but the rest of the island as well.

It was difficult to determine which of them was the most entertaining. It was as if they were taking turns at being the star of the day. They spent time here, time at Nippers and a great deal of time at a unique place called The Landing.

The Landing was simply a makeshift, extremely rustic bar under a cottonwood tree, right on the shore at Fishers Bay. It was the place to gather, especially on a Friday nights, when the local folks showed up with free "munchies" to share. The other reason to show up was to enjoy the antics of Aubrey the bartender. He is absolutely an original, one-of-a-kind. People love his personality, love watching as he chops open coconuts with a big macheté, serving his $3 beers, or using a hand-held contraption on which he has to pull on a chain, much like a chainsaw, in order to get it going to make frozen drinks.

Some folks who knew Aubrey in his other life—the one he lived before he came to the out island—described him as one who was all business, so meticulous in dress that he had the nickname "Mr. Shine," and they swore he had a PhD in something or other. Well, that certainly was different than his Bahamian persona, the one that strolls the island in his bare feet while often sporting a top hat. And the PhD story certainly contradicts Aubrey's claim that he dropped out of school at age twelve.

He does tend to business, but it really takes a backseat to his tending to fun. He now has very long, rather unkempt hair, wears baggy pants and old t-shirts. He owns one pair of shoes, but I was told they don't exactly match, and he wears them only when he has to go to court. I don't really care if he has a PhD or is a grammar school drop out, he is as intelligent as anyone I know, and as well-loved.

The four sisters and Aubrey even decided they were probably related, having the same father but different mothers, or different fathers same mother and separated at birth. I can't recall exactly what crazy notion they settled for, but they certainly felt a kinship.

One sister brought along some colored banners attached to sticks. I know there is a name for such playthings, but for the life of me I can't remember what they are called. She stood around the pool trying to teach others how to use them. You swirl them around, jump over them, skip through them, wrap them around your body, or make them do your bidding in many other ways. No one, including yours truly, had any success in making the tricks work, but it certainly provided for gales of laughter.

Another sister decided to teach us all a game called "Butt Bucket." Since it is just a little risqué, I shall not attempt to describe it. But let me tell you that almost everywhere you went on this island someone was playing "Butt Bucket."

I think the most outstanding entertainment came when the youngest sister took a trip down our little dusty roads in the back of Aubrey's pickup. This truck is held together with baling wire and electrical tape. It is painted in a variety of colors just splashed here and there with no rhyme or reason. In the back is an old broken-down plastic chair with only three legs. This turned out to be the seat of honor for the sister who was on a mission with Aubrey.

They needed to go to the Harbor Corner grocery store to replenish some nonalcoholic bar supplies. Aubrey left the other three sisters in charge of his bar as the two of them took off. Around the island they went, singing old show tunes at the top of their lungs. It was amazing that they both knew all the words. They sang and sang until they pulled up in front of the store.

"Quiet," said Aubrey. "The gentleman who runs this store is some kind of minister. We should act nice and polite and show some dignity so we won't offend him."

Quiet down they did until they started the trip back. They did not offend the "minister," but continued to entertain everyone else they met along the way.

These sisters were determined to do a repeat visit in the near future. They claimed they would be ready for us once again. And I thought that with a little bit of advance notice the island might well be ready for them.

One of the sisters managed, in between all their antics, to paint a beautiful watercolor scene of our courtyard. It is now safely at home waiting to be framed, to be returned to hang in a special place. I shall have to find that place so it is hanging apart from all the wall murals our granddaughter painted.

Charlie recently arrived and had a joyous reunion with his "wife" Madison. While she was waiting for his visit, she told me over and over how she had missed him. She said, "I can't remember what he looks like, but I sure remember how he sounded." I wondered if she meant LOUD because that certainly would have been an apt description.

They very easily picked up right where they left off a year ago, keeping constant company. They walked around the pool holding hands, and every once in a while he'd softly pat the top of her head. It was fun and fascinating to watch. We probably wouldn't feel quite the same if they were ten or twelve years older. Most likely we'd still be watching them, but perhaps a lot closer—and for very different reasons.

Madison is just a bubbly, fun-loving little girl who completely enjoys her visits to Guana. Every summer had been filled with happiness, except for this one. Charlie, Madison and her sister Mallory were on the dock, each sitting there dangling their feet in the water and wiggling their toes. We had what you might call a resident barracuda who everyday just hung around underneath the dock. The kids were delighted to see him swim towards their feet then quickly swim away. It was a game they were playing until apparently the barracuda got tired of the game. In he swam, but this time instead of swimming away he attacked. He grabbed Madison's foot, chomped down, and bit her severely. She was hobbling down the dock, bleeding profusely. The adults were all in a panic but she kept calling, "It's okay, it's okay. I'm a Christian!"

She was taken to Marsh Harbour where she received seven stitches in that tiny little foot of hers.

It was hard to believe how brave she was through this whole frightening episode.

Someday in the way distant future, I would be delighted to have Madison as a REAL grand-daughter-in-law.

While she was on her way to the doctor's, some folks fishing on the adjacent dock actually caught the barracuda. This prompted Charlie, who was extremely upset, into action. He ran to the kitchen, grabbed a knife, and headed out. Running as fast as he could, he shouted, "Don't let him go, he hurt my friend. Don't let him go, he hurt my friend. He has to die!"

And there I stood, shouting just as loudly, "Charlie, don't run with that knife, don't run with that knife!" At that point he didn't hear a word I was shouting. Not that it would have made any difference—he was on a mission! Luckily for the barracuda, and to Charlie's dismay, they released this "enemy." Charlie had no choice but to slowly and sadly saunter back to the kitchen to return his lethal weapon.

Occasionally there was a third buddy tagging along with the happy couple, and her name was Monica. Monica was Nora Mae's seven-year-old daughter who often came to visit. She came to stay with her *Mummy*, just as Sandra's grandchildren came to stay with her.

Bob and I sometimes worried about crowded conditions in their living quarters, but they all seem undisturbed and happy as could be. They had TV, the swimming pool, and could fish off the dock, so for them it was probably like going away to summer camp. All these kids were well-mannered and never seemed to get in the way of the work that had to be done.

The first time Monica saw Charlie, not knowing who he was, she pointed me out and said, "See that white woman over there? She owns this place and I can get anything I want for free."

The next day she climbed out of the pool, plunked herself down at the bar and just waited. When I asked if she would like a Coke, a Sprite or some orange juice, she answered, "No, thank you. I just think I'll have a *FROZEN VIRGIN STRAWBERY DAIQUIRI.*" Although it is one of my least favorite drinks to whip up, I decided I had better make her one. Who am I to spoil a child's fantasy?

The latter part of the winter, the spring and even the early months of summer, the rooms at the Inn were fully booked, and the cottage rentals were consistent. We had some new and rather controversial guests as well as many repeat guests. The repeat guests were the old friends that made week after week seem like an ongoing family reunion. There were just too many for me to attempt to mention them all, but I feel I should share the Greg and Betsy adventure.

This delightful young couple had been guests every year since the Inn became ours. For most of the years Betsy put on a fashion show. She would take over the walkway to model her own designed bikinis, which she also made. They were clever, unusual, eye-catching, and in some cases almost startling.

Other guests who had shared the same vacation time in years past would immediately ask her just what time the show would begin. The ladies didn't want to miss it and needless to say neither did the men. But now, all of a sudden Betsy decided to do something different. Instead of modeling her creations, she decided, as she exclaimed, "to do something special around the place."

"Gerry, how would you like it if I painted some hibiscus on the walls that circle the pool?"

"I really don't know, but perhaps if you did a couple on the concrete post that leads into the bar I might have a better idea."

Greg and Betsy Painting Hibiscus

Out to the shed we went and found some leftover paint. Amazing, but they really were the colors she thought we should use. Two hours later the bar posts were decorated, and after my applause and everyone else's accolades, she and Greg were off and running.

She drew the flowers on the pool walls and Greg, with the help of other guests and yours truly, painted the background. We started mid-morning and by dinner time the project was complete. What once had been just plain concrete walls were now brightly colored with her artwork. Guests who were staying with us as well as those that came for lunch or to use the pool all commented on the improvement. Almost everyone loved it. The only exception was Uncle Leonard.

He sat on his stool grumbling that it made us look like something from Nassau—not like what we really were! He sat for a couple of days facing the other direction so he wouldn't have to look at the "mess" we made. He only grumbled at me because he really liked Betsy and wouldn't for the world say anything to her that might hurt her feelings. I didn't let his comments get to me because I knew that before the week was out he'd be over it, sitting at the bar on HIS stool and facing the way he always did.

We not only had repeat room guests but numerous repeat guests who were constantly there for lunch. We called them the Old Faithful. There were those who lived on the island either full-time as locals or the second-home owners who came for mostly the winter months. There were also those who acted as rental agents for the various properties and always brought their new renters out to meet us and enjoy one of our specialties. We had one second-home owner who always brought his guests out to Seaside for our Cracked Conch. Cracked Conch is a popular dish and is served most everywhere, but this loyal fellow declared ours was the best anywhere on any of the islands. He would call first to make certain that Sandra was in the kitchen, because it was the way she cooked it that made it different and better than any he had ever had. If it happened to be her day off when he called, he would simply wait until she was back on duty.

We had another popular favorite called the Flying Dog. It was interesting how that all came about. Janet and Dave had a cottage on a cove a little distance from the Inn. They named their cottage and their boat The Flying Dogs. Their permanent home was in Florida, but they managed to fly over to Guana on a rather routine basis. Whenever they made the trip, they did so in a chartered plane so they could bring their two Golden Retrievers, Josh and Fran. So I guess you know how the name Flying Dogs came to be.

They often came to Seaside for lunch and one day asked if we could make a special kind of sandwich. It sure was simple enough, actually just a grilled cheese with a hamburger patty inside cooked to your liking and grilled on Bahamian bread. When it was served, a fellow sitting on the opposite side of the bar asked if he could have just what they were having.

The following day a friend of his came, sat at the bar and said his friend had really enjoyed his lunch the day before and described the meal. From then on it snowballed and with so many asking for that special sandwich, we decided it was time to put it on the menu. And in honor of our friends who had first given us the idea, we called it a FLYING DOG. It became without question one of the absolute favorites.

There was another guest who came for a grilled cheese sandwich. He'd ask for mustard, a slice of onion, and a cheaper price because he brought his own cheese. When he requested we put that mustard, onion, grilled cheese deal on the menu as a special and use his name, we respectfully declined. I suppose we could have listed it with a footnote that said, "For a cheaper price bring your own cheese!"

Since the van wasn't working and I couldn't manage to drive the old broken-down truck Bob had bought as a bargain, he decided to buy me a golf cart. And a new one at that. I didn't want a second-hand anything—we'd had enough of those. It was beautiful, bright red, with YAYA'S RIDE stenciled on the front and side.

One day Bob came in with a glum expression. "You had better go out back and take a look at your pride and joy," he suggested.

So out I went and there it sat, wrecked all to hell. The wheels were splayed apart, one going in a northerly direction the other headed south. It had never dawned on me to take the keys out. They were always in the cart and the cart was always parked in our backyard. Guess you might say it was a lesson learned the hard way. It had only been mine for about three months.

Fritz grabbed a cup of coffee from the walkway and asked it I had a minute or two. He really wanted to talk to me.

"Last night," he said, "my son's friend went out and was gone for quite a while. I'm not sure where he went or how he got there."

"Let me guess, you think he might be the one who took YAYA's RIDE?"

"I have my suspicions but am not certain how to confront him. I read in your book WINDY HILL about some of the ploys you used when you needed information from some of the kids who got into trouble. Do you think you could think of something, some way?"

"That was a long time ago, Fritz. But maybe I can figure out a way to get to the bottom of this."

It was just a couple of minutes later when I knocked on the room door with a pad of paper and pencil in hand.

Even though I was seething inside as I looked at the little shithead in question, I smiled and calmly, but with some authority, said, "I have to ask you a couple of questions. "I need to know exactly how the accident happened. What time was it and where did it take place?"

I could tell from the look on his face that he was the guilty party.

When at first he didn't respond, I continued. I sat down with the pad of paper in my lap and the pencil ready to go.

"I will really need all of the details so I can report it to my insurance company."

So, he gave me all the details, at least those he could remember. Apparently he had been drunk as a skunk.

Fritz encouraged him to contact his Father get some credit card information so he could help pay for the repairs. The young man cooperated but his Father didn't.

"To hell with that," his father responded. "Let them pay for their own repairs."

At that point Fritz offered to help, saying he felt somewhat responsible. We respectfully declined but thanked him for his generous offer. Where in the world did this new Fritz come from—this new friend and supporter?

It was a good thing we had a few little details to turn over to the insurance company because in the end they were the ones to pick up the $2,400 tab.

I am not really a gambler but then maybe I am, at least when it comes to football games. I wouldn't be silly enough to bet chocolate bars but did end up betting something worth a little more. Not much more, just a little.

One of our guests, W. Paul Scrupski, was an avid Philadelphia Eagles fan and certainly knew how I felt about the New England Patriots. Once he was at home and the football season started he began an intensive e-mail campaign. He teased me, he taunted me, he made fun of the Pats and he challenged me. He tried to convince me that they were really a fly-by-night, Johnny-come-lately team. We bet online, back and forth, and the loser had to send the winner a coffee cup with a team logo. Although the Eagles had a pretty good team, they weren't quite good enough. I never had to send out a coffee cup but I sure got some coming my way. In fact Sandra confiscated one of those precious mugs. She thought I had enough so I wouldn't mind. Selfish me, I took it back.

It was really fun, all that bantering back and forth. And I really like W. Paul, really appreciate his wife Barbara for tolerating all our nonsense, but most of all I really love my Patriots and Tom Brady!

CHAPTER 27

Weddings, Events and Celebrations

We've owned the Inn for almost six years now. Sometimes it seems as if it was just yesterday that we arrived, other times I can just barely remember what our life had been without it. I do remember clearly that there were days when I looked out at the beautiful and calm aqua blue waters of the Sea of Abaco or sat for a few minutes and watched the surf pounding the shore on the Atlantic side.

Then I'd say from the bottom of my heart, "Thank you for leading us to this little bit of paradise. We are grateful for the new challenge, for this unique opportunity," and I would feel truly blessed. There were also days when I looked at the same scenery, gazed at the beautiful little Inn and said very simply, "What the hell are we doing here?" Those feelings didn't last too long because there was always something exciting and worthwhile to take up our time and adjust my attitude. Just take weddings for an example.

Weddings were becoming quite popular, and although I had a tendency to feel like I was the mother of the bride rather than simply the innkeeper, they were wonderful and very successful.

Steve and April arrived a couple of days before the rest of the guests, truly excited that the resort was just for them, their family and friends. And the day was absolutely perfect.

"Is the weather always like this?" they asked.

"Just about," I answered.

"Does it rain often?"

"Well, don't worry about that. If we get rain it won't last long. Maybe an early morning or late afternoon squall and it'll be over. At least that's typical for this time of year."

All this glee was followed by four days of solid rain. We were socked in, so to speak, around the clock. The wedding guests arrived on a chartered ferry, all smiles and excited, even though most were soaking wet and the bride's grandparents and groom's sister were without their luggage.

"Don't worry," I assured them, "tomorrow will certainly be better."

The rain still came, but thankfully the grandparents' luggage also came, so there was something to rejoice about.

The ceremony was to be held on the beach, which was clearly not an option for Saturday—the day they had chosen. I no longer just had that "mother of the bride" responsibility feeling, but I was beginning to feel like Mother Nature herself. Although their spirits weren't dampened, mine were sure hitting the skids.

"Why are you worried, honey?" Bob asked. "They look like they are having a good time."

"I know, but what about the 'bride's big day, that once-in-a-lifetime day?"

It was clear that I couldn't change the weather, but maybe I could change the schedule. If we didn't have the reception following the wedding as is usual and customary, could we have it before the wedding? So what if they couldn't get married Saturday—we could still have the party. A little backwards but it just might work.

After a brief consultation with the bride and groom, we planned the evening affair. We set up the reception in the dining room instead of the courtyard—a little crowded but quite cozy and at least out of the rain. Some of the guests made a few little speeches and of course with a captive audience I had to put in my two-cents worth. Short and sweet but I just let them know how great I thought they all were, and it was heartfelt.

The inside rescheduled affair was a great success, but the real good time came when everyone decided to go outside anyway to dance in the rain. Some of the older guests who claimed they hadn't danced in years delighted everyone as they "boogied" around the pool. After all, this was a wedding party and you are supposed to dance at weddings.

Sunday morning, it was warm, muggy, and overcast, but no rain. There were an abundance of clouds that at times seemed to be moving rapidly, as they do often in this part of the world. At other times they were stalled and looked like they would hang around forever, or worse yet open up once again. The wedding had to be today because the guests leave tomorrow, so now it was time for some major decisions.

The groom informed me that they were going to aim for four o'clock. I went into the kitchen to let them know so they would be prepared for the wedding dinner. Now the time changed to three o'clock, so back to the kitchen I went. Well, maybe they shouldn't be taking any chances, so now two o'clock sounded good. Back I go, to confuse the cooks a little more. At one o'clock, they announced the wedding would be at one thirty.

They had chosen a special spot on the Atlantic beach side, which was about 450 feet from the Inn. Our white chairs had already been marked with great name tags and beautiful bows, but now they had to be carried over and placed in a semi-circle on the chosen spot. The groom decided the bride should have a carpet of sorts to walk on across the sand, so up came the carpet from our walkway to be carried over. Hustle, hustle, hustle. But it was not a problem because everyone chipped in carrying over whatever. All set up and ready to go and no, it didn't rain—in fact the sun came out and gently warmed the entire ceremony.

The 'bride's grandfather, a judge, performed a wonderful service, adding personal touches that addressed both the bride and groom, and the usual phrases about love and commitments were presented in a unique way.

I always cry at weddings and this one was no exception. I cried not only because it was truly moving, but also a little bit out of gratitude because the damn rain had stopped. There were the champagne toasts around the courtyard bar, lots of jokes, amusing family stories lots of laughter and quality time spent waiting for the kitchen to get everything ready. They did a marvelous job in spite of the several different time frames thrown their way.

The dinner was a huge success, and now it was over. Over, except for one small detail. Because the judge performed the service and wasn't sanctioned to do so by the Bahamian Government, the marriage wasn't legal. That little detail they'll tend to once they arrived back in the states.

That was not the first time we had a wedding that resulted in the bride and groom not actually being married. But those weddings were done with the full knowledge of everyone involved. The brides and grooms wanted to be here, wanted to be surrounded by family and friends, and wanted the whole affair to be unique. They would bring along a friend or family member who was authorized to marry couples in the good old USA. They would get their Bahamian marriage license, go through the ceremony exactly as they wanted it to be, and then do the necessary paperwork once they returned home.

Others engaged the Commissioner from Marsh Harbour. He was personable and did an excellent standard-type service. The cost for a marriage license was $40, and the cost for the Commissioner was $300 plus the round trip ferry fare. Those costs and arrangements did not seem to pose any problems. What did pose a problem, however, was if a couple had their hearts set on getting married at sunset. For some reason—political, moral, religious or just plain tradition—anything associated with the marriage ceremony had to be completed before the sun went down or it invalidated the whole thing. Sure wish I knew why.

Some people have suggested that the ceremony has to be done in the daylight so no impostor could sneak in. Maybe it was some sort of assurance that the bride wouldn't marry the wrong guy. I checked with many sources including religious ones and they all confirmed that before sundown was the rule!

Artistic Wedding Ring Presentation

Wedding on The Beach

Miss Emily's Wedding Cake

Beach Wedding Embrace

The next morning as I stood on the dock to say my goodbyes to Steve, April and their families, I noticed the groom's sister holding tightly her luggage, which had only arrived late the night before. This was the time when they vowed to all return to celebrate the birth of Steve and April's first child. I watched as they boarded the ferry, and still watched as it headed out and rounded the bend. The sadness I felt was real. How dear they were, and because of their upbeat attitude, it was an affair I shall not readily forget. Apparently they have also remembered us because after just over a year had passed, we received an ultrasound picture simply titled "from Steve and April—fetus—11 weeks and two days."

We got more ultrasound pictures of expected little ones from former guests. I was even asked to suggest names. I did a lot of thinking about what special ideas I had and when I settled on a couple of neat wonderful names, I'd e-mail them. I quickly got notes back, always with a thank you and sorry but no thanks. No one liked my ideas, which was hard to believe. Certainly for a little girl there would have been nothing wrong with a name like Geraldine Flora!

We also received numerous baby pictures. Bob and I would sit around, stare at them for a while and try to remember what their parents looked like. Most of the time one of us would come up with a description— some unique feature that would trigger the other's 'memory, then we could put all the pieces together.

That wasn't necessary to do with the pictures we received from April and Steve. Their darling daughter Ashleigh looked to me like a tiny April. She was a beautiful tiny blond. There were pictures of her on a bench, outside sniffing a flower, alone or with her Mom and Dad. How blessed they are.

As a bonus they even sent a picture of the entire family that made those happy memories of the almost rained out wedding, the soggy guests arriving, the lost luggage and their constant upbeat attitude really come alive.

All our weddings have been special and all a little different. But there was one that was so unique I really want to share it with you.

Madison and Charlie met right here at the Inn. There are a lot of us romantics who still believe in love at first sight and knew this was it. We watched in awe as their relationship developed. They did everything together—walked the beach, swam in the pool, ate lunch side by side, and honestly took care of one another. After a couple of weeks of this togetherness, it was Madison's older sister Mallory who innocently declared that if they were so much in love maybe they should think about getting married. That was all they needed to hear—no hesitation, no thinking about it—they both agreed.

Now you would think that a spontaneous marriage would involve at least a few problems, but not this one. It went like clockwork thanks to the bride's sister. She carefully planned and was in charge of the entire affair. She gave instructions to the bride and groom and was the one who walked Madison down the walkway to meet Charlie at the head of the stairs, standing exactly where she had told him he should stand.

Both the bride and groom were a little anxious as she performed the ceremony and had them repeat their vows. She did an excellent job and it went rather smoothly until the very end when she announced it was time to kiss the bride and the groom fell to the walkway in what seemed like a dead faint. Thankfully he was revived very quickly. Madison just kneeled down and said, "It's all right, Charlie, please get up," and he did. But from that point there was a subtle change in the relationship.

Even though they still were considerate of one another, Madison soon began to take a little more care of Charlie than he did of her. She was there with a towel for him when he got out of the pool, watched carefully as he ate, encouraging him to clean his plate, and if he was out of her sight for any length of time she simply went around to all the guests asking, "Has anyone seen my husband?" She had slipped into the role of a concerned wife with a natural ease.

Months later, at home in Florida when her family was discussing the pros and cons of young girls dating older men, she asked, "Is my husband older than I am or are we the same?" The answer was "You're the same, Madison. You are both five years old."

Even with heavy equipment during the road repairs all over the place, people could still get to us, and we could still get to the Settlement. That meant that we could get to the wedding all of us had been talking about and waiting for.

Again, as is almost always the case when something special is happening, just about everyone on the entire island would be there, and dressed in their finest. The ladies were wearing cool and colorful summer dresses, the little girls in pretty outfits with matching ribbons and new shoes, and the men, at least the men in the wedding party, were all elegant in their tuxedos—all of them with the exception of our friend Uncle Leonard. No tuxedo for him, but no t-shirt and shorts either. Cathy must really have put her foot down because he looked very nicely dressed in long pants and a long-sleeve pink shirt. Of course he managed to abandon his ""finery for his usual attire at the very first available moment.

All of my subtle efforts to convince him that wearing a tux would please his son and the rest of the family and how I really wanted a picture of him had failed. I remembered him grinning at me and saying "Mama, all your flattering BS will get you nowhere!" How true that had been. The wedding was beautiful, very well done. The service was special, the food excellent, and Cathy and Leonard not only gained a daughter-in-law but another delightful little granddaughter and a grandson as a bonus.

Not all weddings are what you might call usual and customary. I attended one held at Sunset Beach Resort and it was certainly a little different. When the preacher asked, "Will you take this woman?" a loud voice from the gathered guests shouted, "I will—I'll take her. Let me take her!" When the crowd quieted down and the preacher got to the part of the service where the groom is asked if he will love, honor, etc., the same voice cried out, "Don't believe him—he's lying. Don't believe him!" The preacher continued, the crowd became respectful, stopped laughing, and the service was finally concluded. However at the reception, the friend of the groom who had tried so hard to be part of the service wasn't served any more alcoholic drinks. I don't think it really mattered to him too much because he was taking a little nap on one of the chaise lounges.

Weddings weren't the only special occasions we celebrated. We have had a great Super Bowl Party, Valentine's Dinners, Easter Buffets, St. Patrick's Day Affairs and rehearsal dinners. The first ones are the most vivid in my memory, perhaps because if you have done something once you don't' worry quite as much about the second or third time around.

"We should have a Super Bowl Party," Bob had encouraged.

"That would be great, honey, but how do we do that with only one TV and a satellite card that sometimes works and sometimes doesn't. And even if it's working we never are able to get the major networks?"

"Let's see what we can do. You get on the VHF and announce we are having a Super Bowl Party, and I'll work on the rest."

"Great!" I was thinking. "What should I announce? 'Come on over for the big game, which you might, or might not be able to see'?"

However, I did as requested, several times throughout the day as a matter of fact, each time watching all the scurrying around in the courtyard. I decided early on that if what Bob and several of his helpers were doing didn't work, I'd either deny that it was my voice on the VHF or I'd swim out and hide on our boat until the riot was over.

Bob had located a couple of TVs he could borrow, got his hands on miles of extension cords, spliced this to that and that to this, and even located a satellite card he was sure would work. We were in business.

There was a TV for the dining room, one for the courtyard, and one for the bar, all coming in bright and clear, even before the crowd began to assemble. Of the sixty-some guests that joined us, only one was a Rams fan, or only one had the courage to admit it. Larry, the lonesome soul, said it was only because he had a substantial bet on the Rams and hated to lose.

It was later that I learned the bet was for two lousy candy bars. The Pats hats and shirts were everywhere, so it was hard for me to believe he'd risk life and limb for a couple of bars of chocolate. It must have been an ego thing.

Most of the game I was rushing around serving snacks and drinks and trying desperately to keep track of the bar tabs, but when cheers erupted, I rushed to a TV to see the big play on a replay. That was good, but not quite good enough. Determined to see the finish, I straightened my Pats shirt, made sure my hat was on tight, grabbed a little stool and plunked myself on the floor in front of the TV that was at the bar.

"Okay," I shouted, "if anyone needs me just call my name."

Whenever there was a brief lull the whole bar erupted with shouts of "GERRY, GERRY, GERRY!" which made it sound like we were all part of a Jerry Springer show.

"Okay, enough already. If you want something, just fix it yourself," and that's just what they did.

Needless to say the entire evening was a great success. People claimed they could hear the cheering way around the bend and into the next cove. The fact that my Pats were victorious gave me great pride, but not quite as much as I felt for my genius husband who had managed to pull the whole thing together.

The Valentine's Dinner was a different affair. Reservations were required the day before, and times were assigned in order to make certain everyone could be given all the attention they needed and deserved. I had decided on a surf and turf menu. It included a nice-size steak, a Bahamian lobster tail, three of those wonderful coconut shrimps, along with a large fresh salad, rolls and dessert. I needed to announce it only once over the VHF when the reservations came rolling in. We had to cut off reservations at 45. Although we could do all the prep work well ahead of time and every party had an assigned time, it still meant turning over the tables, resetting, and trying to make sure no one was waiting in the woodwork or standing in line.

We have a small dining room, and an even smaller kitchen, so believe me everyone had to bust their *bungies*. It was our stroke of luck that Larry's friend Beth was visiting. She just jumped in with both feet doing *beaucoup* legwork. It was another lucky break that Glenn's fiancée (at least the fiancée of the day) Rachel was also on hand. She teaches hotel administration at the university in Nassau and added some elite finishing touches. When I saw her shaking out the napkins and putting them on the laps of our guests, I thought to myself, "Wow, this is just like a real restaurant!"

I was too busy in the kitchen and dining room to go anywhere near the bar, so Bob and Leonard did the tending, which was probably a good thing. Even without my pouring the drinks, Bob was certain we were into a losing proposition. A dinner like the one we served would have easily cost $45 to $50 here in the Bahamas, and I had set the price at $35, which was bad enough according to all those who were watching the bottom line. But to add insult to injury, I had also announced that the wives or sweethearts could eat free.

We got rave reviews to which Bob responded, "Why the hell not; they got a damn good deal."

So while I was still counting the accolades, Bob was still counting the expenses versus the income. "Someday, honey, you're going to have to learn to stop giving things away," he said, and how right he was. Someday!

The next grand celebration was to be for St. Patrick's Day. Of course St. Patrick means nothing to Bahamians, but I figured there were enough Americans, even Irish-Americans around, that we could entice a pretty good group to join us for an old fashioned corned beef and cabbage affair. The first thing of course was to find corned beef. Dear God, what was I thinking?

There was none to be had anywhere except in cans, and that surely wouldn't do. Not only couldn't we find any anywhere, but we got very confused blank looks when we tried to describe what we were looking for. After exhausting all possibilities, I suggested we call our son Scott who would be coming down and ask him to bring about eighteen pounds, packaged and wrapped, in a cooler.

I had no way of knowing that eighteen pounds of corned beef would feel like fifty pounds to carry, nor did I realize it would cause my daughter-in-law Gigi real anxiety. She was certain security would stop them and accuse them of carrying body parts. After all that, I did learn that corned beef was available on the island as long as you knew just what to ask for.

I wish I could also learn what to do when something was on sale, priced as two for $5, and I only wanted to buy one. In Marsh Harbour that was not allowed. No matter how I explained I only wanted one, if the price was two for $5 I had to buy the two. In those situations, I guess it was just up to me to decide what in hell I would do with the extra one.

The corned beef arrived, as did some CDs with Irish drinking songs. We found some decorations at the party store in Marsh Harbour. Of course they weren't the bright vivid green one usually associates with St. Patrick, but I decided that the light teal color was probably close enough. Now all I had to do was to remember how to cook corned beef.

It had been a long time, my memory isn't as good as it used to be, and I sure didn't think it was a time to be guessing at the recipe like I have a tendency to do. I decided to call my Aunt Muriel back in the states for some necessary instructions. She told me that my Cousin Laurie was the one usually in charge of St. Patrick's Day dinners. The next step was to e-mail Laurie and when she e-mailed me her instructions my memory was jogged and I thought, "Of course. That's how I remember it." However, just to ensure everything was cooked to perfection I turned to the Internet. There I found a recipe like Laurie's and like I remembered. So that was that! Of course I learned later that my cousin hadn't remembered how to cook a corned beef either, so she had turned to the Internet. At least we were all cooking from the same webpage.

"Who is this guy you be doing this for, Miss Gerry?" Sandra asked as I took over HER kitchen.

I explained who he was the best I could.

"How you be cooking those tings?" she asked.

I explained the best I could.

"You'll need to be adding some sauce and baking them after a while," she stated with some conviction.

"Nope. Sandra, you just keep boiling them with bay leaves and peppercorns for a few hours until they are tender, and skim the top every once in a while."

"That be true, that be it? That be true, Miss Gerry? TRUE?"

I knew at that moment I needed to stand guard over those simmering pots or lord knows what additions might have been made.

Everything was perking along, I was feeling pretty good and somewhat confident when Larry mentioned the O'Malleys.

"They are coming tonight, you know."

"Great," I answered, "real Irishmen."

"Yes, and you know what Mr. O'Malley said? He said he hopes you don't boil the hell out of the beef."

Mr. O'Malley usually had strong opinions and never hesitated to express them to anyone who would listen. And since I really wanted to keep the O'Malleys as friends as well as patrons, all kinds of anxiety began to set in. Man, what if I did what he said he hoped I wouldn't do? I also wondered how many other gourmet corned beef cooks would be joining us for the buffet.

Fortunately all went well, but the compliment I received from one Mr. O'Malley was what really topped off the evening. "Cooked to perfection," he grumbled. Mr. O'Malley has recently passed away, but I venture to guess that he'll be thought of often and certainly remembered every St. Patrick's Day.

"Miss Gerry, you know that guy you did the special dinner for, whatever his name be, and whatever day it be? Well, next year I can cook those tings whatever you call dem and do it very, very good."

"That's excellent, Sandra. Next year it can be your affair."

"See, Miss Gerry? I can learn something from you, just like you need to learn most everything from me."

There had been other special affairs, other things like special birthday parties, anniversary dinners and weddings. Although we were not hosts for one rather large wedding with sixty guests, we did have the honor of serving dinner to forty-five of them the night before the wedding. We set up under a large tent we had recently erected for just such occasions. Polly, a new addition to our team and just the kind of person I had hoped for, was in charge of decorating. She found beautiful conch shells, spray painted the outsides with silver paint, and also sprayed fronds with the same paint to create centerpieces for the tables. She decorated the entrance to the tent with netting and nestled in some of the fronds. With flowers, candles, and pastel table cloths, the setup was as charming as could be. We took many pictures, not just of the decorations but of the buffet table with the large selection of appealing Bahamian dishes, including lobsters piled high. We took pictures of the bride-to-be, her intended, and other guests as they ate, drank, and danced until the wee hours of the morning. I'm sure we took at least sixty or seventy pictures that I couldn't wait to see. However, it looks like I'll not see any of them because Bob lost the camera.

I had such warm memories about the weddings we hosted that I was no longer anxious about the ones booked for the future. Well, perhaps I might be just a little bit anxious, but I had finally out grown my "Mother of the Bride Complex." In truth I was more relaxed because I finally understood that although we at the Inn certainly had a role to play, it was really the setting that made these affairs extra special. The newlyweds continued to let us know how wonderful it was to have had their own personal, private resort for the ceremony and celebration. They claimed that having their own little corner of paradise was the best way possible to start a new life together.

It is also fun to think about the honeymooners. There were those who on occasion joined other guests at the courtyard bar, jesting and relaxed enough to laugh at the jokes that targeted any newly-married couple. They just knew it went with the territory. They didn't mind because they also knew they would have their alone time in a quiet room away from the rest of the world. There were others that we hardly ever saw except for meals, or sitting on the dock watching the sunset, or later at night snuggling as they stargazed. And it sure would be hard to forget the young wife who was so delighted because when she and her new husband walked the deserted beaches on the Atlantic side, they didn't encounter another single soul. The fact that their footprints side by side were the only ones in the sand made it seem to her just like they were in a movie.

CHAPTER 28

A Very Special Bride

Carrie began to e-mail me in April. We communicated almost daily from April until the big day in February, and touched base on everything possible. Her notes were always filled with optimism and humor and she sent pictures of her and her "boyfriend." Before too many weeks passed I began to think of her as the "little one."

She and the groom arrived a few days early and kept us all well entertained. His name is Gerard but she had nicknamed him BooBoo, so that's what we all called him; and when she called for Bob it wasn't just Bob, it was BobEE, a name that some here still shout out occasionally. Her family and friends were all from Canada, his from a small rural town in France. He informed us that it was the first trip his family had ever taken anywhere, and we learned right away that they spoke absolutely no English. This prompted the Canadians to refer to them as the "Frenchies," but always with affection.

Her group spent quite a bit of time at the courtyard bar, listening to music, singing along, telling stories, and teasing each other. His walked the two and a half miles to town and back, at least once a day, and spent time frolicking in the sea, even though it was February. After they had finished their exploring and frolicking, they would briefly join the others at the bar then everyone would speak French. They had no problem communicating, joking or laughing together. I was the only one who didn't know what was going on, but laughed anyway. Sometimes not being able to understand the words doesn't mean a thing, because laughter and happiness have a way of being contagious.

The wedding was as near perfect as could be, and so was the celebration that followed. Right after the cutting of the wedding cake, a group of local folks came to join in. They had brought a big jug of that famous *Coconut Blast* for all to share in—yet another toast to the bride and groom. They just wanted to make sure that this couple had something unexpected added to the memories of their special day. What was more powerful than the taste of that homemade drink was the taste of some typical Bahamian hospitality.

After Carrie and BooBoo returned home, we continued to communicate, not as frequently, but still quite often. Then there came a period of time when nothing was heard from the "little one," until I received an e-mail from her best friend and maid of honor. Carrie was ill—seriously ill. She would be hospitalized for a lengthy period undergoing a strong regime of chemotherapy and radiation treatments. My heart sank, the tears came down, and God knows that prayers went up. Their happiness of just a few months ago—their joy, the belief that all was right with the world and always would be—must now seem surreal.

There was no way I could contact the "little one" and I was just plain afraid to contact any other family members. Call it being a coward, or call it being in denial, whatever it was I ended up just putting my head in the sand. I held positive thoughts, held her in my prayers, and had faith that all would be fine. Knowing Carrie as I did, it couldn't be otherwise. She had her faith, her determination, and her constant upbeat attitude. She had all the things that make healing possible.

Several months went by before I heard. This time the message was from the "little one" herself. She simply wanted to let us know that everything was going fine. The tumor had shrunk by 85%. There would be a few struggles ahead, but nothing she couldn't handle. She ended by sending me a picture of her with her hair just beginning to grow back, thinking I might get a laugh or two.

It wasn't long before she sent another picture so she could share with us their recent purchase. It was of a delightful log cabin, nestled at the end of a long tree-bordered snow-covered path. There was smoke curling from the chimney and the entire image was one of peace and serenity. How I hoped that the peace and serenity, which filled the picture, was filling their hearts and souls as well.

Then came another picture it was one of their new "kids," Bonnie and Clyde. They were two beautiful Black Labs, six months old, and described as very lively. I was truly honored that she had decided these "kids" would know me as Auntie Geraldine!

I can still vividly remember that February Wedding .I can still hear the laughter of her family and friends as they sat around the bar telling stories about one another, joking and singing. I can still picture the groom's family who were fondly called the "Frenchies," wading out of the cool sea drying off to get ready for their walk to town and back.

And I can still name most of the locals who showed up with jugs of that horrible *Coconut Blast* to use as a special toast for this special bride and groom. Was that just yesterday or years ago?

Now she is gone. Carrie, my "little one" is gone. In spite of her spirit, her determination and her faith, she lost her battle with cancer. I think about the picture she sent me of that neat little cottage at the end of the snow-covered lane. It had looked so warm and cozy. Now I wonder if it is now cold and empty. I think of her husband Boo Boo and know that he also must feel cold and empty.

How wonderful it would be if he could find her sweet face in the sunrises, be able to recognize her laughter in the songs of birds, and see her beautiful smile in the sunsets. That way, he would know that she is always with him.

I have asked myself over and over the question so many ask when they lose someone they care about. Why, why, for what good reason did YOU let this happen? Of course there is never an answer—at least not one that we mere mortals can understand. It just happens. That's it, it just happens.

CHAPTER 29

Much More than We Bargained For

The dinner we had hosted for the forty-five guests had been such a hit that the 'bride's family decided to do some promoting. They were aware of a wedding that was to take place on the island and contacted the family. They strongly suggested that Seaside Village would be the place for a dinner and a party the night before the wedding. They gave them our e-mail address and then informed us of what might take place. They were extremely pleased to have given us such a positive recommendation, but not nearly as pleased as we were that they, Ginger and Peter, held us in such high regard.

The bride-to-be, her Mom and sister paid us a visit. They looked us over, checked out the tent, and sampled several things from our menu. They were pleased with what they saw, and also liked everything they had tasted. In fact they were close to deciding exactly what the evening's menu should include, but there were a couple of problems.

First they wondered how to include just about everything they had sampled, and second they were not the ones actually in charge of the dinner. The groom's family would be paying for this special affair, so ultimately, they would be the ones calling the shots. From then on I was to contact them for suggestions, recommendations, and approval of the menu, and to finalize all the plans.

The 'bride's family was from the South. They were familiar with the Abacos, where things are done differently. They understood that wearing shoes even at a wedding was certainly not a requirement or even expected. They were fun-loving, extremely carefree and had an "almost anything goes" attitude.

The 'groom's family was from the North, New York City to be exact. They had never been to any of the Bahamas Out Islands and had an entirely different set of expectations, so let the fun begin.

We chatted on the phone a while and their initial request was for white linen tablecloths and napkins. My first thought was to try and explain that the whole affair would be outside under a tent in a very casual setting and perhaps bright colored linens might work better. But if white linens were what they really wanted, that's what it would be. Provided of course that I could find enough of them somewhere around.

Next was the issue of wines. When you are working with real wine connoisseurs and they ask what kinds of wine we serve, the appropriate answer is certainly not, "Well, we have red and we have white!"

At first the groom's Mother began to list some wines they might like to have, while her husband coached her from the background.

"Stop all that chattering," she told him. "I can't concentrate on what I'm saying."

Finally she suggested that he take over the phone since he was the one who knew exactly what they wanted. Now he was on the phone and she was coaching from the background. All this time I was trying to write down the names of some of their favorite wines—wines I had never heard of with names I could barely spell.

The next day I headed over to Marsh Harbour to wander through the wine section of the largest liquor store anywhere in the Abacos. I had my hastily scribbled note in hand and tried to match my spelling with the names that were actually on the bottles. I hadn't had the time to put in my contact lenses and had forgotten to bring my glasses. This added more uncertainty to my frantic search.

In one of the many phone calls I explained that the wine we served was called *Undurraga* and it seemed to be enjoyed by everyone. However, when they learned it was from Chile they resisted. They would settle for California Wines as long as they were from the best vineyards, but their real preference was for French wines.

Now I had a compound problem. First I didn't know, and still don't know a "good vineyard" from a not-so-good one. Second, this was the time when we were having all the trouble with France before going to war in Iraq. Even if it wasn't my party and I wasn't paying, I still didn't want to be buying any damn French wine.

I walked back and forth between the aisles, squinting to check for names I had listed and jotting down the prices of anything I vaguely recognized. After a couple of hours I caught the ferry back prepared to call and make a full report.

"The price of this wine is $48 a bottle, this one $36, there are two or three others that range from $29 to $31."

There was complete silence on the other end of the line. Neither one was chattering for the first few seconds. I guess shock can do that to you.

"Oh my, that's about three times the price we would have to pay here in the states."

"Sorry," I answered, "but this is the Bahamas."

The final decision was to talk to the 'bride's Mother. She could bring what they needed over on her boat. That meant I would be left out of the loop. I wouldn't have to worry about the wine any more—probably a good thing since it was apparent there were other things to consume my thoughts. The guest list had begun to grow. First there were to be fifty, then fifty-five, then sixty, then sixty-five, and finally an overwhelming seventy-three.

I spent a great deal of time counting. I counted plates, counted silverware, counted chairs and tables, champagne flutes and wine glasses, white linen tablecloths and napkins. I physically counted things in the daytime, and mentally counted them again when I tried to go sleep. It didn't matter how often I went through this exercise, I still came up with about half of what was needed, except for the white linen napkins. I had only ten of those.

Then Ginger called.

"Well," she asked, "are you going to be doing that night before the wedding party for the folks I sent your way?"

"Well, we sure are going to try, but this time there will be seventy-three guests instead of forty-five!"

"Oh my," she responded. "Do you have everything you need?"

"Only about half of everything," I explained.

"Well go to our house, and in the shed there are folding tables and chairs, grab them and I'll see that my nephew gets you a key to the house. Inside, upstairs in the owner's closet, you'll find plates, salad plates, wine glasses and champagne flutes. Take whatever you need."

She even went on to apologize because she had lent her silverware to a family member for a special party so none of that would be there for us.

Now I ask you, who needs a Taylor Rental Service when you have an angel like Ginger looking out for you?

We now had most of what was needed and the rest I could find at home and carry down with me. Table cloths didn't present any problems. They were reasonably priced and in abundance, but the same wasn't true of those darn napkins. Not only were they scarce, but they cost nearly $3 apiece and I needed sixty-three of them.

Now it was the 'bride's mother that came to the rescue. She found some for 89 cents, grabbed them, and piled them on her boat along with a thousand other things she was toting over.

Setting up the tent was left to Larry, Beth and me. Bob had already made a tremendous contribution by working for over a full day with a sail repair kit, hand stitching a tear in the tent top. Now it was our turn to place the tables and chairs to see what kind of seating we could arrange. It didn't take too long for us to realize that there was no way seventy-three people would fit inside, even if we "greased them," as Larry suggested.

We had built an outside deck for the DJ and decided if we set up tables and chairs in the adjacent areas, left that side of the tent open, and placed torches all around, it would work. All we had to do was pray for good weather. If rain posed no threat, it would be the wind we would have to contend with. Trying to figure a way to keep tablecloths in place with the wind blowing really presented a challenge. Beth and I talked over several alternatives. We were aware that there were some kind of clips you could place on the corner of the cloths to weight them down. We were also aware we would never find any such things here in the Abacos, so we decided to invent our own version.

I dragged out the sewing machine to sew little pockets on all the corners of the cloths. Beth scurried around to gather up all the fishing weights she could find. I left just a little opening in each of those pockets so we could tuck those heavy little balls in place. We gleefully began to do just that. We were sure feeling creative and clever. After we'd completed about four cloths, Beth suggested we run out to the tent and see how well our idea worked.

The cloths went down, the wind came up and it was a total disaster. As those cloths whipped around those little steel balls ripped right through my carefully designed corners and were bouncing all over the place. It sure hurt our egos to have to admit that our clever little scheme was useless.

Now we had to ask the guys to put up the side to the tent that faced the sea to block out the wind—there was no other choice. The rest of the afternoon, without even a little breeze that could reach us and with the sun blazing, it felt like we were working in a sauna.

The bridal party brought over beautiful floral centerpieces for the tables, so everything was ready to go. Appetizers consisting of conch fritters, grouper fingers, deviled eggs and veggie platters with a variety of dips were served in the courtyard and around the bar That is where everyone gathered until the "no-see-ums" decided to join the party. Now everyone had to fix their plates and dash to the end of the dock to escape those pesky little gnats. We were just grateful that they didn't follow the crowd to the tent. The wind had died down, so the side was rolled up, allowing for a gentle bug-free breeze to flow through. It was absolutely perfect.

The buffet included lobster tails, blackened grouper, coconut shrimp, chicken tenders, peas and rice, Caesar salad, and vegetable kabobs. Sandra was a little up-tight about the kabobs. Although she made great chicken or shrimp kabobs, she wasn't too confident about doing ones that had plantains and fresh pineapple chunks. However, with a little help and a lot of encouragement, she did an excellent job. Needless to say she was as proud as could be. We also had key lime tarts for dessert—smaller versions of Sandra's key lime pie.

Beth, Renee and I managed the buffet table. Bob and Larry ran back and forth from the kitchen with refills when necessary, Glenn handled the wine and made many other drinks, and Sandra stood alert and prepared as queen in her kitchen. There was plenty of good food, many speeches, and lots of laughs. With just seven of us, and borrowed necessities from our friends, we had managed to pull off an extremely successful affair.

One of the highlights was when Sandra came to the tent and received a standing ovation. The other was the glowing praise from the groom's parents.

I had tried to explain over the phone and through the e-mails what island life was really like, that we were off the beaten path and very casual. They told me that they had heard all that, but still hadn't been sure what any of it meant. Now they knew, understood, and were absolutely delighted with the whole experience.

The next day would be the wedding. Bob and I had been invited both to the wedding and wedding dinner.

The wedding on the beach was wonderful. They had chosen a near-perfect spot and all went as planned, except for one little snafu. The bride was very tall and extremely elegant in her beautiful long gown with a small train. As she stood on the shore to repeat her vows, the ocean decided to send in an extra big wave. Now the contest was between the ocean and the bride's mother as to who would reach the bride first. The mother made a frantic dive forward reaching her daughter just about the same time the wave did. There was little damage, the gown was just damp around the edges and the mother only slightly embarrassed, but it certainly provided a few seconds of unexpected entertainment.

Next was the dinner. Not only were we to attend but so were Sandra and Glenn. It was to be held at the 'island's newest restaurant, one that had been modeled after a four star restaurant in the states and named the Blue Water Grill. Consultants had been hired to help with the design, and they had actually hired a gourmet chef from Austria. The setting was absolutely beautiful, everything bright spanking new, and I expect nothing had to be borrowed.

I wondered what Glenn was thinking as he watched four bartenders, not mixing all types of drinks as he had done, but just serving the wine. I wondered what Sandra was thinking each time those doors to the kitchen opened. She could see all the amazing state-of-the-art stainless steel kitchen equipment, and I'm sure she marveled at the five or six people in there helping the chef. I know what I was thinking as I watched all of this along with the seven or eight people who were doing the serving.

"Dear God," I thought. "This is our competition and it sure is a far cry from our 'rinky dink' kitchen, small staff, Sandra, and a tent."

I tried to fairly judge the meal. The salad was excellent, perhaps one of the best I had tasted. I even decided to remember just what was in it and try replicating it back at the Inn. The rest of the meal was satisfactory. The presentation was wonderful, but there were some things on the plate that, although they looked pretty, were hardly edible. Steak was the main entrée, cooked to Bob's liking but certainly not to Sandra's.

"Look, Miss Gerry. Look at this. They not even cook dis right. It not even be rare. Rare is red but this be purple in the middle. I be *ceris*, Miss Gerry. I can't eat this!"

She decided to send it back and they brought her another one just like it, or perhaps the same one. I'm not sure. In any event, she decided to take it with her and cook it some more when she got back to Seaside. Most of my steak just stayed on my plate and so did Glenn's—they just weren't very good.

I must, however, give the owners credit. This was the first big event for this restaurant. In fact they were still putting on some finishing touches late that same day. They were brave, did a good job and I'm certain there were many others who were more impressed with it all than we were. Maybe it is natural to have a jaundiced eye when viewing your competition.

Since that time, the restaurant has changed hands. Now they have a very creative and young American chef who does a marvelous job with each of their undertakings.

This is a small island and there are only three places to eat. When tourists come ashore, they really want to try out what is available and since we were on that list, I decided not worry about who else was doing what and tried not to be envious of all they had to work with. We'll just keep plugging away. Besides, it also helped to remember that so many of the wedding guests told us that of all the affairs they had attended, their night under our tent was the very best. That included the groom's family, who decided they were in love with Seaside Village, that little white Inn with the red roof that was "off the beaten path."

CHAPTER 30

Another Spontaneous Move

Our little Inn was quiet until the very end of January and the first week of February. We would then be hosting a yoga retreat organized by an instructor named Quinn Sales. We would have all the rooms filled, a couple of cottages and the favorite place of most renters, the Yellow Ocean House.

Shortly after we purchased the Inn we also bought the Yellow House. That was another one of those spontaneous happenings that is difficult to explain.

We had switched attorneys from the ones we had been struggling with in Nassau to another gentleman in Marsh Harbour. It just so happened that he owned the land adjacent to the Inn. It was land that went from the Sea of Abaco to the Atlantic Ocean where a neat yellow house sat high on a bluff.

Bob told us that this attorney wanted us to look at the Yellow House, thinking we might be interested in that as well, as the land that went with it. "Sure we might be interested, but everything we have is tied up in the Inn, so why bother?" was my question. That was right, but Bob thought that at least if we went up and took a look we could honestly tell this guy we had done so. Then we could tell him it wasn't anything we could handle right now. We just were not in a position to buy it.

Up the little lane we went—Bob, Janet, Lisa and I. We immediately loved the Yellow House. It had four bedrooms, two baths, a great kitchen, dining area, great room, and views that were beyond compare. Being up a little high, the cottage provided views of the Sea of Abaco from almost any point, and the Atlantic Ocean was right there lapping at our feet. There were steps leading from the cottage patio down to the ocean, where the beach was unbelievably beautiful.

The Yellow House

"Okay girls, lets go," said one impatient father/ husband. "Now I can call our attorney and tell him we have been up and looked it all over."

"And," a couple of us said, "you can tell him we ARE GOING TO BUY IT!"

"Are you crazy? How in the hell do you propose to do that?"

"Not sure," I answered, "but we'll figure a way."

And figure a way we did. Lucky for us the place was a very popular rental, especially with repeat guests. The rentals could take care of our hefty monthly payments to the bank, at least some of them.

The Yellow House was a favorite with the yoga group as it had been with many others. They found that the sounds of the surf, the salt breezes, and the rolling waves added to their peace and contentment. It was a spiritual place.

With the yoga retreat onsite, things had to change slightly. They provided most of the breakfast foods, which consisted of cold cereals, yogurt, nuts, granola, wheat germ and fruits We set it up as a buffet and provided hard boiled eggs, breads or muffins of some kind, juices and, on their insistence, Starbucks coffee. For lunch they were on their own, but we provided dinner.

Dinner always began with a large salad that was served individually and then a buffet. Jan and Lisa both came down to be on hand to help with this group. They were the ones who actually planned the nightly meals and did most of the cooking. Of course that delighted both Sandra and me. Neither one of us was a vegetarian and suffice it to say not too excited about learning how to stir fry stuff with tofu!

And as for Bob, the first time we had hosted this group he was at home recuperating from a hospital stay. He informed me that if he hadn't been home for that reason he'd be hiding in New Hampshire anyway. He explained that he just wouldn't be comfortable watching a group of ladies putting their behinds up in the air and their legs over their heads. He also thought it hilarious that females who were involved in yoga were called "yoginis."

Yoga at The Yellow House

After several phone conversations he finally admitted that he didn't have the foggiest notion what yoga was really all about, so of course he asked me to describe it to him. Well trying to describe all the aspects of yoga is difficult indeed. I tried to explain the meaningful exercises, the total relaxation, the peaceful feelings and the spiritual aspects.

"Try to think of it this way. If they are in a relaxation mode, lying on the dock, they let the warm sun and the gentle breezes not only caress the outsides of their bodies but they pull those feelings deep inside as well. They let the quiet lapping sounds of the waves erase all worrisome thoughts."

"Why don't you just tell me simply what the goal is!"

""Well, it's to stay focused, to be calm and energized at the same time. It's like getting in touch with your whole being as well as the world around you." Not a very adequate answer but the best I could do.

"Okay," he answered, "Now I SEE!

"Sure," I thought, "that's just what the blind man said."

The girls really added to the overall experience for these guests. Janet was available for her CranioSacral healing sessions and Lisa did spiritual readings for those who signed up. They also spent a great deal of time planning for and making special little favors that they passed out to these guests on a daily basis.

For the most part, the participants took their sessions very seriously. They would start out on the dock for sunrise meditation and a workout. They would close with a workout again out on the dock as they watched awesome sunsets. There was only one occasion that gave us grief and put us in a defensive mode.

One of the yoga guests was caught red-handed shoplifting from our little Guana Gift Shop. Amazing as it may seem, this lady was a high-ranking Canadian official. We kept it as quiet as possible so the entire group wouldn't be tainted by this one bad apple. Quinn, the organizer and leader of this retreat, handled the situation quite deftly. She used her power of persuasion to assure the locals involved that this "lady" would not be around to finish the retreat and most assuredly would never be invited back.

There was one other time when I detected a small group that perhaps wasn't so totally committed to the yoga efforts as the rest were.

"I have a great idea," said one lady sitting at the bar with three of her friends.

"Let's just sit at the bar, have a few Jolly Bobs, stay up late and say to hell with that sunrise shit." That they did.

But truthfully those were the only rebels I ever noticed and they only rebelled that once. I guess feeling whole and healthy won out over having a miserable Jolly Bob hangover.

The others truly loved this retreat as did we and it was obvious that the whole experience had a rejuvenating effect.

It was time to prepare for another wedding. This one was estimated to have forty to forty-five guests, a good number—one that was certainly easy for us to handle. There should be no reason for anyone to get uptight or push panic buttons, except perhaps for Larry. The groom's parents were good friends of Larry's. In fact just the previous year Larry and Beth went for a lengthy visit to their home in Alaska and had what was described as a wonderful get-together. Now they also considered Beth to be their friend and certainly would include her as an invited guest to the wedding. Sounds simple doesn't it, but believe me it could get mighty complicated—not for us but for Larry.

CHAPTER 31

Headaches Over a Wedding and Heartaches Over Beth

Whenever Beth was not on the island, Larry had a tendency to, shall we say, find temporary substitutes. Although we were pretty protective of Beth, we kept our comments and our moral platitudes to ourselves. He was, as he described himself, a single healthy male, free to do as he pleased. Besides, his dalliances were usually short-lived, ending most of the time when husbands showed up. Now he was involved on quite a different level.

He had just about moved in with someone who didn't have a husband. In fact the only time he came back to his room at the Inn was when she threw him out, and that did occasionally happen.

Now with the wedding fast approaching, we were all wondering how he'd juggle all of this. He hadn't been honest with Beth, but certainly she must have known something wasn't quite right. He never seemed to be around when she called, and her calls often went unanswered until the next day.

I was quite certain that with Beth coming for the wedding his new friend would not throw him out. In fact I suspected she'd hang on tighter than ever. She really did keep close track of where he was at any given moment.

One of the young local fellows asked how long we thought Larry would put up with being "pussy whipped." I guessed it just depended on what the rewards would be. I was wrong. When he explained that she couldn't come to the wedding with him because she didn't even know the people, it didn't sit too well. After a crying screaming fit, she did throw him out. That sure was a lucky break for Larry. Now he could give all his attention to Beth and pretend to her and their friends that things were as they used to be. He even stayed on her boat with her, took some time to go fishing with her, and doted on her just like in the old days.

"Damn you, Larry," I thought. "Beth is such a perfect lady—she would do anything for anyone." How we all hoped that she would find someone who would treat her right and really value her for who she was. The problem was how much she really loved Larry. As far as she was concerned he was her one and only. "Damn you, Larry! Damn you!"

All of us with the exception of Uncle Leonard tried to be polite to Larry's new friend. Leonard, true to form, would simply take off. She certainly was aware that she wasn't everyone's favorite, but that didn't give us license to be rude.

Whenever Larry did come back to the Inn, she usually showed up just a few minutes later, right behind him, hanging around, acting like a victim. As she said in a crybaby voice: "Nobody likes me and that is really not fair. It's not like I broke up a family or anything. After all, they only saw each other two weeks out of the year."

I couldn't believe that she actually thought that was the case. On this small island everyone knows exactly what goes on. She had to know that for the past four years Beth came and stayed a couple of months at a time. She had to know how often Larry went to the states to visit her, how they took numerous vacations together and how they had been in the process of looking for land to buy together, or more likely for her to buy for Larry so he could finally build his house.

The second time she tried to pull that poor-victim role on me I felt obligated to explain to her just what the relationship had really been. But please don't ask me why, maybe the island isolation made me think

I had the right to stick my nose in wherever I chose. However, during that conversation it dawned on me that she knew it all but just didn't care.

There were other things that were none of my business and I know I was being defensive of Beth. She was such a sweetheart, and a real lady. So when Larry's new friend engaged in public displays of almost pornographic affection, it really bugged the hell out of me. I shall not attempt to describe some of the antics—this is a good place for you to use your imagination. But it was obvious she was staking out her territory.

As possessive as she was of Larry, it was very interesting to learn that Larry wasn't the only player in the game. The other one that we soon became aware of happened to be a friend of Larry's. Larry knew he wasn't alone and stated openly that he didn't care. Well, this is a small island with not much available, so I guess sharing is the friendly thing to do; and as kids, didn't we learn that when we were playing we should take turns? That, after all, was only fair. Maybe I should ask the Barefoot Man to write a song about Guana's Fair and Sharing Guy.

As for his friend, when the situation became clear to him he just graciously bowed out. But until that happened we were simply amused by the stories about the trio that floated around the island. It reminded us of our junior high school days.

The day of the wedding finally arrived. There were quite a few last minute changes requested by the groom's mother. It was very clear that she was calling the shots. In fact it was understood that she was the one who had chosen the wedding spot, but had not given any clear thought to the distance most guests would have to travel. That triggered a lot of behind the scenes grumbling.

The bride also had a mother, but not a very assertive one. The groom's father, who was divorced from his mother, came just for the day of the wedding and then left quite quickly. Not exactly a warm family scene. But regardless, the affair went off without a hitch. However, I found some of the comments a little puzzling.

"This was great. I can't believe you pulled this off!"

"Wow, this was really first class. Who would have thought you could do it."

"What a surprise. This was really nice . . . and really unexpected!"

I had no idea what they had expected, but apparently something quite different than what we provided. If they had been really aware of what had gone on the day before, I could probably have better understood their comments.

The day before the big event we decided to close the bar and dining room to the public. That was not an uncommon practice for us when we were about to host a wedding. It was an effort to make sure we had the time to get the place really spruced up and everything ready to go. Knowing that these were friends of Beth and Larry only intensified our efforts. I'm not sure how it all happened but the more we announced to the public that we were closed, the more the people came.

Boatload after boatload and golf cart after golf cart of hungry and thirsty people arrived on our doorstep. Of course, you don't turn them away. In fact you feel obligated to actually hang around, see they are well taken care of and even chat with them a little. That meant that other things you were committed to do would have to wait until later, in fact much later.

We had one of the workers rake up all sorts of dead bushes and leaves. He added them to the usual paper and boxes that were to be burned. It was a great day for it. There was only a light wind and it was blowing away from the resort. We thought that was a real lucky break. However, after the fire got roaring, the wind picked up, changed direction and the smoke blew right into the tent. Right into the tent where we were supposed to be decorating for the wedding tomorrow! The only thing we could do was shout to the worker, "DON'T THROW ANYTHING ELSE ON THAT FIRE!"

We kept shouting the instructions 'NO MORE, NO MORE," and he kept piling things on while smiling and nodding his head YES. Bob had to race over to the burning pile, stomp his feet, shake his finger, and engage in other demonstrative efforts before the message was finally understood.

Just as all of this was happening I was standing at the bar chatting with the guests and Lisa approached me.

"Can I speak to you, Mom?"

"Sure, what's up?"

"Well, can we talk over there?"

So over I went to the other side of the courtyard.

"Mom, we have a dead mouse smell in the dining room!"

"Oh my God, how could that be? We've never had that before. Are you sure that's what it is?"

"Yes, I am really sure. The housekeeper found this mouse in the back of the closet under the stairs. He was really small but dead as a doornail, and smells very bad.

Once inside the dining room I needed no more convincing. "Open all the windows and the sliding glass doors, turn on the fans and the air conditioning. Let's see if that helps."

Lisa suggested burning incense might also help. That did help—until the dining room caught on fire. Thankfully it was a relatively small fire that we got under control before there was too much damage.

Now all we had to do was hang around until the guests who weren't even supposed to be there because we were "closed" finally decided to call it a night. Once they left, we would still have a long night ahead of us.

As I mentioned before, the wedding went off without a hitch. Looking back I might concur with one of the guests and wonder how we were able to pull it off.

That small fire in the dining room had seemed really threatening and had gotten everyone's adrenalin soaring. But certainly it was nothing compared to what occurred a couple of months later.

Lisa had come back to the Inn to help relieve me of some of the workload. Instead of my working from 7:00 a.m. until at least 11:00 p.m., seven days a week, we could take turns. She would handle breakfast and lunch, then I'd step in to help with the afternoon bar crowd and dinner guests. If we were swamped, either with dinner reservations or a large number of fun people wanting a drink or two, she would automatically put herself back on duty.

Her usual routine was to take a very early morning walk before the breakfast hours began. This one morning it was raining a little bit so she decided to change her routine and walk after breakfast. Thank God she did. I was in the small hallway-like pantry off the kitchen. Lisa was hanging around the kitchen with Sandra and her Dad. I had asked Bob to come to the kitchen to light the oven. Over and over I had tried but could not get the igniter to work.

Bob went through the same exercise with no better luck, so now out came the big old kitchen matches, followed immediately by a large BOOM.

Sandra was crying, I was rooted to the spot, and Lisa was yelling.

"Hold still, Dad, hold still!"

"I'm all right, Lisa, I'm all right."

"Damn it, Dad, you are not all right. You're on fire!"

And so she banged away, slapping out the fire that was burning his beard, on his head, up his arms until it was all under control.

She had maintained her cool and did what needed to be done, which is more than I can say for Sandra or me. But once the danger had passed, she fell apart. She was crying and shaking all over.

"Come here, Lisa, come with me, come to our room, relax sweetie, sit right here," I pleaded as I hugged her. But that wasn't working, so I had a brilliant idea.

"Here," I said, "smoke a cigarette."

Now wasn't that a neat suggestion from a mother to a daughter who is a nonsmoker? I have no idea what I was thinking.

Instead of smoking, she went into the office, called home, and told her siblings they would all have to chip in to buy Mom and Dad a new stove.

I stayed in the room and smoked.

She came back to help me trim the singed part of her 'Father's beard, eyebrows, and what hair he had. Even as we were doing those repairs he was still claiming that Lisa had over-reacted. It wasn't until afternoon when the big blisters began to show up that he changed his tune.

When Beth heard about the incident, she sent a $100 donation to help with the purchase of the new stove.

Once we finally figured out the problem and determined we really didn't need a new stove after all, I tucked her donation in an envelope and will see that someday she gets it back.

CHAPTER 32

Not Hosts but Guests and a Crisis

We weren't in charge of all the weddings on Guana. Sometimes we were simply guests. That's what happened when our friends Bruce and Judy decided to get married.

It was at a recent wedding when Bruce simply turned to Judy and said, "Maybe we ought to do that." Now how is that for a romantic proposal?

Everyone close to them was surprised and delighted, none more so than Judy, I suspect. After all they had been live-in partners for twenty-plus years. Now he had proposed. So, let the planning begin!

The invited guests would include family and friends from all over the states who would need travel instructions and housing accommodations. Who would share which cottages and where took a lot of careful consideration for obvious reasons. Placing people together who were not quite compatible could sure put a damper on the affair.

The friends who were already second-home owners on the island and the rest of the general population would be the easy part. It would only take one general announcement at the Pot Luck Supper or at a Nippers Pig Roast to let the whole Island know that EVERYONE was invited to the wedding and reception.

There were still a multitude of details to be addressed, but all of us knew without a doubt that they would be handled by "General" Judy. Our only role would be to stand by and wait for instructions. That system worked well, especially since the wedding was actually going to be a four-day affair planned for all the visiting friends and relatives.

On Wednesday we all met at Sunset Beach Bar and Grill for the Pot Luck Supper. Those of us who had kitchens available cooked extra dishes so there would be plenty for the off-island guests. I think the bride-to-be brought more food than any of us just to make sure everyone was well fed. The setting was perfect for getting to know who was who, and clearly the party was beginning.

Thursday we converged on the Blue Water Grill for their Pizza Night. It was quite a crowd but handled without too many mishaps. The same folks were there that had partied the night before. In addition to the some close island friends, there were sons and daughter-in-laws, daughters and son-in-law, grandchildren, and nieces and nephews from both sides. There were sisters, sister s' husbands, old friends, and even old bridge partners.

It is no wonder I was still trying to sort them all out. When we had a house full of kids and some ruckus would start, I'd simply shout, "Okay, whichever one you are, knock it off," so I guess it's fair to say I was still running true to form. Remembering names is not something I do very well.

Friday was Chicken in the Bag night at Nippers and, keeping with the program, we all gathered.

Saturday morning a small group gathered to decorate the gazebo where the wedding would actually take place. It belonged to Joe, a friend. Lights were strung, flowers put all around and netting and bows here and there. Lights were even placed to border the small path that led from Joe's house down to his charming delightful gazebo that sat right on the shore of the Sea of Abaco.

When evening came, the affair was a little different, and a little more personal. Mag and Wendy, good friends of the bride and groom, hosted a night before the wedding dinner.

They provided the main entrées and some of the rest of us provided a variety of dishes including desserts. Guests filled the house, the sunroom, wandered around the yard and walked the dock. As a wild guess I would estimate there was a crowd of about seventy-five people—and I could actually name about twenty of them, but sadly most of those I could name were not the newcomers.

Sunday was the big day and the weather was actually perfect. Both of the previous Sundays there had been pouring rain, but Judy swore she had prayed to St. Jude for sunshine and knew her prayers had been answered. I believed her, but others swore that it was simply the fact that Mother Nature hadn't dared to defy "General Judy."

I wrote a little ditty for Bruce and Judy to try to capture the essence of the big day. Suffice it to say that I'm sure as hell no Jason. But I tried, so here goes.

IT REALLY IS QUITE SILLY TO TRY AND MAKE A RHYME,
BUT A SIMPLE MIND WILL TRY IT WHEN THEY HAVE A LOT OF TIME

A FOUR-DAY WEDDING WEEKEND, WHO THOUGHT IT COULD BE DONE?
BUT EVERY DAY WAS PLANNED, A LITTLE WILD, BUT LOTS OF FUN.

THE WEDDING ITSELF WAS BEAUTIFUL BUT DIFFICULT TO DESCRIBE,
THE GRANDCHILDREN DRESSED ALIKE, AND THEN THE LOVELY BRIDE.

DOWN THE LIGHTED PATH THE SMILING CHILDREN SLOWLY GO,
AND THAT'S WHEN FOR MOST OF US THE TEARS BEGAN TO FLOW.

THEN CAME A RADIANT JUDY ON THE ARMS OF BOTH HER BOYS,
BRUCE IS WAITING IN THE GAZEBO, FILLED WITH PRIDE AND JOY.

THE SERVICE WAS WONDERFUL, MEANINGFUL, SHORT
AND SWEET.
THEN THE GUESTS WHILE DRYING THEIR EYES BEGAN A
SLOW RETREAT.

OFF TO RIDGE HOUSE WHERE THE RECEPTION WILL
BEGIN,
A HUNDRED FIFTY PEOPLE GATHERED TO CELEBRATE
BEFORE THE EVENING'S END.

THE APPETIZERS WERE SO ABUNDANT GUESTS THOUGHT
THAT WAS THE DINNER,
THEN OUT CAME THE PRIME RIB AND LOBSTERS, SO
FORGET ABOUT GETTING THINNER.

I GUESS THERE ISN'Y MUCH LEFT TO SAY
ABOUT "JUICE" AND "BRUDY'S" SPECIAL DAY
EXCEPT
CONGRATULATIONS TO MR. AND MRS. WHITE.

MAY THE REST OF YOUR DAYS BE FILLED WITH LAUGHTER,
LOVE AND LIGHT.

The reception was wonderful, catered by Judy's son-in-law. He owns
and operates Party Caterers in Ft. Lauderdale, Florida, so there was no
question that he knew just what to do. There was live music, plenty of
dancing, loads of laughter and only one thing that folks were grumbling
about.

A young man who often comes for a stay on the island showed up
with his dog. And, as most dogs would have a tendency to do, he
kept hanging around the buffet table looking for handouts or scooting
between the guests legs looking for dropped morsels. Several guest
shouted "GET THAT DAMNED DOG OUT OF HERE!" The
owner took him home but really to no avail because this DAMNED
DOG returned just a few minutes later.

This time, however, he didn't hang around the buffet table. Instead
he just began to circle the small table that held the wedding cake. The
guests that were observing this were quick to respond.

"HURRY, SOMEONE GRAB THE DOG. GRAB THAT

DAMNED DOG. HE IS ABOUT TO DEVOUR THE WEDDING CAKE." So, he was brought home again, with the owner being told that unless he could come back without his dog he shouldn't come back at all. I am not sure where or how he locked him up, but just a short while later he returned with a big smile, minus the dog and offering an apology. That apology helped a little, but there were still some unforgiving people that did little to make him feel welcomed.

The party went on in full swing. Out on the very large deck most of the guests were dancing, some singing, and others sitting around with plates on their laps and eating their third or fourth helpings. Only a handful sat in the living room where the topic of conversation continued to be about the DAMNED DOG and speculation about how his owner, the newcomer, would really fit on the island.

Most of those on the deck weren't even aware of the prior situation, and if they had been they probably couldn't have cared less. There was, however, something that would happen shortly that had everyone caring.

"GERRY, GERRY!" Someone was yelling. "Did Glenn ever have seizures when he was working for you?"

"My God, NO," I answered. "Why? What's wrong?"

"Something has happened to him, something BAD! He was talking to some of the guys when all of a sudden be began to slur his words, his eyes glazed over, he began to drool and it looked like his left side was immobilized. Now he is unresponsive and it all happened so fast."

A STROKE? Could it possibly be a stroke of some kind? It seemed unbelievable. Glenn was a young man in his forties and always seemed to be in good health. "How could this happen?" I asked, "Could this be real?"

Real it was. Judy is a nurse and recognized what was happening and so did Captain Nick, one of Guana's rescue workers. Even though Nick had been celebrating right along with the rest of us, he immediately came to attention. All his skills and training just kicked in. He knew just what to do and went about doing it.

The rest of us scurried around looking for aspirin, thinking that would help—something we had heard about on TV.

A couple even raced over to Graceland, the nearest place to Ridge House. Carol and Farmer Bob had left the party early, so they might have just what we needed.

In the meantime Nick went to work. He radioed Johnny at Nippers to tell him they needed his boat. He radioed the Marsh Harbour medical clinic to inform them of the problem and to ask for their help. He also gave them an estimated time of their arrival at the government dock so they could be waiting.

Some of the men helped load Glenn into a chair and lift him into the back of the pickup truck. Three or four of them also got into the back of the truck determined to help in any way they could. Among these helpers was the dog owner.

When a couple of the "grumblers" saw what was happening, they couldn't resist commenting.

"Where in hell does he think he's going?"

"Why is he going along? He hardly knows Glenn."

"What does he think he's going to do?"

"I'll tell you what he's going to do," came a quiet response. "He is a pilot, his private plane is on the landing strip at the Marsh Harbour Airport and he has volunteered to fly Glenn to the hospital in Freeport. That's what he's going to do!"

Amazing for some people how quickly a person can be transformed from a villain with a dog to a hero with a mission.

They reached the government dock in record time and picked up the nurse from the clinic who was there to help with the transport. They also got to the airport in record time, loaded their precious cargo and headed for the hospital. Captain Nick and the nurse were the only ones to make that final leg of the trip. They, along with the pilot, stayed for hours with Glenn as the necessary and numerous tests were taken.

The rapid response and doing the right things was certainly in Glenn's favor. Although we were told the recovery would take months and there were no guarantees, the prognosis was favorable.

He was flown to a hospital in the states for additional, more intensive tests, back to the hospital in Freeport for a brief stay, and then back to the states. He would be staying with relatives in the US for a while longer so follow up studies could be done.

The favorable prognosis was correct. It has been a lengthy road to recovery but he has done remarkably well. He has gained the full use of his left side and his speech, although slow, is no longer slurred. If fact he is just about where he used to be.

When he woke up that first day in the hospital, he saw three concerned visitors gathered around his bed and the atmosphere was anything but friendly. They identified themselves as one HIS WIFE, another HIS SWEETHEART and last but not least HIS GIRLFIRIEND.

It was somewhat of a miracle that having all three of them in the same room in a confrontational mood hadn't pushed him over the edge.

CHAPTER 33

Personal Storms and Party Planning

In the past the folks on the island gather to decorate the fig tree with Christmas lights to begin very festive holiday events. One thing that they added was a Christmas parade, to be held on December 23rd. Everyone decorated their golf carts or bikes and there were even a couple of small trucks thrown in for good measure. They started at Nippers for appetizers, went on to Seaside Village for salads, then down to the Blue Water Grill for the entrées, and finally back to the brightly-lit fig tree for desserts made by all the great Guana cooks.

We were home for the Holidays so we missed the entire affair. However, Sandra and her helpers did a great job with the various salads they served. Listening to her being praised was a real Christmas gift. It had been such a success the plans were to make it an annual event.

This year as in the past we would be leaving for home on December 16th. So the party planners very graciously changed the date from December 23rd to December 15th just so we could be here to participate. They also changed the menu a bit.

We would still begin at Nippers, but this year they were going to have a large roast beef, bake a ham, and slice it all up thinly so folks could make little tea sandwiches. They would also provide numerous other goodies. Seaside Village would be the next stop and would provide soup instead of salad. My brilliant idea was to make a good old fashioned New England fish chowder.

On our next visit home I ordered forty pounds of fresh haddock that we dragged back in a cooler and tucked safely in the freezer. I checked with the small grocery store here on Guana to be certain they could provide me with enough quarts of half-and-half. I thought that most of the other ingredients wouldn't pose a problem, except perhaps for the salt pork. So that prompted me to drag down a few pounds just to be on the safe side.

I was really excited about making that chowder—it is one of the few things I can cook really well. But it just wasn't to be ...

The date was changed back to the original December 23rd. There were so many folks coming to Guana for the holidays who were looking forward to this big night that the planners didn't have a choice. Once again we would not be here to share in this festive community affair. Like last year, we would be spending Christmas in New Hampshire and be back before New Years—at least that's what we thought. However, we spent many more days than planned at home, with Bob in a hospital bed, and the kids and me by his side.

It all started when Bob was on the small slanted roof outside the dining room at the Inn. He was crouched in a screwed-up position for quite some time trying to replace a cracked dining room window. My major concern of course was that he'd slip and fall. That didn't happen, but his time in that untenable position really caused a great deal of pain in his hip. It also looked to both of us that one leg ended up shorter than the other.

"Maybe you can help me, honey," he said."

"Okay, I'll try," was my simple-minded answer.

So he lay down on the tile floor of our room, stretched out flat on his back, and I began my medical assistance. I braced myself against the wall, grabbed the short leg and pulled as hard as I could.

"Do it again," he said. "Only this time, give it a good yank!"

Several more good yanks and he still had one short leg.

"Why don't you call Janet and ask her what to do."

Janet is now a certified CranioSacral Therapist. We were both aware of the people she had really helped with her Energy Bodywork, so I gave her a call.

I tried very hard to remember exactly what her instructions were, but with my memory there sure was an element of uncertainty—that plus the fact that Bob questioned every little thing I tried.

"I don't think you listened to her closely enough. Are you sure that's what she told you to do?" Or, "I don't think this is how Janet would do it!"

Well, damn I wasn't Janet and I probably wasn't remembering correctly just what she said. The only thing I was sure of was that I didn't have the foggiest notion what I was doing.

"Dad, I think we should get you to a chiropractor," I suggested.

"How the hell do we find one of them?" he questioned.

"Let's just try tomorrow morning's Cruisers Net."

We did just that and came up with the name of Dr. Koch. The next morning we climbed on the ferry and headed for Marsh Harbour. We weren't certain how to find his office but trusted that our faithful cab driver Joe would know.

The first visit was fairly routine. The Doctor didn't do any yanking or pulling; he just worked very gently on Bob. It eased the hip discomfort and I swore to God that both of Bob's legs were now just about the same length. There would, however, be a need for a return visit. This time I would let Bob go it alone.

When he returned from the second visit he had a piece of paper that he showed me. On it Dr. Koch had written, "Aneurysm in the abdominal aorta."

Neither Bob nor I really understood the full implications of those words. Even when Dr. Koch instructed Bob to get to his own Doctor the minute he got home, telling him not to waste a single day, the two of us were still oblivious.

We arrived home late at night on December 16th. The following day, Bob's birthday, he underwent a series of tests. The next day he was admitted to the Manchester Medical Center. The medical professionals refused to let him out of their sight. They explained the situation to us and drew some pictures so we could understand.

Most often when an abdominal aorta aneurysm reaches 5 to 5 1/2 centimeters, the patient is monitored closely and prepared for surgery.

Bob was sporting one that measured over 8. Needless to say, that's when the seriousness of the situation dawned on me, but not necessarily on Bob.

As Lisa began to call her brothers and sisters to tell them about the current events and that their Dad was being hospitalized, he raised all kinds of objections.

"What the hell are you doing, Lisa? This is no big deal, the whole world doesn't need to know!"

"What is the matter with you, Dad? These are your kids I'm calling, and they sure as hell do need to know!"

It was only after our conversation with PJ in Colorado, who informed us she would be on the next plane home, did he acquiesce. After all, if our daughter, who is a nurse practitioner, felt it necessary to be here, he decided it just might be a bigger deal than he thought.

And a big deal it certainly was. It involved an operation that lasted over seven hours, home after eight days in the hospital, and a return to the hospital for another week after only three-and-a-half at home. The second visit to the hospital was because his bowels had frozen and everything was backing up. He actually weighed 28 pounds more than he did when he went in for the surgery. I guess a crude person would claim that if he wasn't full of shit already, he was now filling up quickly.

They put a tube in his nose, down his throat and into his abdomen and began to vacuum around the clock. After the fourth day they cut down the procedure to only four hours a day. Now we began not only to wait for things to happen naturally but to begin hands-on therapy.

Janet took the lead, utilizing her CranioSacral expertise and led the rest of us for some hands-on exercises and hand holding prayers. I was also hoping that my Poop Surprise Basket would provide some additional motivation. Every time he did a little something on the pot he could pick out a prize from the basket I had filled with prettily-wrapped surprises. The very last surprise at the bottom of the basket was a nip size bottle of vodka. "Come on, honey," I cheered from the sidelines. "Surely that will help you do what needs to be done." It was the same trick our daughter Bonny had used when she was potty training our grandsons, but of course vodka had not been one of their prizes.

In the long run, we felt certain it was the hands-on therapy and the prayers that did the trick. We found it amusing that as the nurses observed our hands-on efforts they scoffed and made minor derogatory remarks. The Doctors however had a completely different attitude. In fact at least one surgeon expressed the opinion that what we were doing was probably more important to Bob's recovery than anything they were doing or could do.

Through it all Bob was an excellent patient. My only problem was trying to get him to slow down once I had him home. He muttered a lot about my keeping him a prisoner and most of the discussion centered around his not being able to drive.

"You can't drive, Bob, until you have your follow-up visit with the Doctors."

"The hell I can't," he answered. "When I was getting checked out of the hospital the nurse said I could drive any time and as soon as I wanted to."

That was most interesting since there had been three of us in the room to escort him home and he was the ONLY one who heard that.

During the convalescence period I took to sleeping in the guest room so as not to disturb him. On his third day home I quietly went into his room to see if he was awake and ready for his coffee. He wasn't there.

"Oh my gosh," I thought, "he has gone downstairs already, and by himself."

Down to the kitchen I went and he wasn't there either. It seemed ridiculous for me to check the garage but I did, and he wasn't there either, nor was his Ford Explorer. He had driven himself downtown to a local coffee shop to join his "buddies" for breakfast. He felt pretty smug when he finally drove in but not so smug when he had to sleep for the rest of the day. God love this stubborn old Yankee I'm married to. God love him.

Bob survived, and so did all of his caretakers. PJ really enjoyed needling her high-priced medical co-workers. After all, she chided, her Dad had comprehensive medical exams every year when he was home in the good old USA and yet it took a chiropractor in a third world country to discover his problem. It was a problem that could have easily cost him his life.

Through all of this Bob was clearly my priority and consumed my thoughts and prayers. But when it looked like all was going well,, my thoughts traveled over a thousand miles away to that little Inn of ours in the Bahamas.

The Christmas parade went on as scheduled. A few phone calls with simple instructions helped Sandra and Larry put together a marvelous New England-style fish chowder. It was a humbling lesson for me, proving that I don't always have to be onsite, or in control for things to go right. That was one bridge successfully crossed. "Great," I thought, "but now what about New Year's Day?"

I think it was about the middle of November when a group of us "girls" sat around the bar remembering and discussing the great success of the recent Halloween party. Terri was the real driving force behind that effort. I actually was in New Hampshire when she e-mailed me to ask if I were still interested in hosting a Halloween bash for the kids on Guana. Of course I was, but when I asked if she had any idea what I should drag back with me for this special deal she simply answered, "Nothing, I have it all," and believe me, that she did.

She was a great party planner, organizer, and traveled to the states frequently so she had access to about anything you might want to get your hands on. In addition to boxes and boxes of decorations, she also had a group of delightful Guana volunteers in tow to do just about everything. We had about two hundred little ghosts made out of white garbage bags that we hung from the trees along our little wooded lane. Right underneath them we hung snap lights that you simply had to shake to activate. We got them all glowing just before the kids started our way.

The tent had been transformed into a fantastic haunted house, and there were decorations everywhere. Big kids, little kids, parents, grandparents and varied and assorted adults came dressed in costumes. Every family brought some "munchies" and there were trick or treat bags for not only the youngsters but the old timers who had a sweet tooth. There were games and contests with prizes for everyone. It had been the great memories about that Halloween bash that prompted us all to start planning for a New Year's Day party.

We decided that first we should designate Guana Seaside Village as the "Official Recovery Center," or the "First Aid Center," or better yet, the "Thirst Aid Center." We could have little medical stations set up here and there where we served life-saving *Bloody Marys* and maybe wear some kind of nurse's caps with red crosses on them. Or maybe we could all manage to get our hands on some hospital scrubs and wear those.

Breakfast would be limited to the Bahamian favorites of boiled fish or chicken souse served with Johnny cake. Then we decided we would have a nacho bar with all the fixings set up on the walkway for the lunch hours. Everyone could just load up their own plates. Then later in the afternoon we could have a large buffet with all the foods you are supposed to eat for good luck in the coming year.

"Don't forget the black eyed peas."

"Oh yeah, we'll also need collard greens and ham hocks."

"And pork—we have to have pork"

Well I sure could take care of the pork, but as for some of the other suggestions I hadn't the foggiest notion how to fix those gourmet selections!

Someone could try to find colored wrist bands. If we set someone up to keep track of the tabs they could pass out a different colored band as the guest paid for either the breakfast, the nacho bar or the buffet. It would make it easier to keep track of who paid for what. They might almost look like hospital bracelets, enhancing the theme we had proudly developed.

The guys could rig up some TVs in the courtyard so people could watch the football games, and maybe we should ask everyone who is coming to decorate their golf carts like they were in the ROSE BOWL PARADE!

We would have to let everyone know. Advertise early, put flyers all around and hit the Cruisers Net morning after morning.

Oh dear Lord, my head was swimming. I had a headache just trying to digest the scope of this magnificent plan. Even our friend Janet who had volunteered to take care of the black eyed peas, and Pat who was going to do the collard greens and ham hocks, and another Pat who swore to be on hand to help, didn't do much to ease my need to go take a nap. At least I wasn't alone; they were all feeling excited but also a little overwhelmed. They decided they would also head home for a nap of their own.

Now the time for the big party was fast approaching and here I was home in New Hampshire, where I would surely be for a few more weeks. Having Larry and Sandra in charge of making a chowder was one thing, but leaving them and Glenn all alone to do all the work for this grand affair was quite another. Each time I called the Inn they would tell me how excited everyone was and how many folks were planning to join them on New Years Day. It was for information purposes, or so they told me, but truthfully it sounded more like a cry for help.

Our daughter Lisa decided now that her Dad was out of the hospital and her daughter Hilary was on school vacation, she'd be free to go down to Seaside and pitch in. In fact Hilary could go and help as well. It really sounded like just what we needed. Not just helping hands, but Lisa could sort of lead the parade and see that the volunteers didn't give Sandra a "hissy fit" when they stormed her kitchen.

When Lisa stepped off the ferry in Guana, she was greeted by more than a couple of folks who were showing some concern.

"Hey there, Lisa, glad to see you. How's your Dad? How long will he have to be in the hospital this time?"

This was how she found out her Dad had been readmitted. She called me as soon as she got to the Inn. I tried as hard as I could to reassure her that everything was going to be all right. I could tell by her responses that she was not convinced.

The big day was about to happen. From all reports, everyone had a really wild time on New Years Eve at Nippers. Johnny always goes all out when he throws a party. There were hats, horns, party favors and fireworks. In fact some of the fireworks came right up on the deck, so party goers had to hop, skip and jump out of the way. There was also the added attraction of a naked man jumping over the bonfire on the beach.

And, if you can believe this, Bahamians who are always really slow with most everything had the countdown to midnight at 11:50 instead of 12:00. Everyone hooting hollering and blowing their horns 10 minutes ahead of schedule. Tomorrow, New Years Day, it would be our turn.

By eight o'clock, the bar was full. Folks couldn't wait to get their Bloody Marys and have breakfast. We thought we had clearly stated the breakfast would be limited to the Bahamian specials of chicken souse, boiled fish and Johnny cake. It really was what most wanted, but then there were those who decided they needed something different. One ordered a special all egg white omelet, others ordered our special breakfast sandwich they had heard so much about. Some wanted French toast and others just plain bacon and eggs. It doesn't sound like too much to accommodate and usually it wouldn't be, but today was a different story. Even this early, the kitchen was in an uproar trying to get things ready for both the nacho bar and the buffet, so every time Glenn stepped in with a new breakfast request staff and volunteers alike were ready to throw him out.

I learned a little later that they were already upset with Glenn because instead of ordering nacho chips he had ordered taco shells. It was just plain luck that someone discovered the mistake before the stores closed for the holidays. Of course the stores in question were in Marsh Harbour. So they had to call our favorite cab driver, have him hunt for the chips, and try and charge them to the Inn. And if that didn't work, then he'd pay for them himself and we would reimburse him.

Next, we had to make sure he got them on a ferry and have the ferry captain notify us over the VHF that our chips were aboard. Let me tell you, nothing is easy. But it worked, in fact it worked so well that three big cartons came over on the boat, and a year later we still had a carton-and-a-half left.

They also (fairly or unfairly) blamed Glenn for the cheese fiasco. Part of the plan for the nacho bar was to have a crock-pot filled with melted cheese right out there on the bar. But apparently no one could figure out how to melt that 30-pound clump of cheddar sitting on the kitchen counter. Everyone assumed Glenn had ordered it because when asked, Sandra simply answered, "It wasn't me"." So who else could it be?

Our friend Mike who does catering in the states came to the rescue by explaining that they simply had to either grate or shave some off the block and melt a little at a time. He also explained in detail what they should order next year if they really wanted to simplify things.

If we do it again, hopefully someone will remember his advice.

About ten o'clock when Lisa needed a bathroom break, she had to resort to using the men's room. There was already a line at the ladies', but isn't that the way it is when two or more are gathered?

The thing that struck her when she stepped inside the door was the picture of her Dad. Seeing that picture gave her an overwhelming feeling of sadness and she began to cry. Suddenly she was really afraid we were going to lose him.

She could hear the phone ringing and wondered how she could scoot by the guests and get into the office unnoticed. She dried her tears, blew her nose, put her head down and simply ran for it.

"Guana Seaside Village," she answered as usual.

"Honey, you do not have to worry about me. Just stop it, because I am fine!"

It was her father calling from his hospital bed. He said what he needed to say and just what she needed to hear. And I really don't think the timing was coincidental. Lisa was able to go out and continue on, and on, and on!

One of the first things she did before she really got rolling was take off the silly-looking hospital scrubs. She and Glenn were the only ones wearing them, thanks to a donation from P.J., but when people kept asking why they were dressed like that, they gave up. Our carefully thought out party theme apparently went completely overlooked.

There were guests in the pool, in the courtyard, in the dining room, on the walkway and standing eight to ten deep behind the bar. There was a volunteer keeping the tabs, but it took Glenn, Lisa, Beth, Uncle Leonard, and our volunteer friends Pat and Janet to keep the drinks rolling.

There were quite a few interested in the Rose Bowl and they gathered around the limited TVs. However the best TV for watching the game was taken over by a couple who changed the channel so they could watch figure skating. I guess I don't have to tell you that they were soon persuaded by Lisa and many others "to get with the program."

By all reports, it was one "hell of a day," with the last of the guests leaving at 3:00 a.m. Folks were looking forward to a repeat happening next year—same time, same place and the good Lord willing. *Both* of the Reluctant Inn Keepers had hoped to be there, not only to work and to enjoy the guests, but to also celebrate a little. All the reports of that day made me think back to last year's New Years Eve and to some other very interesting events.

There had been no lack of excitement—we had plenty of that—only it was a little different in nature. Last year Glenn had once again been in trouble. However it had nothing to do with ordering cheese or the right chips and everything to do with a couple of his women. 'Of course he did his best, and continues to do his best, to keep them hidden from one another. That's no mean trick, especially when their numbers are legion.

We had met his fiancée Rachel at our very first Valentines party. We all thought she was a first class lady. She had come to visit Glenn quite often but then suddenly just faded from sight. Every time we asked Glenn about her he just remained silent. It was several months before we learned from someone else what had happened.

Rachel lived in Nassau and when Glenn went there for some type of political convention and failed to tell her he was even in town, she got a little more than perturbed. It really was Glenn's ego that trapped him. After the speeches, he hopped up on the stage to shake hands with all the big wigs. A budding politician, Glenn really wanted to be noticed. Well, he was noticed all right. This convention was being televised and Rachel was just sitting home alone watching the whole scene unfold' on TV. Guess he should have called her.

It didn't seem to really concern Glenn. After all, he had several other fiancées to keep track of. His women were everywhere—some saying they were married to him, others saying they used to be married, some just wanting to get married, and a number of them just wondering where he was because they were waiting somewhere for him to show up.

I have a hard time figuring out the attraction. Granted he is nice looking, very neat, spends a fortune on his clothes and always uses plenty of cologne, however, that can't be all of it. I figure he must have a hidden talent that far surpasses the ability to climb trees for coconuts.

Last year one of his new "loves" was a pediatric nurse practitioner. She was from New York and had made the trip down to spend New Years Eve with him. On the ferry from Marsh Harbour to Guana she met many friendly people and chatted with them all the way across. During that 45-minute boat ride, she shared a lot of things about herself, including the fact that she was headed to Seaside Village so she could spend the holidays with her new boyfriend Glenn. She had no idea that Glenn had a long-standing girlfriend right there on Guana, nor could she possibly know that before the night was over that girlfriend would know all about the "intruder" from the big city.

It was just after midnight when all the banging and slamming began. The Guana girlfriend was bound and determined to find Glenn. First she went to his apartment in back of the office and found it empty. The next step was to bang on all the guest room doors.

"Come out! I know you're in there!" she shouted as she banged on each doorway.

Our Janet was the first to respond.

"All that banging and shouting is disturbing our guests. Get off this property NOW," she ordered. It was while she was trying to get that message across that the phone rang.

"Happy New Year Jan."

"Hang up, Lisa. There is a crazy lady running amuck down here."

"Well, take her out Janet. 'That's what you are supposed to do when a crazy lady is running around. Just take her out!"

"Sure. Easy for you to say since you're over 1,000 miles away! Happy New Year, Lisa. Now hang the hell up so I can handle this."

And handle it she did.

At least the girlfriend stopped ranting and raving and banging on doors and left the premises.

It is hard to believe that Bob and I slept through this whole fiasco. I vaguely remember the sound of someone banging on doors, but guess I thought I must be dreaming or just chose not to get involved. That part about not getting involved held until the next morning.

Once everything had become quiet and back to normal, the girlfriend decided to return. This time she quietly came in the back way into Glenn's apartment and proceeded to really raise havoc.

She had soaked his bed with water, cologne and shaving cream. His drawers were emptied and upside down. And in the bathtub, Glenn's expensive suits and favorite silk shirts were just floating around. It took some time and some strong arguments to convince Glenn not to call Marsh Harbour police and request they come over and drag her away. We finally got him to agree not to press charges. Bob would have a talk with her to explain she was not to set foot on our property ever again, and if she did we would be the ones to call the authorities.

I couldn't help but wonder who would be cooking him the special meals he requested on an almost daily basis. Or who would pick up his laundry and dry cleaning and bring everything back just the way he liked it. I wondered who would pitch in and pay some of his bills when he found himself in a bind. Clearly his new friend from New York would not be in position to do most of the above, but perhaps she could pitch in for the last part.

A couple of years later when we were all at a potluck supper at the Guana Beach Resort, the local girlfriend cautiously approached us. She had a lot to say and directed most of it to Janet. She was sorry, really sorry, for the damage she had done and for upsetting our family. She explained that every time she saw one of us she felt very ashamed. Janet and I both told her that it was in the past and we could tell she was sincerely sorry. We were ready to forget the entire episode, and she was no longer banned from the property. She really was grateful and thanked us profusely for accepting her apology. However, she did add that if someday we found Glenn dead, we would know she did it.

The second week in January, with Bob home from the hospital (for good this time) and on his way to a full recovery, it was safe for me to return to the Inn. Not an easy thing to do but safe nonetheless. The kids were close by and would really tend out to their Dad's needs, so I headed south.

The thing about my return that stuck out most in my mind was the number of people who greeted me with "Hello Miss Gerry, welcome home, and how is Mr. Bob doing?" This greeting was from the local folks.

Others that were boaters or second-home owners asked about Bob, showed their concerns and said they were glad to see me. But none said those words that had so overwhelmed me, "Welcome home, Miss Gerry!"

There was no question that we needed a new van badly. I think Bob was the only one who was dragging his feet. Can't blame Bob, he is the one who fought with the bottom line day after day, but he was home and I was there when opportunity knocked.

A gentleman in the Settlement had just taken possession of a van he had ordered over the Internet. His idea was to run a taxi service here on the island, but Glenn's idea was to have him bring that van out to the Inn so I could take a look at it. Of course, it looked wonderful. All the doors opened, all the windows worked and even though it was not a new van, it sure looked it. And the price was right.

We took some pictures, e-mailed them to Bob and then I gave him a call. Much to everyone's surprise, he gave us the go-ahead without a single objection.

It really didn't take much to transfer the vehicle to us. I wrote up a paper that stated I was going to buy it, the seller agreed that he was going to sell it, and we both signed it. Then all we had to do was stick a Bahamian postage stamp on that piece of paper to make it a legal document. We almost had our almost new van.

There were a couple of things that gave me a little concern. First the steering wheel was on the wrong side of the vehicle—well perhaps not exactly the wrong side, but the opposite side from what I was used to. And this van was quite a bit wider than our old wrecked one was. I would have to convince everyone who would drive it that they had to stay right in the middle of our little dirt lane. Otherwise, the bushes and overhanging trees would scratch the top and sides badly. In no time those scratches would all be rusty and our new treasure would soon look like the old junky thing that we were ashamed to use.

It was time for Bob to return to the island. He had made enough progress for the doctors to give him the okay. No one was any happier than I was because it sure got lonely without him. Of course there were big hugs when he got off the ferry and a kiss or two.

"Come on, Dad, I want you to see our nice new van."

"Pretty neat," he said. "Think I'll drive it back to the Inn."

"Well, it's kind of tricky, honey. The steering wheel is on the wrong side and it is a lot wider than our other van. Why don't I drive and you can watch what I do."

"I can't believe this. You want me to watch you, to learn how to drive this thing? What a joke that is!"

"Okay," I answered. To have said otherwise would have been futile.

Into the van he got and the first thing I had to caution him about was to go SLOW. Damn, I forgot SLOW is not in this man's vocabulary. No more than, "Don't run, don't run," is understood by little boys!

The first thing he did is hit some corners trying to get out of the Settlement, so I knew we are in big trouble. He hurried along like there was no tomorrow all over the paved road, one side and then to the other, until we got to the dirt lane.

"Dad, you are going to have to go very slow and stay right in the middle," I advised.

"Stop backseat driving. I know what the hell I'm doing and where I am supposed to be going."

I didn't think he was supposed to be going right smack into a tree, but that's just what he did. Now the new van had a big dent and was missing a light on the passenger' side.

I had been so glad to see him, but he'd only been back fifteen minutes and already I was so ticked off at him that I could hardly see straight.

"Okay," I ordered, "from now on you are only allowed to drive the old junked up van. Stay out of this one. This one is MINE." That lasted about a day and a half.

Bob really does have a reputation for his driving. In fact there was a sign on a tree at the Inn that stated RESERVED PARKING FOR BOB ONLY. No one dared park in his spot, and most cautioned others that because he really did park there, they should park their carts as far away as possible. Someone even bought a sign for the windshield of our cart that read BEWARE OF BOB!

Then there was also Craig, a very creative local fellow who sawed down the tree Bob hit, dug up the trunk, painted it vivid colors and wrote on it "BOB'S TREE." It was a conversation piece around the bar for quite some time and almost everyone smiled or laughed when they looked at it—everyone except me.

Around 6:00 p.m., three days after Bob returned, people began showing up at the Inn. Golf carts all over the lawn and small boats at the dock brought about 90 invaders. All were carrying pot luck casseroles, appetizers, and desserts. It was a surprise party to say WELCOME HOME MR. BOB! The food was great, but the number of caring friends and the feelings of fellowship overwhelmed both Bob and me. It made us believe we really belonged.

Friends in The Courtyard

CHAPTER 34

An Almost Wedding

We had been planning for another wedding, working closely with Matt, the groom. The planning had been going on for nearly a year. Each time a new idea cropped up we would explore the possibilities.

First, Matt's best friend, who was a chef in a four star restaurant, wanted to prepare the wedding dinner as a gift to the bride and groom. He would be responsible for it all, soup to nuts. What I certainly needed to know was what kind of soup and what kind of nuts.

I e-mailed Matt and explained that I would need to have the complete menu ahead of time so I could tell his friend what would, or perhaps more importantly would not be available. If he needed out of the ordinary ingredients, we could search for them while we searched for the ordinary.

I also explained the kitchen set-up. Although we managed quite well day after day, it had limited working space. I wondered if a chef from a four star establishment might find it a little disconcerting. We had never allowed an outside chef to take over before, but if it was what they really wanted we would do our best to make it work.

E-mails went back and forth on an almost daily basis. After a couple of weeks I got word that they decided to scrap that idea. Matt's friend the chef would just have to find something else as the unique wedding gift. However, another brilliant idea was surfacing. The day before the wedding they would roast a whole pig.

Could we get our hands on a seventy-to-eighty pound pig? Did we have a grill and spit large enough to cook it? If not, could we dig a pit to cook it in? What could we serve as side-dishes? Could we decorate the courtyard and serve it there—save the tent for the wedding dinner the next day?

"Okay, let me take one thing at a time," I simply answered as follows:

"Yes, we can get a big pig."

"No we do not have a grill or spit or contraption of any kind to serve as a cooker."

We have no idea how to dig or line a pit for cooking, but if we ask a friend of ours named Aubrey, hopefully he'll dig one for us. We would have to oversee the process to make sure he places it as far away from our pretty beach as possible."

If it was to be a pig roast in the courtyard and around the pool, I anticipated decorating with colorful plastic cloths, candles, a few wildflowers and serving on heavy duty colored plastic plates.

"Matt," I asked, "please let me know the bride's favorite color and the colors she would like us to use so I can begin planning for the fun stuff!"

I was excited thinking about how bright the courtyard would look. I could picture all the bright colors, the colored candles on the table, and the native flowers we would gather. I also pictured how the little lights wrapped around the courtyard palm trees would enhance the overall effect. That was a lot more fun to think about than pig cooking.

We had another two or three weeks back and forth on this pig thing. He really wanted to have us dig the pit and his friends do the cooking. But I persuaded him otherwise. We should just let Aubrey pick up the pig, cook it, and bring it back to us at whatever time they designated. He seemed comfortable with that arrangement and finally agreed. He also told me his friends seemed really happy with that solution. I was sure they were, but not nearly as happy as I was!

As for the color theme in the courtyard the groom informed me that he was certain his bride wanted everything white—linen tablecloths, linen napkins and dinner plates. I explained that would surely be the scenario for the wedding dinner the next day. However, I thought that perhaps a little more informal setting would be appropriate for the pig roast.

He was so intent on making sure his bride had everything just the way she wanted it that I knew white it would be.

As for the side-dishes, they only came up for discussion three or four times. I had promised Bahamian macaroni and cheese, potato salad, cole slaw, peas and rice, baked beans, tossed salad, hot rolls and dessert—there wasn't much else I could add to the pig. The groom just needed to be reassured, kind of like over and over.

I decided that there would be no more borrowing of Ginger's plates. Instead I hunted for some at the shops at home. I got a great deal on some very pretty white ones and bought seventy-five. That should be sufficient for any future weddings or parties, at least for the time being. Everyone who came to the Inn from home was instructed to carry as many as they could without going overboard on the airline weight requirements. A month before the wedding they had all safely arrived at the Inn and were lined up in our room.

I also decided to prepare many of the basic things ahead of time. Lisa and Janet were coming down to help with the wedding, but I really wanted to spare them some of the "Mickey Mouse" chores so I began to tackle them in any spare time I could find.

Count out the silverware, polish and wrap them so they would stay bright and shiny and I could feel comfortable knowing there were enough pieces of the same pattern for every place setting. That may sound like something I should just automatically know and could take for granted, but it really doesn't always work that way.

There was a time when I couldn't figure out what was happening to all our luncheon plates. First we had plenty—more than enough. Then all of a sudden we didn't even have enough to get us through the lunch hour. I had to stand at the sink frantically washing plates. It took a long time before it dawned on me that we really could use paper products at lunchtime. Just about the time I decided on that simple solution and ordered cartons of paper plates, the mystery was solved.

When a staff member left us and we were cleaning her room, we found forty-six of those plates under her bed. How that happened or why or what she intended to do with them none of us could figure out.

Now surely you can understand why I didn't want to have a last minute surprise where the silverware was concerned .So I carefully counted a second time and then lined them up right along with the plates.

Next came the big thing—the really big thing: IRONING.

Linen tablecloths, mounds of napkins carefully ironed, folded with great care and stacked along with the dishes and silverware. As long as I'd come this far, I thought I might as well keep going and line up the decorative candles and holders right next to everything else. The room was getting a little bit crowded but I was sure pleased with myself. I now had the most essential things all together in one place.

All that was left to do was to talk to Miss Emily about the wedding cake to make for the bride (whose name was also Emily). The wedding cake had always been a gift from us to the bride and groom and I always had the pleasure of picking out the design. Then of course we would have to place the order for the extra food supplies that would be necessary, including that seventy-to-eighty pound pig. But that was about it. I was feeling quite smug and happy about being ahead of the game, but Bob sure wasn't smiling.

"What's the matter, honey?" I asked.

"I'm watching the weather. There is a hurricane brewing, and right now it sure doesn't look good."

"Well, things can change, can't they? We still have over a week to go and hurricanes are always changing course. Don't they most often miss these outer islands?"

"It seems like that was the case for a number of years, until Floyd hit about five years ago. Since then, these little islands have had more than their share of hits. You had better get in touch with the wedding party, and I would suggest doing it today."

"Oh damn," I thought. We had been communicating back and forth for months, making plans, changing plans, arranging for all the room accommodations, reviewing menu choices, and checking out color schemes so the wedding cake could be decorated to please the bride. We went over details right and left making sure everything was as they wanted and ensuring we could provide what was on their list. Then along came FRANCIS.

This first big hurricane of the season to come our way was projected to hit us beginning the night we had planned for the pig roast and then full force the following day just in time for the wedding on the beach.

Of course we were very disappointed. We had hopes of making their special day something that would be beyond their wildest dreams, but I could not begin to imagine how Matt, Emily, their friends and family were feeling right about then. It wasn't just a matter of putting everything on hold; they had to be told that the entire affair was canceled. We would work with Matt to notify guests. We also would assure everyone that the deposit for accommodations would be refunded and we'd start that process immediately. Hopefully the airlines would be as accommodating with ticket refunds as well.

I couldn't imagine what they would all be doing, but I know I would be packing away the white linen tablecloths and napkins (that I had so carefully ironed) along with the candles and the other table decorations. We would cancel the pig and the wedding cake, take down the tent, board up the rooms, hunker down, and pray for the best.

CHAPTER 35

Protecting the Inn, Adjusting our Attitudes and Taking Cover

The weather was being closely watched by all the family at home, they were tracking Francis just as we were. That naturally resulted in phone calls over and over again. All the kids saying basically the same thing: "Ma, Dad, GET THE HELL OFF THE ISLAND!!!!!"

I simply told them I was sorry but their father wouldn't leave so I was staying with him. Janet and Lisa had airline tickets to fly down and help us with the wedding. Now the wedding was canceled and they decided on their own to use those tickets to fly down and help us face the hurricane! I have no idea what they thought they could do, maybe stop the wind from blowing. Anyway, by the time they showed up it was too late to stop them. They thought it was really funny that they were the only two people on the airplane flying in and everyone else was flying out. "Idiots," I thought, but I sure was glad to see them. They turned out to be not only moral support but also helpful and necessary workers.

Getting ready for a hurricane is more than just boarding up windows.

It is gathering up anything that could possibly act as a projectile; storing all the outdoor furniture in one of the rooms you might deem to be safe; climbing all the coconut trees and chopping down the coconuts; and dragging all the bar stools, the CD player the special radio, the amplifiers, the cash register, the popcorn machine and anything else at the bar that is movable to the inside. The rest you secure the best you can, and try and cover what's left in hopes that damage might be minimal.

We had to move the vehicles to the back of the Inn, to get them away from the Sea of Abaco. We were bound to get some water surges because the Sea of Abaco was like our front yard, only steps away. We couldn't take them too far to the rear because the Atlantic was only about 350 feet behind us and there was no way of telling where the most damage would come from.

Our location was wonderful for vacationers, ideal in fact. On the brochures and on our Website you could clearly see it couldn't be better. The ocean or the sea—the choice of where you wanted to play—was yours. You really could have the best of both worlds. That's why we called it a little piece of paradise. However, when a hurricane was headed our way and we were saddled between that sea and that ocean, I'm not sure what in the world we should have called it. We went around the Inn again and again to make sure we hadn't overlooked anything. We continued to search all the nooks and crannies while Bob stayed high on his ladder cutting down the last of the coconuts.

Time to pack up food items, water, clothes, flashlights, battery-operated hand-held VHF radios, personal things like toothbrushes, combs, medicines and passports. All that was really left for us to do was to adjust our attitudes and find the courage to take off and leave our Inn behind us.

We had decided to stay at the apartment under the Ridge House. Even when Floyd blew the roof off the main house, everyone in the apartment had remained safe—a little frightened perhaps, and wet, but nevertheless safe. So that is where Bob, the girls and I headed, along with the brothers Chet and Shawn, who were dear to us.

Chet and Shawn are accomplished carpenters and have other talents as well. Chet could repair almost any vehicle, bodywork included—a talent I suspect he learned from his Daddy. Shawn is a skilled fisherman, sometimes gone for weeks at a time during crawfish season, earning enough to see him through the off-season times. He is also an extremely talented artist who can create beautiful pieces using only what nature makes available on the land and in the sea. Both are delightful and entertaining. They were the first locals, with the exception of Uncle Leonard, to come our way and feel comfortable being here.

They were putting the finishing touches to a house being built privately. It was the sixth one adjacent to the Inn and considered part of the Village. At the day's end they would come together to the courtyard bar for a beer or rum drink. Then they'd share with us some of the things that happened during the day. They both spoke rapidly, with a heavy Bahamian accent, and quite often interrupted each other. But always their dissertations were filled with abrupt laughter. Chet would often be laughing so much that he'd have to lay his head on the bar. And of course we would laugh right along.

"What did he just say?" someone would quietly ask.

And of course no one was quite sure. We were after all transplants, new ones at that, and some locals (not all, but some) speak with such a heavy Bahamian accent that it takes a lot of getting used to and a whole lot of careful listening.

Although Chet was a few years older than Shawn, you could almost mistake them for twins and they were always together. They worked together, partied together and even lived together along with the girl Chet had married. Then the trouble began.

Simply put, Shawn began sleeping with Chet's wife. Needless to say, that was not to be tolerated, especially under the roof they shared. It not only resulted in different housing arrangements but a divorce and a wedge between the brothers that was to last much too long. They still came to the Inn, would sit at opposite ends of the bar but never utter a word to each other. There was no longer the laughter. Just quiet times. It was actually painful for us to watch, believing it was tearing both of them apart. I tried some intervention, but to absolutely no avail. Either the split was too deep, I had completely lost my touch, or they thought I was probably too old to really understand. However, whenever Lisa or Janet came to the Inn, they did their best to intercede. We all thought of both of them as friends.

"Mom, I don't know if these guys will ever get back to being on speaking terms again," Lisa confided.

"They were so close," I answered. "I can't believe this is happening.

Just keep talking to them whenever you can. You could probably break down the barriers."

"I don't think that will happen. Yesterday, trying to make Chet see that he really cared for his brother, I asked what he would do if he saw him just laying in the middle of the road."

"Step over him and just keep going," was his answer.

"I told him I couldn't believe that."

"Well, maybe if I saw someone coming along I might tell them to check out the mother f--- lying in the road, 'cause he might be dead."

Although it concerned us greatly, I explained to the girls that there were three or four other sets of brothers from the older generation that hadn't spoken to each other for years. Maybe it was just an example these two were following. However, neither girl was content to let things stay as they were

After both Lisa and Janet made many attempts to bring the brothers together, it became clear that it would take more than the efforts of mere mortals. What was needed was an act of God, or a serious intervention by Mother Nature. That's exactly what happened that September.

As Francis neared, everyone who had stayed on the island was already boarded up and most had hunkered down. Then we all heard an announcement on VHF 16: "Anyone who doesn't feel like locking themselves in just yet, come on down to the Sunset Beach Bar and Grill for a last minute drink with your neighbors."

It was rather hard to believe because we knew that Captain Easy, who was in charge of this place at the time, had already closed up his bar, battened down his hatches, stored the furniture, and locked up the liquor. However, his bartender Ray had convinced him to take down a few of the boards, drag out a couple of chairs, broadcast the invitation and wait to see who would show up. And who showed up was almost everybody that was left on Guana Cay.

This was very early Thursday evening. It was calm, quiet, absolutely beautiful, but with a different and eerie feeling—something I am hard-pressed to describe. The atmosphere was just different—that's about it. People who usually hung out at the bar were racing around chasing kids in made-up games. Folks I knew that really didn't even like each other that much were hugging, hanging on, and promising to help one another if help were needed.

I asked Captain Easy to drag out a reasonable chair for me to sit in, something like a throne so I could play queen and people would have to curtsy when they passed by me from the walkway to the bar. Stupid, I know, but at the time it sounded like a fun idea. When it dawned on me that the Captain was the only one bowing, I decided a different game was in order.

"Anyone know how to play spin the bottle?"

It immediately became obvious that spin the bottle had not been a Bahamian childhood favorite, but the explanation on how to play was certainly simple enough.

Lisa refused to join in and so did the one brother, Shawn, but that really didn't matter. The circle was quite large enough. I had only thought: that if Shawn joined in and sat in the circle with his brother Chet, it might serve as an icebreaker. That was about as smart as my queen on the throne idea.

There we were, all sitting on the ground with an empty beer bottle in the middle of the circle and my grand announcement, "Let the game begin!"

But before we actually began the spinning, I told Shawn that the next time I saw his Father I was going to tell him that his son wasn't a very good sport. At this point, since Shawn was over thirty, who should care? But Shawn's Father keeps a close eye on his boys—always wants to make sure they aren't causing trouble or bothering people. He wanted folks to like and respect them. My comment was meant to be a joke, but before I could even get out a chuckle Shawn passed me his cell phone.

"My Daddy's waiting to hear what you have to say."

I was really taken back and could only mumble that we were just playing a simple game and Shawn wouldn't play. I had thought it would be understood as a joke and that would be the end of it, but unfortunately for Shawn it wasn't. Days after Francis blew over and had come and gone, Shawn was still in trouble with his Daddy.

"The next time you are with those people and they want you to play a game you'd better do it. That's the polite thing to do, and you'd better play fair."

Poor Daddy. If he only knew what spin the bottle was all about.

That wasn't the only problem I caused. Whenever it was my turn to spin, I always grabbed the guy next to me regardless of where the bottle stopped. Poor Sid, he was a newlywed but his wife was in Florida out of harm's way. Now here he was being accosted every time that bottle stopped in front of me.

The first time I grabbed onto him I got a big laugh, so of course that prompted me to repeat the performance; and since he was right next to me, I didn't have to get up and walk over to anyone else. Hopefully his new bride would understand once she got back and people tattled on me. There is no question that on Guana she will get a full report, and I dare say it will be exaggerated and perhaps a little more than slightly

I think it was about 8:30 when we began to say our goodbyes, good lucks and God Bless you's to all around us. We headed to our Ridge House shelter. There was Bob and me, the girls, Rustin (the head maintenance engineer from Dolphin Beach Resort), and both the brothers Chet and Shawn.

We were finally in, and just waiting and wondering what we were in for, when the rain began. It was pretty gentle at first and so was the wind. I was thinking that maybe it wouldn't be so bad after all. It was about this time that Paul showed up with his little dog Spot. He had decided there was no way he was going to ride out this storm all by himself, so here he was. He knew he'd be welcomed and he was and so was Spot.

The girls fixed some snacks, brought out the game, loaded questions and turned on the TV so we could track what was happening or about to happen. Bob and I were the first to retire and things were still not bad. All I could think of was, "So far, so good." Those thoughts lasted until about midnight.

I hung on to Bob and exclaimed, "Oh honey, this is awful!"

"I know sweetie. Remember, I went though Floyd."

"Everyone says it's like a freight train going through, but it isn't. It's like 1,000 singing tea kettles all whistling at once."

I could see things flying by the window, all kinds of things, but that wasn't nearly as disturbing as the high-pitched screaming sound. It was shattering and seemed to be endless. There was no point in trying to sleep or even rest. Everyone else had already gathered in the small kitchen-living room area, so we just piled in as well.

Some wise guy greeted me with, "Good morning, Yaya. Glad you got up because your tea is ready." At least it brought a laugh.

The island lost power very early on in the game. That came as no surprise counting the times we have lost power when there wasn't a storm or even a cloud in sight. Thankfully Ridge House had a generator that helped us stay in touch with others who also had generators. We could also communicate with those that were using battery-operated VHF radios

At first the calls were simple. Just checking up on one another and trying to make certain that the folks you knew and cared about were doing okay. Then after a while they got simple in a different way. I mean really simple!

Lisa announced that the evening special at Guana Seaside would be shrimp scampi and reservations would be needed by 5:00 p.m. That started the ball rolling. There were some witty responses to her announcement, followed by folks making jokes, all in good taste, and someone entertaining us by singing some good old country western tunes. It certainly helped keep spirits up.

The only announcement we didn't quite get was from Larry's new friend. She simply said that she had just finished a nice warm bath. We all wondered what in the world that was supposed to mean. It doesn't take much to entertain you when you are a captive audience, nor does it take much to have your imagination run wild.

We played some games, told some stories, snacked some more, trying desperately to ignore what was happening outside. Then the younger ones decided to put on a relaxing DVD. That will work, I thought, but *Pulp Fiction* was not exactly my idea of a relaxing film.

I tolerated it but begged for something different the next time. They understood, agreed and promised that the next one would be more to my liking. So I sat there, huddled up and without comment quietly watched *Scarface*.

Unfortunately the phrase from the movie, "Say hello to my little friend," rented a space in my head and I heard it over and over—in fact I still hear it once in a while. But at the time it was good competition for the outside howling.

The apartment is small, two bedrooms, one bath, a Pullman like kitchen and a living space with a computer, desk, small pull-out sofa and a futon. Right above the futon is a small window that actually only opens onto a space under the upstairs porch. The space is surrounded with lattice work and is very sheltered.

"I know," suggested someone who was really bored. "Let's go out, hang on tight, and crawl into that space. What a great place to watch this show!"

So out they went, leaving Bob, Spot and me behind. At first the thought of them heading outside scared the living daylights out of me, but that didn't last long. I had only to kneel on the futon, peek out the window, see them all safe and sound in that cozy little space and then I was kept quite busy taking orders. They treated that window as if it were at a fast food drive-in somewhere, and of course expected me to be the bartender, cook, and waitress.

"We would like to have a Miller Light, one rum and coke, and some crackers and cheese, please."

A few minutes later came another order.

"Could you possibly cook a couple of hot dogs, pass them out the window with two more beers and some of those brownies?"

And so it went. Bob was relaxed, I was busy, Spot was content, and the "kids" were enjoying a safe front row seat to observe Francis and speculate what possible damage might be occurring.

They could see Susan's house on Susan's Cove, Blue Berry Hill, the home that was recently featured in the *Coastal Living* magazine and the point where our friends Janet and David had their cottage known as The Flying Dogs. They watched for quite some time and still really couldn't make any determination. It looked to them that The Flying Dogs was the one taking the most direct hit. Actually that proved not to be true, but because Janet and David were the ones we felt the closest to, they absorbed most of our thinking and concerns.

Finally, with everyone tucked back inside, we heard reports that the sustained winds of 140-145 miles per hour would occasionally gust up to 160. The rain was falling at an unbelievable rate, the screeching sounds continued and I noticed that we were about to get a leak in the ceiling.

"Hey guys, someone better poke a hole in that little bulge in the ceiling."

"No way, Yaya. We can't cut a hole in the ceiling—that would really be destructive."

"Well, if you don't do that, then the whole damn ceiling is going to come crashing down."

I had dealt with ice back-ups on our roof at home winter after winter that resulted with ceiling leaks. I really did know what I was talking about and what to expect.

Finally convinced, they slit a hole in that bubble and then had to jump out of the way of a massive waterfall. Down it came, and out came every bucket we could find.

They had big buckets, large plastic baskets, a whole variety of anything that would hold water, and the guys formed an assembly line. Fill the bucket, run to the shower, empty the bucket and back for a refill. It was hard to believe that they kept at it for as long as they did. They fought the fight for hours.

It was about 3:00 a.m. when it became apparent that they were fighting a losing battle, so they just gave up. As the water began to build up, everyone evacuated the living area and crowded into the two backrooms. Walking from those rooms to the bathroom was an interesting adventure. It meant wading through water above 'the ankles and for some of us actually mid-calf.

This is going to be hard to believe and probably one of those situations where to find it hysterically funny you had to be there! But Shawn, the guy who wouldn't play spin the bottle, decided to provide us with a little amusement. He put on swim goggles, a pair of fins and began to snorkel, or attempt to snorkel, on the floor and through the kitchen. It is a memory that I am sure will come to each of us anytime we hear the word hurricane. His brother Chet laughed right along with the rest of us, but amazingly they still weren't talking.

We were all quite concerned about what was happening to the upstairs part of this Ridge House. If we were flooded down here, then there had to be major water damage upstairs. This great place belongs to friends of ours who happened to be away in New Mexico. We couldn't begin to imagine what they would have to face when they returned. It was at this point that Bob decided to go outside, climb the staircase and try to determine for himself just how much damage Francis had already caused.

"It's still raging out there, Bob. What are you thinking?"

"Don't worry, honey. I can hang on to the railing, and when I get topside I can brace myself against the side to the house!"

"Why in hell won't you listen, you stubborn old Yankee? Every single report pleads for people to stay inside. INSIDE, INSIDE, OUT OF HARMS WAY!" GET IT?" It's not like you were one of the kids crawling under the porch and into a sheltered space. You will be in wide open space trying to climb stairs—steep stairs no less."

"I'll be right back," says he, as if that had been an intelligent well thought out answer.

We knew there was no changing his mind, so Lisa took Paul aside and devised a plan to protect her father.

"You go first," she told Paul, "then we will put 'Bobby' next, and I'll be behind him. That way he'll be protected from both sides."

"Oh great!" I thought, "Now I don't just have my husband to worry about, but a daughter as well."

I really didn't want to watch this expedition. I felt like running to one of the little bedrooms, covering myself and pretending I was somewhere else. Of course those screaming teakettles wouldn't let that fantasy happen, so I decided I might as well stand guard and watch from inside. I did and believe me it wasn't pretty!

Bob has broad shoulders, long arms, rather big hands, good-sized feet, but skinny little legs. I think it was this last physical attribute that really got him in trouble.

He just began to climb those stairs when Francis swept him right off his feet. Thank God for Lisa's protection plan. She grabbed her Dad and so did Paul. They put him upright and helped him climb the rest of the stairs.

At the top of the landing Bob and Paul somehow managed to cross to the middle of the porch area, but it was as if Lisa had gotten trapped in a wind tunnel.

Paul sensed she was in trouble, grabbed her hands and held on tight. Lisa's feet left the floor, went into the air and straight out behind her. She went flying half way across the porch until she slammed into a picnic table and landed on the floor with a thud. Thankfully she was only bruised slightly. That encounter with the picnic table kept her from being blown off the porch and into the wilderness somewhere. She told me later that this was the only time she had ever been frightened.

I refused to watch them coming down. I curled up with Spot, saying prayers, and didn't open my eyes until the door into the garage opened and the three staggered inside.

That would be it for the time being, I pleaded. No more being outside in that shelter under the porch and having me play cook and waitress through the window. No more outside business to check for damages. In fact no more outside for any reason until all this wind and rain was over. This just wasn't fun anymore. This time they agreed, thinking it would end any minute. It really wasn't my fault that instead of rapidly moving on Francis stalled for hours.

Bob and I sat together, each trying to read a book of some interest. I bet you can guess how that went. When we weren't talking about the Village, it nonetheless consumed our thoughts. I knew it wouldn't be long before Bob couldn't stand it a minute longer. By noon on Saturday he was ready to move on out.

"It's pretty quiet now, honey. I think it is safe enough to go check out the Inn. You stay here and I'll go on over."

"I think you're right, Dad. Time to check things out. . ." responded Lisa, "and I'll drive you."

They loaded themselves in that big wide van and started out. The Inn is only about a mile from Ridge House and everything was clear until they got to the end of the paved road and hit our "picturesque" little dirt lane.

They managed to travel the entire length of the lane, or what they assumed was the lane, by stopping every few feet to clear away branches and debris. Larry met them with a chainsaw and a machete, then he and Bob just hacked away at fallen trees and bushes to make a path to Seaside Village. The water was up to the doors on the van, but it kept chugging away.

Lisa said it was like a ship making a big wake. We were amazed and proud as could be of that van. It was wonderful and ran as smoothly as could be for the next couple of weeks, but of course it hasn't run since.

Lisa suggested I be a little bit prepared for what I'd see when they finally got the rest of us back to the Inn.

"It's not good, Mom, it really is not good."

Damage to The Courtyard

Not good was the understatement of the century.

There were gaping holes in the roof, which resulted in water damage in most of the rooms. New walls would be necessary, new ceilings, new mattresses, new curtains, new spreads, new rugs and all the rooms would have to be repainted. Hopefully we could find a way to salvage Nicole's murals.

The upstairs dining room was destroyed, the flowers and plants in the courtyard wiped out, everything behind the bar like the icemaker, the coolers and anything else we didn't or couldn't have moved would have to be replaced. The pool was filled with sand and there were shingles, roof parts and lights from the walkway along with unrecognizable debris just scattered everywhere as far as the eye could see. We probably should not have worried about the coconuts. They were right there on the ground next to the trees, which had been uprooted and blown down.

A window in one of the bedrooms at the Yellow House had caved in so it was no surprise to find the curtains missing, the mattress soaked and the entire room filled with sand.

It was a little surprising, however, to find ankle-deep sand through other parts of the house. Hard to explain but there it was, piled up along the windows and sliding glass doors, looking a lot like snowdrifts. Just about everyone who had a home on the ocean side was experiencing the same thing.

Although I felt heartbroken, there wasn't time for tears. No one was hurt and we had much to be thankful for and plenty to do.

The girls, Bob and I, and all the guys who had stayed with us at Ridge House decided to get started. Paul was the only exception. He had a new house on the ocean at the other end of town. He'd have enough shoveling of his own to do.

I couldn't believe how hard everyone worked. Jan, Lisa and the guys just went nonstop gathering large pieces of debris, dragging parts of the walkway and the roof to different piles they had set up in the courtyard. They had a pile for plastic stuff, old shingles, walkway lights and ceiling pieces. A pile for things we could burn, a pile of things we could bury, and last but certainly not least a pile to be dragged to the dock for a freight boat to haul away.

I worked also, but nowhere near their pace. Most of my contribution was gathering shingles, off the beach, out of the sea, and up and down the shoreline, then dragging them back to the right pile. Even that effort left me feeling pretty "wrung out."

Some of that tiredness was due to the physical labor but perhaps even more because of my inner emotional turmoil. I wasn't about to let the girls, Bob, or our young loyal friends know how close I was to throwing up my hands and saying "To hell with it!"

So I smiled, laughed and plugged away. Watching all of them, there was no way I could be a quitter. And besides I was still very much in love with our little Inn and realistically knew that when the chips were down all of us would do just about anything it took to make her better.

Bob was laboring hard on the swimming pool, shoveling out what sand he could, trying to protect the filter, the plumbing and whatever. He also had a generator that could perhaps work temporarily if he came up with some innovative repairs. As for the two water makers that were no longer working, there was nothing that could be done. Guess we should be thankful that while Francis hung around he had dumped nineteen inches of rain so our cisterns were full.

We worked for hours and it wasn't until late afternoon that we finally decided where we'd all bunk for the night. There was damage in all the rooms, but rooms 1, 3, 4, and 7 were livable.

Bob and I went to room 3 because that is where we were staying before all this hit us. The ceiling was missing in part of the bedroom and all of it in the bathroom and shower area. It was pretty much the same picture in those other three rooms as well.

Ceiling tiles were hanging down and there was plenty of dampness everywhere. But all in all they were in much better shape than the other rooms. The girls chose room 4, and the three guys bunked in room 7. All of us needed to pick up ceiling tiles along with clumps of wet insulation, sweep out the rooms, and open all the windows and doors in a feeble attempt to dry things out.

All of a sudden it dawned on us that we hadn't seen Chet, Shawn or Rustin for the last half hour or so. We discovered they had retreated to the kitchen and were busily preparing a special Bahamian dinner for all of us. All three were busy either chopping stirring, adding spices or tasting whatever was in that big pot to make sure it was all going right. I smiled with gratitude as I listened to the brothers talking about making their Mummy's favorite cake for dessert tomorrow night. We were grateful for a delicious dinner, but even more grateful that the feud between the brothers was finally over.

We played some cards and listened to calls on the VHF. It was just like the old days when I was a kid and folks used to listen in on those telephone party lines.

The first was a call from Larry's friend to the "girlfriend." He had stayed with her through the hurricane and was apparently planning to return.

"I have some lobster's. I'll bring over and cook us dinner!"

"Well, thanks but I think I'll just have a peanut butter sandwich."

"Fine, I like peanut butter. I'll come and join you."

"Uh, uh. I think I want to go to bed really early!"

"Okay, I'll just bring the lobsters over in the morning and make us some lobster omelets."

"Well that's not a good idea because I want to sleep late!"

It was then Larry's turn to get on the VHF. He hailed a couple of his friends and kept repeating that if anyone needed him he'd be at Seaside Village. Just hail him at the Village . . . remember he'd be right there at Seaside. As soon as he put that message out over the airwaves he was off and running.

The girls watched him as he sloshed through puddles with a garbage bag full of his belongings slung over his shoulder. They offered to give him a ride and he agreed as long as they didn't tell anyone they saw him headed to her house. Of course they couldn't wait to tell me and even though such intrigue is hard to keep under wraps, they didn't tell anyone else. It didn't matter because Larry's friend figured things out for himself. This is probably just about the time he decided to bow out of the trio.

CHAPTER 36

Everyone Pitches In

The call went out the next day for a general island clean up. Those with pickup trucks were to canvass not just the Settlement, but the entire island. They were to pick up downed tree limbs, bushes, branches and whole trees, then haul the debris to a chipper parked, ready and waiting. Volunteers were needed not only for the hard labor of loading and unloading the trucks but to prepare lunches for everyone.

Lisa decided she'd volunteer for the hard labor. Not Jan and me, we settled for being cooks. The clean up started at 8:00 a.m. and went until 4 'p.m. The food was all set up under the fig tree and there was plenty. Even with all the confusion, folks remembered to bring soft drinks and paper products.

Lisa described what hard work it was unloading the trucks but was determined not to give up until the job was finished. She shared with me that a couple of male helpers were fascinated because they never saw a woman work the way she did, and they told her so. After that comment there wasn't a chance in the world that she'd quit, no matter how tired she got. She told me she just kept saying to herself "no more trucks . . . please no more trucks." I'm not certain exactly when she started that mantra, but after forty-three truckloads the job was done.

Under that fig tree, there were numerous offers of help. Everyone was asking just who needed what. There was the fellowship, old and new friendships and the awareness that everyone's houses were wide open and not a soul had to worry about looting. All of that plus the blessings said before lunch just reinforced what a special place Guana Cay is.

The daily routine for the next week and a half was just about the same and every evening we enjoyed a different Bahamian dish. The boys were great cooks but not too good at learning new games. We certainly didn't play any more spin the bottle foolishness but settled instead for different kinds of poker, and even tried the old Prince of Wales game.

When it got to the point that all the work left to do was structural in nature and us "girls" couldn't really be of any more help, we graciously offered to get out of the way. How happy we were when everyone thought it was a great idea for us to head for home. Now the trick was how to get off the island.

Both the girls had return tickets on American Eagle over to Florida, and from there American to Boston, but of course almost nothing was flying out of Marsh Harbour. American just kept saying tomorrow, or maybe tomorrow, or maybe the day after tomorrow. Once we had decided to leave, the fact that we couldn't was really frustrating.

Someone said they thought that Calypso was flying, and they knew someone who knew someone who worked for that airline in the states. Now if they could only find someone with a cell phone that worked, they might be able to get us aboard a flight. We waited and waited until late afternoon when the word came down that we were all set. The three of us had seats on the only flight out tomorrow.

It was an early morning flight so that meant catching the really early ferry, provided it was operational. That could be doubtful since no one was really going much of anywhere. After several VHF contacts with the ferry company, we settled for the answer that, "Maybe they might be running or maybe not."

That was good enough for us. We could simply pack a few things in carry-on bags, wait at the dock, and hope for the best. That is exactly what we did, and when we spotted that dear old ferry chugging towards us, we knew we were on our way. Leaving Bob behind was the only thing that kept me from jumping with joy.

I knew that Bob was depressed. Last night he sat on the edge of the bed and told me he wasn't sure how much more he could take. He had to stay behind to deal with the insurance adjusters and customs people, find the necessary supplies and have them shipped over, and struggle to get the extra help he and the guys would need. Knowing he was feeling so down was really troublesome.

"Dad, I really don't mind staying here and letting the girls go on home. I am sure there are some things I could do," I said in a sincere offer.

"No way," he answered, "I want you out of here. You are depressing the hell out of me."

And all this time I thought it was the hurricane damage and tasks that lay ahead that were getting him down.

The ride from the ferry dock to the airport in Marsh Harbour was traumatic for all three of us. We rode in silence as we looked at the destruction that was everywhere. Entire marinas were wiped out without a single dock remaining. One of our favorite spots to grab a quick lunch when we were in town was in pieces, many of which could be seen casually bobbing in the Sea of Abaco. Across the street at another favorite spot there was a large sailboat that had been blown ashore and was sitting there in the outside eating area. It sat there upright as if it were waiting for service.

Trees of all sizes were down, scattered here and there. Try as we might, we could not spot a single flower. There were no Oleanders, Bougainvilleas, Hibiscus, or even a single Yellow Elder, the national flower of the Bahamas that grows like a weed. The landscape on both sides of the road had just about recovered from the hit it took from Floyd five years before. Now it must begin all over again.

When we reached the airport it was obvious why none of the larger planes were flying. The major part of the runway was so flooded that it looked like a lake. There was a tiny bit of runway farther down from the terminal that had almost completely dried out with just enough length for a smaller aircraft to take off. Not really ideal, but manageable. There would be only one flight a day for the next few days. Lucky for us that was the flight we were booked on.

We took out our passports and credit cards up to the Calypso desk only to be greeted with a blank stare from the ticket agent. "I have no reservations for any of you. In fact your names don't show up anywhere on my lists."

"How is that possible? Someone in the states got word to us that we were all confirmed for this flight."

"Well, whoever that was didn't know what they were talking about."

"Is there any room at all on this plane?"

"I will have to check, but I know there certainly isn't room for three."

At this point I told the girls to wait and see if any seats became available, if so they should grab them. I'd simply go back to the Inn and stay with their Dad. In the meantime I strolled over to the American Airline desk and began to chat with the agent there. She didn't have any idea exactly when the American Eagle would be able to get either in or out, but it looked like at least another three or four days. Then I heard Janet call me.

"Mom, come on back over here. He just this minute got three cancellations, so we can all go."

Before we boarded I gave the agent a good-sized tip and thanked him for his patience and his efforts. Lisa thought I was out of my mind.

"Ma," she said, "do you really think he just this minute got three cancellations?" He was waiting for one of us to grease his palms. A little extra for him under the table! When it looked like it wasn't working and he saw you talking to that other agent, he all of a sudden came up with three seats."

Of course I didn't believe it and really wondered how in the world this child of mine had become so cynical? In fact I told her she should be ashamed of herself for not having more faith in people.

Once we were seated, I looked around the nine-passenger plane, saw two other travelers, four empty seats, and Lisa grinning.

We flew into Ft. Lauderdale then had to take a taxi to Miami to catch our homeward bound American flight. Because of all the delays and other problems, American upgraded the three of us to first class. Nice touch, but it hardly mattered since we all slept most of the way to Boston.

It was of course great to be home where everything was still in one piece, nothing inside was soaking wet or beginning to mildew, and no ceiling tiles or insulation bits were hanging down in the rooms as

I entered. There were no assorted piles of debris. And both vehicles worked just by turning the keys. That was the upside. The downside was the fact that there was no Bob and a very limited way to communicate with him.

Following Francis, we got messages home by using the only computer on the island that was still functional. The owners very graciously offered their home to be the e-mail center for anyone who needed to get messages in or out. It was a very generous effort on their part, especially since they were dealing with their own personal hurricane damage.

Walking through their main living area you would see several large boards where there once had been windows that looked out on the ocean. You were also painfully aware that you were traipsing through sand that was almost ankle deep. How long they would be able to keep their house open as a message center was certainly a question. However if they continued to stay there and both their computer and their generous offer held up, then Bob would be able to contact me once every few days without abusing their hospitality.

CHAPTER 37

Bad News about the Yellow House and Insurance Companies

The insurance adjuster came to the Inn, reviewed the damage and gave Bob a really unbelievably low estimate as to what they would be willing to pay. Then the battles began. It meant reviewing everything that had been destroyed and documenting every single replacement cost. Just as it looked as if a reasonable and agreeable compromise had been reached, the company changed the adjuster.

Now the new man was quite determined to do his own review. Bob was certainly discouraged but the change, which meant an unreasonable delay, had also made him angry. That was not good news for the insurance company. Bob had been very cooperative in providing the company with whatever documentation they requested and had been a model client. Now he was tired, fighting mad and wanted to get some of the repairs underway. They just didn't realize what it meant when his ears turned red, but that meant good news for us. When Bob got done with the new round of "negotiations," we actually came out much better. It would, however, be a while before any actual payment came our way.

Since it would be critical to replace the roof as quickly as possible, I was responsible for finding the financial resources and a way to transfer them to Bob so he could at least order the necessary materials. At this point in time, everything you needed had to be paid for upfront. My task was not as difficult as I had assumed it would be. Bankers at home were very helpful. They listened to my tale of woe, seemed to grasp the urgency of the situation and made all the necessary arrangements to have funds transferred in a timely fashion. However, not timely enough to reach Bob before Hurricane Jeanne did.

Back he went to the Ridge House downstairs apartment. This time he wouldn't be with quite such a crowd; he hunkered down with our friends Bruce and Judy, who were the actual owners. They had been on what they had hoped would be an extended vacation in New Mexico. Instead of returning around Thanksgiving, they were forced to hurry back to check out the damage Francis had caused.

I was really pleased Bob would be with them, not only because they are good company, but because Judy is also in command of any situation she finds herself in. God help Bob if he decided to step outside before it was all over. He'd receive a worse thrashing from Judy than he would from Jeannie. She is a no-nonsense lady and I had no doubt she'd keep him under control.

When the worst was over and it was safe to return to the Inn, Bob and Larry hooked up some kind of gadget to the computer that enabled them to make phone calls. The trick was to wait until the other person finished talking before you spoke. Actually saying "over" when you were done made communicating a little better, but still not good. The echoes, static, feedback, and delays made these calls frustrating as hell. But even if I could only understand half of what was being said, just hearing Bob's voice made it all worthwhile. At least I could tell that he was alive and well.

I was just coming in from shopping when I noticed the message light blinking. My visit to the store had been a rather lengthy one, not that I needed a lot of supplies, but the novelty of having just about everything at my fingertips had kept me spellbound. Thinking it was probably Bob, I was ready to do a lot of careful listening in order to understand the scrambled and scratchy message he had probably left. It wasn't Bob; it was a friend of ours whose message wasn't scrambled or scratchy but clear as a bell.

"Oh Gerry, I'm so sorry, so very sorry that you've lost your Yellow Ocean House."

Yellow House Hurricane Damage

Harry is a friend of ours and although he lives only a few minutes from us in Maine, we had not met either him or his wife Cathy until we were in the Bahamas. They have a lovely home on the outskirts of Marsh Harbour and when there they spend much of their time caring for stray animals. Working with a limited number of volunteers and with no government help, they developed a whole program for spaying, neutering, and arranging for these cats and dogs to be adopted. At home they have operated a cat hotel for some time, and now also operate a similar facility for dogs.

You'll notice that I didn't say kennel, because these facilities are far from that. Catnaps and Browser Bedrooms are two elegantly furnished all private room "hotels." There are even some two-room suites so pets from the same family can room together Their level of caring is really unbelievable and it transfers from animals to people around them. I guess that explains why Harry gave me the Yellow House message with a catch in his throat.

When Bob finally got to me with the news, he was surprised that I already knew. Harry had picked it up off Abaco Message Board that was listing some of the known damages on the islands. Bob, however, determined the loss in a much different manner. He and Larry had stood on the top of the hill leading to the Village with binoculars in hand.

They thought that perhaps they could assess the damage to the house from a distance, but the surprise was that it wasn't even there. It just wasn't anywhere to be seen. It was just gone.

The kids and I sat around the table reminiscing about all the great times we'd had at our Yellow House. We decided to start sketching what type of house we would build on that land. Looking to the future eased the sadness of the present to some extent.

I came up with almost the same basic floor plan of the Yellow House but I attached two walkways with pod-like units for guests at each end. Others had all types of designs that were fun to review, some were reasonable possibilities, others looked liked they belonged in outer space, and at least two would be wonderful if we had been multi-millionaires. There was one, however, that got all of our attention.

Our granddaughter Hilary had been at her home, which is right across the lawn from our house. After she finished her homework, she decided on her own to sketch what she thought we should build. It got our attention because she had drawn exactly what I had. Both pictures were identical, the same basic floor plan, two walkways attached with pod-like units at each end. Either we thought alike or some telepathic brain waves had traveled about 150 feet across the lawn.

It looked like it would be a long time before Bob could get back to New Hampshire. There was additional damage to the Inn that he would have to document. The loss of the Yellow Ocean House and all its contents would also have to be documented for insurance purposes. So let the fun begin AGAIN!

The task of listing the Yellow House inventory became mine. It was something I could easily do from my kitchen at home. I used the Internet to find the least expensive replacement cost. I outlined everything I could remember. The list included pots, pans, silver, dishes, bedding, curtains, mattresses, furniture, appliances, the VHF, TV, lamps, rugs and paintings. We had insured the contents for $25,000 and even though the total came to $29,000, I decided to leave it at that, thinking they would probably discount a thing or two anyway. Oh silly me! I was soon going to learn a real lesson about insurance companies and how they work. Maybe not all of them, but this one sure had a surprise.

Instead of simply not allowing some of the items I had listed, they were adamant, explaining how wrong it was for us to be paying premiums on only $25,000 for the contents which we now documented were worth $29,000. We certainly had been underpaying them. That was a great big No No, so we had to be penalized. Our "punishment" and the end result was a reimbursement for the contents of only $20,000.

Both Bob and I decided not to fight it. That $5,000 wasn't worth his time, his energy, or his mental stability. There was too much else to be done.

CHAPTER 38

Now It Is My Turn

Home in New Hampshire this October was beautiful. It was only a little cool— not like some other years when it had been downright cold and even some years when there had been snow covering the brightly colored leaves that had not yet fallen. It meant that the little kids could go out Trick or Treating with only warm jackets over their costumes. There would be no need for scarves, mittens, hats or rubber boots.

My cousin Cathy was planning a Halloween get-together for her children and grandchildren, and lucky for me I had also been invited. I was really pleased to be included and although I hadn't slept very well the night before and was feeling a little out of it, I decided that wasn't going to keep me away from the party. That wasn't going to deter me, but something else came along that certainly did.

The restless night before convinced me I might have a touch of pneumonia, so I decided to call my doctor.

"Rick, I think I have a touch of pneumonia so would you please prescribe me some antibiotics?"

"What makes you think you have pneumonia?"

"Well, my chest felt real heavy and the only way I could sleep was to be propped up on pillows. Besides I have had pneumonia before and I remember what it felt like!"

"Well, I absolutely am not ordering any medicine for you. Instead, I want you to get to the hospital right away."

"That's crazy Rick. Why the hospital when I know what's wrong?"

"The hell you do. Stop this self-diagnosis. I'll meet you in the emergency room, and DON'T DRIVE YOURSELF.

"Oh Lord," I was thinking, "this is really nonsense, especially the part about 'not driving myself when the hospital is less than two miles away." But I knew if I wanted to keep him as my doctor, I would have to do as he suggested.

I saw no need to call any of the kids since my cousin Tim was right outside. I' asked him to give me a ride.

He told me just to call him if I wanted him to pick me up. "Great," I thought, "we can go directly from the hospital to his Mom's house. That way I wouldn't miss the Halloween party, the little kids or even dinner."

I was just nice and cozy resting in the little ER cubicle when the kids came rushing in one at a time all giving me holy hell.

"Ma, what were you thinking? You didn't even tell us you were coming here. What's the matter with you?" Even my cousin Laurie came rushing in singing the same tune.

"I didn't call any of you because I'm not going to be here very long. It's no big deal, so what's all fuss!"

Then they started a whole series of tests.

My response was, "Stop taking these tests. Every time you do one, you come up with something else wrong."

So far they had discovered a leaky heart valve, an aneurysm, and the need for a quadruple by-pass. Maybe that explained at least a little why I had felt so tired trying to help clean up after Hurricane Francis.

I was right about not being there in that hospital setting for very long, because a couple of days later I was in an ambulance on my way to the Massachusetts General Hospital.

"Why there?" I asked Rick.

"Because that is where one of the best heart surgeons in the world is. The cardiologist here and I both agree that you need to have the best available."

"Damn," I thought, "what an imposition on the family." I knew them well enough to know they would make an effort to be there with me as often as possible. The traffic in Boston is always a nightmare both coming and going, and the trip not an easy one. Bob would come home from the Bahamas and PJ would have to ask for time off from the doctors she worked with. When she explained why she'd have to come home, they all wondered if she was making up this family of hers. Last year her Dad, this year her Mother! What a bummer!

On the trip down, Lisa followed close behind the ambulance and I could watch her from the small back window.

"Someone tell her not to tailgate" or "Tell her to use the blinkers," and I had a number of other suggestions. I was trying to backseat drive from my gurney. At least it kept my mind off of where I was going and why.

It would be several days before this special surgeon could put me on his operating schedule. Since I wasn't hurting in any way, we made the most of this waiting time. The kids who were there on any given day would join me in the sunroom. We had picnics with food they brought in, played cards and board games and even celebrated Lisa's birthday with a cake and presents. It certainly made the wait easier to take.

Bob came of course, but he didn't have time to join in any of the games. Instead he was constantly on the phone that was right outside the sunroom, which we referred to as our "play pen." The Inn was still in a mess, with the insurance adjusters still dragging their feet and getting supplies in still posing problems.

Trying to get everything in order would have been difficult if he had been back at the Inn, but to try and set things straight over a hospital pay phone was almost impossible. Listening to him struggle, the kids would often remark "Oh damn, poor Dad," and they really were feeling a great deal of compassion. However there were a couple of times when they suggested that one of them go out and remind him that a loud voice and swearing wasn't really appropriate for a hospital corridor.

We decided that booking a room in a hotel close to the hospital might be a wise move. Lisa ended up being a full-time guest; the others including Janet and PJ shared the room off and on. Bonny and Bob booked their own room, and the rest of the kids and Bob continued to travel back and forth, the kids in their automobiles and Bob on a C&J bus.

"Dad, you don't have to take the bus. Come with us. We'll pick you up whenever you want to go and we won't leave until you are ready to leave."

That was a daily argument coming from all directions, but to no avail. Bob always responded by thanking them but firmly stating that he would take the bus. (The young man who owns and operates the C&J bus line is a fellow who grew up with our kids, spent a lot of those years hanging around our house, and remains friends. In fact he still calls Bob "the old man" and me "Ma." Both Bob and I can ride anywhere free of charge at least until the year 2020.) I don't believe that it was because he didn't trust the kids driving; I just think the bus offered him the chance to sit quietly and do some thinking or napping. Besides, why not take the bus—after all he had a free pass.

Finally, after a four-day wait, the surgery was finally scheduled and barring any emergency it would be my turn. Waiting could be a nerve-wracking experience, but at Massachusetts General they do everything possible to make you comfortable. The cardiologist assigned to me came in at least twice a day. The first visit was always early in the morning with a group of Harvard interns making the rounds. Later in the day or early evening, he'd stop by just to check on how well I was holding up. The surgeon also stopped by on a couple of occasions to offer words of encouragement, and the nursing staff was unbelievable. They were there constantly; it was as if I were the only patient that needed their attention.

This entire medical group functioned as a team, and you honestly felt they were a team developed solely for your benefit. Their attitudes were always upbeat and their messages positive. There was only one exception, and it involved a single intern.

Lisa and I were happily playing cards on my bed table when in walked this little intern. We both wondered if he'd lost his team, as it seemed he was just sort of wandering around. We said hello and watched as he read my charts at the bottom of the bed. His eyes flew wide open as he exclaimed loudly, "WOW, THIS IS A BIGGY!"

It was so unexpected that both Lisa and I started to laugh.

"DON'T LAUGH," he said, "BECAUSE THIS IS A BIGGY, A REAL BIGGY!"

We informed him that we already knew but thanked him for his input. After he left we began another round of laughter and both wondered out loud if "BIGGY" was a special Harvard medical term.

Needless to say, the operation was a success or I wouldn't be writing this. After a week's stay I was headed for home.

There had been some intense discussions about exactly where I should be going. The first thought was that I should be released to a rehabilitation hospital and of course I objected strenuously. Thankfully they listened to what I really wanted and that was to go home. They made arrangements for a nurse and a physical therapist to pay home visits. They outlined a lot of conditions that I would have to abide by if they were to be comfortable with this decision.

The first was to be certain I had someone with me around the clock for at least the first two weeks. I was to follow the instructions of both the visiting nurse and therapist. There should be no visitors or phone calls during this same period of time. Watch what I ate and make sure the foods were only those included in a heart-healthy diet, on and on. They also would enroll me in the therapy program at the local hospital, and I would have to participate on a daily basis once the cardiologist at home gave me the go-ahead.

I got all set up on the pullout sofa in the family room. It was comfortable and I could watch all the comings and goings in the downstairs and especially in the kitchen, which has always been the hub of any activity.

Lisa had this large sign that read "The Queen is not accepting any visits from her subjects today," which she placed in front of the French door leading into the family room. Everyone monitored the phone calls. Although it was easiest for Lisa to be the constant watchdog, all the others also took their turns. If they weren't "Ma sitting," they were cooking the things they thought I should be eating and, eventually, driving me back and forth to therapy sessions. It seems that Bonny constantly brought dinners that would have fed an army, Janet was the "I'll bring the lunch person" and Lisa took care of breakfast. That wasn't all—the others brought dishes of all kinds and were very guarded about what I could and could not eat.

One day when Scott was my guard, he asked what I would like for lunch. I thought, "Okay, here's my chance. Maybe I can fool him—and the girls will never know." I very innocently asked if he would go to the small store up the street and bring me back a steamed hot dog.

"Oh no, Ma. NO! NO! NO! Honey, you CAN NOT eat that. I'll get you something else!"

I can't for the life of me remember what he fed me. I only know it wasn't the steamed hot dog I was dying for.

Seeing how well I was being cared for, Bob decided it was safe to return to the Inn. But he didn't return alone; the kids took turns joining him. They weren't traveling down to the Bahamas for fun and games but to really pitch in and work their *bungys* off. They sanded, painted, did carpentry and a general clean up. They didn't all go at once but worked out a schedule so when one crew came home another went down. Some stayed only four or five days, others a week or more. Our son Rob and a friend of ours JO went together and their primary chore was to repair the dock.

The last to lend a hand was our son-in-law Bob, who is in the hotel business. He was the organizer who got everyone to follow instructions and do assigned chores, sort of a clerk of the works who even got the hired Haitians working at a steady pace. It was rather unbelievable how fast everything was taking shape.

Of course none of the family had work permits, but the hurricane damage was so pervasive and help so hard to find that it would have been unreasonable for anyone to register a complaint. Even the government would have to acquiesce. The kids who weren't working as repairmen were taking turns at caretaking.

Bob came home for Christmas, but we all knew the visit would be a very brief one. That is when I decided that this year we shouldn't bother to put up a Christmas tree. There was the manger set and other decorations we could put here and there to at least reflect the holiday season. That made sense to me, but certainly not to Scott.

I heard once again "No No, Ma." Only this time it revolved around the fact that he didn't think I should go without a tree. He brought back a perfectly shaped little six-foot tree and set it up in front of the fireplace in the family room.

Instead of searching the back closet, the attic, the garage and the storage bin to try and find our ornaments and lights (and the Lord knows where else), he decided to bring some of his from home.

He and my grandson David did a beautiful job of decorating it. I could just lie there or sit there and really enjoy it. It was a far cry from the tree that a florist had decorated when our house was open for an annual Home Christmas Tour. That tree had been in the hot tub room, was over twelve feet tall and secured with bolts to the open beams. Of course it was beautiful and expertly done all in blue, white and silver, with stars, streamers and flowers—including fresh orchids. But as far as I was concerned it couldn't hold a candle to that delightful little tree. To me it was the most beautiful tree I had ever seen. I loved it.

Bob kept in touch and reported the progress at the Inn on a regular basis. Because of all the extra help the kids had given, he was certain that the Inn would be in good enough shape so that the New Year's Day recovery party could be held as usual.

When the big party day rolled around, Seaside was not only good enough but folks thought it looked better than ever.

It was another absolutely great party. The crowd was the biggest one yet, and the celebrating lasted well into the night. There were many volunteers, including Janet and her family and Lisa and hers, leaving Scott and Bonny to tend to their pouting mother. They traveled down just in case their Dad wasn't up to handling the job of official host. They shouldn't have worried because he really stepped up to the plate. He was everywhere doing all types of socializing and doing things that he had always left up to me and had shied away from. It was not only a great party it was also the grand reopening of the hurricane-devastated Guana Seaside Village.

It was the very end of January before the doctors would give me the okay to leave the country. When they asked about what medical facilities or professional help would be available, they were not too excited by my description of the rescue squad and their pickup truck. We finally reached a compromise.

First I had to promise not to work and avoid all the confusion. They suggested I find a place to stay away from the resort and limit my activities to a simple daily walk. Of course I shouldn't walk if it were really hot or windy. And finally watch my diet, rest, and be faithful in doing my prescribed exercises".

Janet, Lisa and I left New Hampshire at 6:00 a.m. on a very cold unpleasant day. The early departure was necessary if we were going to make the connection in Florida and the ferry in Marsh Harbour.

It was a long day but the easiest one I had yet to experience. The girls were in charge of checking in, keeping track of the luggage and any other logistical concerns. I just went merrily along, pushed in a wheelchair. We were put to the head of all the lines and really got special treatment. I jokingly suggested they should get me a wheelchair everywhere we went, even when I no longer needed one.

We arrived in Ft. Lauderdale a little after noon and our flight to the Bahamas was scheduled for 3:30. We decided that there would be plenty of time for lunch and just hanging out when we noticed on the departure board that there was another flight scheduled for our destination that was leaving in 20 minutes.

We were told that there was room for the three of us on this Continental flight, but they couldn't take us because we had checked luggage on American Airlines that hadn't yet been transferred'. Regulations required that you fly with your bags. At this point the young man who was pushing me around in that wheelchair told us and the ticket agent to just hang on. He left running as fast as he could, got to American Airlines, retrieved our bags, got them to Continental and notified the ticket agent that all was set and we could board.

We had been taking turns tipping the wheelchair agents and I was sure glad it was Janet's turn to tip this one. We arrived at Marsh Harbour a couple of hours ahead of schedule, and there was Bob already waiting.

When we arrived at the Inn, Bob made an announcement over the VHF that I was back and he was taking me to the Blue Water Grill for Pizza Night. The girls and I couldn't understand why he said that; it certainly wasn't anything we were aware of and it certainly wasn't on our schedule. The folks who heard his VHF announcement all showed up at Blue Water Grill to welcome me back. Those who hadn't heard it showed up at the Inn for the potluck welcome home party they had been planning and. The girls concluded that their father really wasn't aware of the party. He just wanted to get me out in the public so everyone could see I was alive and well. And as he would add, "See, she's all better." It really didn't matter—the friendship, fellowship and the welcome home sentiments were all that counted.

The original plan was for me to stay at the downstairs apartment at Ridge House. Somehow the signals got crossed and Ridge House had been rented. It would be a couple of weeks before the apartment was free.

Bob did not think that was a problem. He thought I could simply stay at the Inn in room three. That decision lead to a fierce family debate.

"Are you crazy, Dad? She can't stay there—she'll be out every time she hears guests outside!"

"No, she won't," he responded. "I'll just keep her inside!"

"And when someone asks 'where is Gerry,' you don't think she'll feel obligated to come out?"

"I just won't let her, damn it. I just won't let her!"

"Well, the stress of not letting her out will probably do more damage than if she were outside doing what she thinks needs to be done. You must have forgotten how she likes not only to be involved but also in control!"

A day later, the problem was solved. An excellent opportunity came my way.

It was called Graceland. As you can probably imagine the original owners of this Guana home had been avid Elvis fans but not so the new owners.

Graceland had been purchased by the new owners in a most unusual, fascinating and perhaps risky way.

Carol and Bob were Americans who lived in Illinois, and for a number of years they had vacationed in the Out Islands of the Bahamas. Year after year they rented the very same cottage on Lubbers Cay, and year after year they talked about buying a place of their own. Unfortunately year after year the price of property on Lubbers rose higher and higher, so when they finally decided they were ready to buy, they also decided they had better look elsewhere.

They made their way to Guana Cay and first found a delightful cottage with everything in place, ready to move in without much to be done. The person who was showing them around mentioned a larger place that was for sale a couple of miles north of the Settlement. They decided to take a look and even though it needed a lot of work, they fell in love with the house, the location and the spectacular views. Now comes the risky part.

Bob, who is really a very conservative fellow got on the Internet with a simple question: "Is there anyone out there who is a "Guanawannabe?"

Back came the equally simple reply, "YES" from a Fred and Tyler who lived in Colorado.

Communications between the couples began in earnest. Back and forth, back and forth, until all the I's were dotted and the T's crossed. It can be cumbersome to do business in the Bahamas, even when you're here in the country. Yet these courageous guys managed all the necessary details from the USA and jointly purchased Graceland. The first time they actually met face to face was when they arrived here on the island for a three-week stay together.

What could have been a disaster turned out to be a delight. Each person had their own talent and expertise to contribute, and they agreed on just about everything. Where to place the bar in the kitchen, what type of tile for countertops, which colors to choose for which rooms, which flowers and bushes to plant and how to renovate the downstairs into an apartment. They also agreed that the first step they should take with remodeling was to remove all the Elvis pictures that were painted on black velvet and hanging everywhere.

Bob (who most on the island now refer to as Farmer Bob) and his wife Carol very generously offered me the use of their newly renovated apartment until such time as Ridge House was ready. Not only was the apartment delightful, quiet and peaceful, but my "landlords" treated me like I was from a royal family. They checked on me to see if I was all right or if I needed anything. Farmer Bob built me a little computer table so I wouldn't have to sit at the bar when I wanted to work. There was a day when I wrote for a couple of hours and for some mysterious reason lost all my work. Carol came to the rescue. When she was unable to find my efforts out there in "cyberspace," she immediately got in touch with her son who is somewhat of a computer expert. Certainly he knew more than either one of us. He gave her step-by-step instructions that she carefully followed while I stood by like a baffled computer idiot. Lets face it, I still think rebooting means kicking someone in the butt twice. She was successful and also taught me the valuable lesson of saving what I was working on every once in while. She even showed me where to find the little save button—a button that I didn't even know existed.

My stay was extremely pleasant and since Graceland was about a mile from the Inn, a short walk back and forth was just perfect for me. I'd relax until early evening, walk to the Inn, have dinner and stay the night with Bob. In the morning I'd have breakfast, then stroll back to my haven away from it all. They had given me a perfect gift. I marveled at their natural hospitality and also at their courage.

It was only a year-and-a-half before this time that they had come to the Inn to introduce Carol's sister Janet, another sister Linda, her brother-in-law Ken and her mother. They had just arrived and were in high spirits, all here for a family vacation. Ken commented on the fact that he knew I was trying to write another book and suggested it might be beneficial if I included him in the story. His family laughed telling me that was probably not a bad idea. Apparently Ken was somewhat of a cut-up and often entertained others.

"Okay Ken," I responded. "But, you will have to do something really spectacular if you want to be in my book." Those were words I wish I had never spoken!

It was late afternoon the following day when the guests renting the Yellow House called down to the Inn in alarm. There was some sort of accident right in front of the Yellow House and they were fearful that someone was in serious trouble. Bob and Larry ran up the hill as fast as possible while I hailed the rescue squad. Farmer Bob and Ken had been out snorkeling and were wading towards shore in about waist-deep water. When Farmer Bob turned to say something to his brother-in-law, he was nowhere to be seen. After a brief search he found him floating face down. He struggled to reach him and managed to drag him ashore. That's when the first call from the Yellow House reached us.

Both Larry and Bob gave their best efforts to revive him while waiting for Guana Rescue. I must say the rescue workers were there in record time and worked on Ken for over forty-five minutes, to no avail. Everyone present knew from the beginning that nothing could really be done, but for the longest time the rescue squad refused to give up. Now it was up to Farmer Bob to return to Graceland and inform the rest of the family.

I don't remember who drove him but someone surely did, and when he returned he had Carol, Linda and his mother-in-law with him. Everyone was gathered at the back of the Inn. I knew there was nothing I could do, but I really felt the need to try and comfort the family so out back I went. They were all in shock, and I am sure that each was grieving in their own way. I don't believe that the tears and hugs from just a friend made any difference at all. They were looking at Ken, so still and so blue, stretched out in the back of the truck. I looked also. And just as I was sorry I had spoken those words to Ken the day before, I was now sorry I had seen him in death. The image haunted me for days and I couldn't possibly imagine what the family was going through.

I am not too sure or can't remember how many family members traveled to Nassau. I only know that Farmer Bob was responsible for all the arrangements. He had to charter a ferry to Marsh Harbour and then a medevac plane to Nassau. It took two weeks from the time of the autopsy until all the paperwork had been completed. Finally the authorities released the body so Ken could be brought home for a decent burial.

Well Ken, you are in the book—only God knows that I wish it were a different story. All that is left to be said is that I sincerely hope you are enjoying your new paradise.

Carol and Farmer Bob did return to Graceland and a year later convinced Linda she should revisit as well, which she did. And during that visit she found a kind of closure. Carol's Mother however has never returned.

I moved from Graceland to Ridge House and once again got very special treatment from Bruce and Judy. Even without their caring and concern I would have been really comfortable there. Once it had been a haven from a hurricane and now a haven for recovery. The walk to the Inn was a little more tedious. Although the distance wasn't much farther, I had to maneuver those monster hills from hell. I was just thankful that at least now they were paved.

Bob joined me in the evenings, stayed until the first morning light then hurried back to Seaside. Everyday Judy cooked for us. I should have felt a little guilty, but then Judy cooked for everybody. At times it seemed like she was feeding the whole island—always something a little new added to some of her old standbys. She enjoyed cooking gourmet meals that had caught her attention on The Food Network.

I often wondered what I could do to repay them both, but as far as Judy was concerned I showed deference to her by staying the hell out of her kitchen when she was creating.

It was time to return to the Inn and although I wasn't especially active, it certainly was a good feeling to be back. I arrived in time to enjoy the last week of another yoga retreat and was on hand to witness a very special event.

It had taken me sometime to get up the courage to walk up the path and view what was left of the Yellow House. Actually there wasn't much to see except a few remnants, a piece of yellow siding or a small bit of coral trim here and there. Just enough to remind me that we had recently paid $3,000 to have it painted and that our boys had just as recently finished lattice work all around the base of the house. There were pieces of that latticework a quarter of a mile down the beach.

I had hoped to see a hearty plant or small flower poking up out of the ground where there used to be a conch garden—another a recent addition. Instead of a typical rock garden we only used rocks to outline the garden bed and used beautiful conch shells placed here and there in between where our new plantings would go. Our daughter Bonny, who really is an expert gardener, had gone with me to the nursery in Marsh Harbour to pick out a variety of plants. She was careful to choose plants that would do well in sandy soil, full sun and were of the salt tolerant species. We had a tremendous assortment shipped over and spent days planting them all. Too bad there was no such thing as plants that were hurricane tolerant because now there was nothing, not even a hint of what used to be.

Although I felt sad at the loss, I wasn't the only one. The yoga folks were feeling it as well and decided to do something that might bring about a closure of sorts. Up the path they meandered, arms full of assorted things. They sat in a circle, held hands, had some quiet thoughts then each said something in turn.

One lady had found a couple of pages of a book blowing around. Coincidentally they were from a book she had read when she had stayed there, so she read those pages. Others just told stories about their adventures at the Yellow House, and still others read poems they had written for the occasion.

While the recitations were taking place, each person held a candle. It was an honest to God candlelight vigil, not for the house but to honor the fellowship and the friendships that had been enhanced by that setting. It was simply a candlelight vigil for memories.

CHAPTER 39

Swimming with the Sharks

One of the things that my cousin Sonny really enjoyed when visiting us was fishing. However, I am sure that there were other things that he and my cousin (godchild) Laurie would also think of once in a while. They had been to the Inn several times and were not only great guests but also very helpful. They were always looking for things to do and fit very nicely right into the "Inn Family." They also made the most of their time by swimming, collecting shells and driftwood. They collected so much stuff they had to spend time pondering how much they could carry home and how much they would have to leave behind. Laurie thought that what they left behind would be nice to decorate the walkway right outside their room.

They would take the kayaks here and there and usually be gone for a couple of hours. However, the day they ventured up Joe's Creek, they came back in one big hurry.

"You won't believe this!" Sonny said.

"You really won't," chimed in Laurie. And the story began.

When they were far into the creek they saw a very large bull shark. At least Sonny thought that's what it was. The shark circled around, avoiding Sonny, but then deliberately rammed the kayak Laurie was in. They excitedly told us that he rammed her really hard and then took off.

I didn't want them to know that I didn't quite believe them, so I just went on to explain that there really weren't any bull sharks in these waters. I thought Sonny must have been mistaken. Maybe he just saw an extra large nurse shark.

"Oh no," he insisted, "it was a bull shark!"

Neither Bob nor I were convinced until later in the day when people were buzzing about spotting a bull shark very close to shore. Everyone was really surprised because bull sharks never hang around the Sea of Abaco. But people sure saw one. Guess that should teach me to trust my cousins.

There was another occasion when we all went down to the beach at a favorite place called High Rocks. Bob, Sonny and I were strolling along on the beach. Laurie, however, decided to wade in the water. There she was, just wading knee deep, and right beside her was a nurse shark just slowly swimming in the same direction.

Although we know that nurse sharks aren't thought to be dangerous, that didn't keep the three of us shouting as loud as we could, "SHARK, LAURIE! SHARK!"

Apparently not hearing what we yelled, she just waved, smiled and kept on wading.

This time when we yelled, we pointed frantically at what was cruising beside her.

She took a quick look, spotted what we were panicked about, and made a beeline for the shore. She made me promise I would never tell her mother about this episode; it would give her a heart attack.

Usually we are very safe but as with anything in nature, there is always the unknown. It was an extremely hot Friday when we decided to take our little 22-foot boat and head to Green Turtle Cay.

We walked around the delightful little settlement and noticed that most everything was closed so folks could attend a funeral. There was one neat restaurant right at the top of a rather large hill that was open, so we slowly made our way up.

We placed our lunch order and after an hour went by I called the bartender over.

"These are my visiting cousins," I explained. "They have to catch a plane back to the states on Tuesday. Do you think they'll make it?"

They were not busy at all, but apparently the bartender had just never given our orders to the kitchen. I wasn't angry—after all I know from experience how things can get all *kerplunked* up. How well I know!

It was still extremely hot and sunny as we headed back to Guana, but about halfway a storm broke out. A real storm with rain, thunder, lightning—the type of storms we had all experienced before. This one, however, had the frightful addition of a waterspout. There it was, right in front of us, directly in our path.

"What are supposed to do?" I asked Bob.

"I have heard that you are supposed to jump overboard."

"How much sense does that make? If it can suck up the boat, why can't it suck up the people in the water?"

He didn't have an answer, but while we were struggling with our dilemma we could see the spout veer to the right of us. We were out of the direct path but still close enough to watch the spout suck up a lot of water in its way. I guess this is something else I shouldn't tell my Aunt about.

Sonny loved to fish—usually off the dock or in the surf. Those efforts were never very successful—a lot like Bob's. But on one of his visits, and the day before they were to leave, Larry decided to take him out in the boat and lo and behold there came a grinning Sonny carrying a couple of nice size tunas. One he left with the Inn, the other Sandra packed in ice, placed in a cooler, and since they were leaving the next morning, they simply carried it home to New Hampshire. Sonny claimed he was going to invite his whole family over for a fresh tuna dinner as soon as he got home. Now Sonny has a really big family and I don't quite remember the tuna being that big! But I guess a taste is better than nothing and would go along nicely with some glee and great big taste of pride!

Thinking about carrying home shells and bits of driftwood and other perceived treasures, Laurie never left the island without at least one loaf of Bahamian bread. And she never came back without some gifts for Sandra's grandchildren.

On one of their visits they decided they wanted to contact a business named Dive Guana to arrange a snorkeling trip. Dive Guana is owned and operated by Troy and Maria Albury. They provide the equipment, give you lessons if needed, and make sure your day or half-day trip will exceed your expectations.

I was usually too busy with the Inn to ever get into serious snorkeling. Besides, I am somewhat paranoid. Put all that gear on me and I really freak out. I tried it once a long time ago in about three feet of water. I just put on that ridiculous mask, stuck my head in the water then bolted back to the surface. It didn't matter that little kids all around me were getting the hang of it. I just decided never again. But then minds—even mine—can be changed.

Sonny and Laurie were determined to go, but the only catch was they didn't want to leave the resort and me behind. Bob encouraged me to go, said he'd cover for me at Seaside, so I agreed. But I had a plan of my own. I'd bring a good book, sit on the boat while Sonny and Laurie paddled around, read a few minutes, and once in a while just watch for any pretty fish that might swim by. It was a great safe plan but not one that Maria would stand for.

"Come on now, Miss Gerry. Put the gear on."

"But I really don't want to do this," I whined.

"Don't worry," she said, "I will help you. I will take you to the reef to see my favorite fish."

She can be quite forceful, so like a little kid I obeyed.

On went all that stuff, the mask the snorkeling gear, those cumbersome fin things, and by my choice a lifejacket—just in case.

She jumped in the water first and kept nodding encouragingly as I carefully lowered myself down. Very, very carefully!

Then she took my hand and began swimming to a nearby reef. Since she was holding my hand tightly, my only choice was to also hang on tight and swim with her.. Before long she pointed out what she called her favorite fish. I have no idea what it was but it was vivid blue with shiny dots all over it. Those dots actually looked like glittering diamonds. It was absolutely awesome and I could only wonder how she knew just where to find it.

There were other beautiful fish and colorful coral to see. Before I realized it, she had let me loose and I was all on my own truly mesmerized by all that underwater beauty. The only time I felt even a little bit anxious was when I turned and spotted the boat which seemed to be very far away. So I slowly headed back enjoying myself along the way.

My whole adventure lasted about 45 minutes and when I finally scrambled aboard I was as proud as could be. Maria said she was also proud of me. In fact she was so proud that the next time she would take me to swim with the sharks. I didn't answer her but simply thought to myself, "Shiny blue fish are one thing; sharks are something else. No way, Maria. No way."

CHAPTER 40

Trouble Was Brewing

There was a time when Troy and Maria were frequent guests at the Inn. There was also a time when Troy would pull up to our dock to pick up guests who had reservations for a day trip. Sometimes he'd grab sandwiches to go or he'd place an order 'to pick up on their return.

Suddenly things began to change.

We rarely saw them. And if we had made reservations for our guests to go on a trip, he no longer would come to our dock to pick them up. It was all of a sudden our responsibility to carry them down in the golf cart to the Dive Guana dock. Then of course it was also our chore to pick them up when the trip was over.

At first we weren't too certain what brought about the change, but we finally concluded it was because of some of the new guests who were renting our rooms. Not all on Guana but some, including Troy, found what we were doing so objectionable that it probably couldn't have been any worse if we had been harboring fugitives.

When we had a vacant room or cottage, we rented them to personnel who had been hired by Discovery Land Company. Their primary responsibility was to research the impact of a massive proposed development on Bakers Bay.

There had been only one meeting concerning the proposed project. It was held in the little schoolhouse and had been sponsored by the development company. The place was packed and the presentations were as you might expect. There were charts, graphs, elaborate drawings and numerous experts to testify.

The plans featured custom home sites, beach cottages, boathouse villas, a small commercial center in the style of old Caribbean seaports, restaurants, a grocery store, a 180-slip marina, walkways, paths, boardwalks, and last but certainly not least the main feature—an eighteen-hole golf course. The presentation was rather predictable, and so was the outburst against the project.

Some folks sat quietly or mumbled to one another. Others stood, shouted and paced back and forth in front of the developers. They pointed at the charts and graphs, claiming what they showed was nothing less than the complete destruction of all the wonderful natural resources of Bakers Bay. That was the beginning of a committed and determined group called the Save Guana Cay Reef Association. Terry Picard, a friend and strong environmentalist, described the SGCRA "as a group who was laying the groundwork for environmental protection laws in the Bahamas. They are leaders, taking this young country emerging from colonialism to democracy and daring to challenge Government to take into account the wishes and needs of its people in fashioning responsible and sustainable policy." They could not and would not be taken lightly.

Not all of the locals joined the SGCRA. However, many folks who did join were second-home owners, and even some who had recently purchased property but had not yet begun to build. Much of the money raised for future court battles came from these outside folks.

Bob and I were continually asked what we thought. How did we think it would affect our business? What did we think it would do to our property values? Did we like it? We had no definitive answers to any of those inquiries.

We loved Guana just the way it was—quiet and peaceful. We also knew that most all of our guests came to us simply because we weren't like the high-class, fast-paced resorts of the Bahamas. What the impact would be, we had no way of knowing. But we certainly did know that the island would never be the same.

We did some research and still couldn't determine if there was an environmentally safe way to build a golf course. Was there really a way to construct such a course and ensure that the pollutants would not seep into the sea and kill the reefs? The developers claimed there was a way, and they had the technology to do it. But the SGCRA claimed the developers were liars and the precious reefs would be completely destroyed in no time at all.

There were the same conflicting opinions about the 180-slip marina destroying the fish estuary. We listened to the arguments both pro and con that flared up around our bar. It was really difficult for us at this point to know just what to believe. But it was also at this point that we decided to remain neutral for a couple of reasons.

First and foremost, even though we had been welcomed as guests, this land was not our land and this country was not our country. I asked myself how I would have felt if some project had been planned for good old New Hampshire and all those part-time summer residents from Massachusetts decided they had a right to raise some hell to try and stop it.

We could and did strongly believe that the most disturbing part of this whole plan was the fact that the Bahamian Government was giving over 100 acres of Crown Land to the developers. The land was meant to be held open for any Bahamian who wanted a parcel for his own use, and now it belonged to a foreign investment company. The government did make a claim that they had given nothing away. They had stated that they only granted the developer a 100-year lease. Who in hell would be around 100 years from now to claim it back? The lease idea was a ploy clearly meant to pacify the Bahamians and also a little attempt to CYA.

It was, however, part of the very same Crown Land next to the Inn where the former government had planned to put that damned old "sanitary landfill." There wasn't an organized protest then. People raised questions and when they were told what they said wouldn't matter, that was that. No group was formed, and no money raised for court cases. Looking back, we wondered why. We also knew quite clearly something would end up there sooner or later, and Lord knows what that might be.

The consultants who stayed with us were geologists, botanists, environmental experts, oceanographers and some that belonged to an earth watch organization. We watched them leave early in the morning and return late in the afternoon, and waited anxiously for a daily report. The more we learned, the less concerned we became.

They were taking elaborate measures to protect all aspects of the environment. They established hot houses in order to replace any native plants that might be disrupted in the development phase. They established a mangrove preserve of many acres, they cordoned off potential house lots far enough away from the waters edge so the dunes would not be disturbed, and they showed us a plot plan that really convinced us they were trying to do things the right way.

The plans showed various paths where house lots would be and where the village replica and community center would eventually be located. It also showed in bold black outlines areas where no equipment, golf carts, or even foot traffic was allowed. These were the areas that were determined to be potential turtle nesting grounds.

One morning as two of the young men were headed for Bakers Bay with their knapsacks and equipment, Lisa called out to them.

"You guys going to work?"

"We sure are," came the answer.

"I didn't know you guys worked on Saturdays."

They looked at each other, thought for a while, laughed and answered, "It's not Saturday, it's Friday!"

That response was quickly followed by a voice from someone at a courtyard table.

"IT'S NOT FRIDAY, IT'S THURSDAY!"

That just goes to show you how out of touch you can be when you're in the middle of nowhere.

The following months there were numerous court battles, with each side presenting its case. After the final court hearing and while awaiting a ruling from the court in Freeport, the developers decided they would voluntarily stop all work until the decision came down. I guess they expected, as did everyone else, that it would only be a matter of a week or two.

Week after week after week they waited. With their equipment shut down and their staff sitting idly by, they went back to the court and informed them that they were no longer standing by their voluntary work stoppage. And work began again.

The developers called for another meeting and although neither

Bob nor I was there, it was described as "A Meeting from Hell!" The developers announced that The Fig Tree Foundation would be established to help benefit Guana Cay.

There would be three Guana citizens along with three representatives of the company to act in an advisory capacity. Initially the Bakers Bay Golf and Ocean Club would donate $500,000 to this effort. They were also going to offer Bahamians the opportunity to purchase 20 of the lots owned by Bakers Bay at $50,000 per lot. They would then contribute all of the proceeds of those sales to the Foundation. Areas under consideration for usage of these funds included health, education, and general social needs. They had already identified the payment of past medical bills for a recent widow who would have to spend the rest of her life playing "catch up." They also had agreed to accept all of the ongoing costs for cancer treatment for one of the local residents.

Some residents claimed that the developers were attempting to buy town approval. However this was nothing more than they had done in the past. It was part of their usual and customary policy in all of their developments, whether in Arizona, California. Hawaii, Wyoming, New Mexico or wherever. They strongly believed it was a way of contributing to the quality of life for local residents. Still the cry was, "You're trying to buy us off!"

I am not sure if it was this meeting or not that prompted the emergence of a new petition. The new petition simply stated that the citizens of Great Guana Cay request that the SGCRA limit their claims and opinions to include only the members of their association and not the entire island and other community members. It was signed by 72 citizens, clearly dividing this delightful settlement right in half.

None of this slowed SGCRA down. They decided to take yet another step.

They informed the courts that they were going to appeal to the Privy Council in London to get a formal injunction. The judge told them to go right ahead but they would do so without his blessing.

The Privy Council was, after all, called on most often for extreme cases. Usually it acted something like our Supreme Court. When someone was found guilty of a capital crime and sentenced to death, he could appeal to this Council. It was the only way to keep from being hanged in a public square. That was why it was a surprise when SGCRA was successful. An injunction to cease and desist was imposed.

It was to last until such time as the judge in Freeport issued a ruling.

Who knew when that ruling would come down? Apparently there was no court stenographer in Freeport to transcribe the trial notes. That made it a little difficult for the judge to have something to review and rule on.

Life at the Inn went on as usual except for the added discussions about Bakers Bay. Glenn joined in and since he was the Island Councilor he assumed he should be strongly opposed to the proposed project. After all, he explained, he had been elected to represent his constituents.

I wasn't so sure he should be taking an active role. After all, it was apparent that many, if not most of his constituents were not members of the SGCRA. But if that's where he felt his loyalties should be, we decided that we would try not to curtail his involvement. I asked only that he keep us informed. Let us know if he were going to attend a meeting and just when and where and how long he intended to be gone.

We reminded him that we were running a business and he still had a job to do. After all, we had to make sure that all the bases at the Inn were covered.

"I am so excited," exclaimed one female member of the SGCRA as she sat at our bar one late afternoon.

"Why?" someone asked. "What the big occasion?"

"We are using some of the money from our fundraiser to go to Nassau. We are chartering a plane early tomorrow morning to get us all there."

"Do you have a meeting with the authorities?"

"No, we are just going with a lot of signs to protest outside the Parliament Building. But the newspaper is going to be there, so we should get some pictures taken. Not only that, we might even stay overnight and Glenn, our ISLAND COUNCILOR, is coming with us!"

I looked at this American lady, the same one who had called the authorities to complain about Nippers, and simply asked "OH, so YOU plan to give Glenn the time off?"

I was a bit ticked off, but it really was between Glenn and me. He hadn't mentioned a word about it, and I couldn't help but ask just when he intended to tell us. It was clear that in attempting to be fair we had given him too much leeway. Talk about being easy. It dawned on me that half the meetings we had allowed him to attend were probably not meetings at all.

Glenn did go to Nassau and there was a picture in the paper. It was a picture of about eight adults with four or five of their kids and Glenn. Having his picture in the paper probably made the whole trip worthwhile as far as he was concerned. Maybe not, but it sure did please him.

CHAPTER 41

Swapping One Piece of Paradise for Another

Regardless of all the community intrigue, life just went on as usual. There were the long days and late nights seven days a week. We embraced our old returning friends and had a chance to make new ones. We experienced love, laughter, excitement and fun, lots of fun.

But there was also the stress, lots of stress, and at times complete exhaustion.

It has been truly a grand adventure. And I could still vividly remember the first time as a new owner I saw the Inn from the water. As the boat pulled up to the dock I was overwhelmed. "Oh God," I thought, "how beautiful, how special it really is. A piece of paradise and it's ours—it really is ours!" Now both of us were wondering how long we could hang on or how much it would really hurt to let her go. For a while we would just kept plugging away.

Rick Newman came back. He came again, again and again, but never empty-handed. He always brought toys for the pool, games, and made sure to bring enough balloons so we could fill them with water and bombard fellow swimmers. Everyone, regardless of age, used them for water fights. He usually brought a dear friend named Sylvia. She was a petite little thing and as sweet as she could be. On one occasion he brought her daughter, and often came with his son Brian.

The first time I saw Brian he was a little short chunky kind of kid. The last time I saw him he was tall—taller than his father as a matter of fact—muscular, handsome and no longer a kid.

Rick is a writer and wrote an article praising all good things about Guana Seaside Village. I can't quite remember the exact name of the magazine that published it, but I certainly remember with gratitude all the wonderful things he had to say. I also remember some of the folks who said reading his words had helped them decide to head our way. He turned out to be not just a strong supporter but a dear friend as well.

Bob and I began to talk seriously about selling the Inn. Even though we did this as we walked the beach or in the privacy of our room, it seemed as if the whole island knew. There were so many things to consider—all the pros and cons. We talked about our new friends, our old friends, and all the repeat guests who were making their plans to return. We reminisced about all the fun times, remembered the laughter as well as the frustrations. We relived some of those incredibly long days, exhausting hours and hard work. We also wondered about the staff—how would each of them make out? And as silly as this may seem, I wondered who would occupy Uncle Leonard's stool at the bar.

It wasn't too long before we began to get spontaneous inquiries. One couple approached us with a serious proposal, one that Bob rejected immediately. He explained to them that we weren't even sure we were selling, but he explained to me that they were the last people in the world he'd want to take over Seaside Village. He was certain they were so much like the original owners he was afraid that the locals would no longer be welcomed.

There were several other inquiries, so it became obvious that when the chips were down and we were really ready to move forward there would be no need to involve a realtor. The next folks to approach us were friends of ours—people we were sure could make a go of running the Inn and we would be pleased to see taking our place. As the talks became more serious in nature and some of the buyer's family members got involved, we decided to ask Janet to handle the negotiations. There were several scenarios that were proposed. One involved swapping the land we owned that was adjacent to the Inn for a piece of property they owned. We initially agreed, then they thought better of it. And as several other ideas were presented, including the possibility of our holding a second mortgage, the whole prospect became quite confusing.

There were a lot of communications back and forth, from Janet to them then to us, from us to them then back to Janet. Although at first we were quite excited at this prospect, it was now giving us up to wondering how the whole thing could really work. It was in the midst of all of this that we were approached by the developers who were part of the controversial Bakers Bay Project.

They explained they would like to buy Seaside Village. They would not be operating it as a resort. There would be no restaurant, no bar—it would just be used for housing their staff and they then asked Bob what he thought it was worth, including the adjacent land.

He talked to me, called Janet, told her to let the other prospective buyers know, and then he gave them a price. There were no questions, no dickering back and forth, just a simple handshake and that was that.

When Janet talked to our friends, the fellow primarily responsible for the effort to buy the Inn offered his congratulations. He also shared the fact that what he was really looking for was to run the Inn for a short while then sell it, just as we had, for a reasonable profit.

That was one bridge crossed. And as far as the locals were concerned, I guess it's probably better not having a restaurant, bar or pool to frequent than having them operating 'under management they mostly disliked.

Most who spoke to us told us they were really happy that we had the chance to sell. They believed that with the major health problems we had both faced it was like the Inn was running us instead of us running the Inn. There was one person however who confronted Bob personally and who in a loud accusing voice claimed we had SOLD OUT.

"Now what?" we asked each other. Neither one of us wanted to completely put Guana Cay behind us. We really did feel like this was home, even if it was a second home. Soon we'd have to move out of our little Room 3 and find somewhere else to hang our hats.

How many times have we said things like "Guess the timing was right," "Wow, what a coincidence," and "Hard to believe what just happened." All of those things came to pass while Bob was sitting in the kitchen of a cottage called Wind Chimes and Anita the owner was cutting his hair.

"What are you and Gerry going to do when the sale of the Inn is final?" she asked.

"Just look for another place," he answered.

"Why don't you talk to my husband Al? We haven't really been thinking about selling, but maybe now is the time to give it some consideration."

We both thought Wind Chimes was an adorable cottage and we certainly liked the location. Right across a little dirt road was a beautiful piece of property that I had admired from the first time I saw it. In fact I'd stop to take a good look at it every time my golf cart went in that direction. This piece of land was owned by a friend of Al and Anita's, who lived in Austria. For years Al had been acting as this friend's caretaker, overseer, and executor, as well as doing whatever else needed to be done on his behalf.

"Why don't you contact him and see if he would be willing to sell. If he agrees, then maybe we can make up some kind of package deal." That was what I quietly suggested. But I was hoping, wishing, and envisioning owning the cottage and also that land. I was composed on the outside but my insides were going 90 miles an hour, just like I was doing some internal racing. In the meantime I tried to keep a poker face so my excitement wouldn't show. And Bob, dear Bob, just kept telling me to slow down, take it easy, what will be will be!

Al made several calls to his friend and in no time we had a package deal. A deal that was once again consummated with a simple handshake. One door had closed but another had opened. That is always the way— as long as you don't let the closing one hit you in the ass and are willing to walk through the new opening trusting that it's just meant to be.

CHAPTER 42

More Government Blunders and Legal BS

It was time to sign the legal purchase and sales agreements, one for the Inn and another for the cottage and land. Now it was up to our attorney to set the wheels in motion.

The first step in any real estate transaction is to present the documents to the Bahamian Investment Board for their review and approval or disapproval—whatever their decision might be. We had no idea how often they met and quite frankly I don't think they knew either. It seemed apparent that they didn't have a schedule, or if they did it was without any rhyme or reason. It was now you see them, now you don't; or more aptly put, now they are meeting, now they aren't. There was nothing we could do but sit and patiently wait. And wait we did.

All the wonderful handshakes had taken place in June. The legal purchase and sales agreements had been filed in September. Fourteen months, three weeks and two-and-a-half agonizing days later, we finally received the Investment Board approval.

The package deal with Al and Anita was contingent on the sale of the

Inn. Now that this first hurdle was over, we all felt like it was time to celebrate. But not so fast. Something else was standing in the way. Our attorney called Bob and dropped the bombshell.

"Bob, you know the piece of land adjacent to the Inn that was part of the package? Well you have no proof of ownership!"

"What do you mean? Check with the tax people. We have been paying taxes on that parcel for the last six years."

"That doesn't prove a thing. Nothing has been filed that really shows you own it, so we can't move forward with this sale."

"What in God's name is wrong with him?" I asked Bob. "He ought to know we own it—after all, we bought it from HIM! Tell him to check his damn bank deposit slips."

None of that mattered. It was as if nothing mattered. Here we were once again in limbo.

This attorney blamed the Nassau attorney who had handled the original transaction six years ago. He claimed that the guy in Nassau hadn't properly filed the papers. I wondered if that meant he had forgotten to add the Bahamian postage stamp. He went on to explain that there was nothing he could do—it was all up to Bob to straighten it out.

Bob spent endless hours on the phone to Nassau. He was told the attorney would be in at 9:30, but of course he wasn't. He was then told to call back at 10:00, but by then the attorney was in a conference that would last about an hour, so he should call back then. By the time he called back the attorney had already gone to lunch, so he should try at about 3:00—and he did, only to find that the attorney had left for the day. He placed hundreds of phone calls, sent numerous e-mails and numerous faxes, but to no avail.

The only possible alternative was for Bob to fly to Nassau and camp out on the doorstep until someone got the idea that we were ceris. It was a Saturday morning when we came to this conclusion, and Bob on the spur of the moment just picked up the phone and began to dial the Nassau number.

"Why are you doing that?" I asked. "If you can't get him during the week, what makes you think you'll get him on a Saturday morning?"

"Just a hunch," he answered. "Maybe I'll catch him off guard."

And lo and behold the man himself answered the phone. Bob explained that Monday he'd be in Nassau before noon and expected the attorney to set up whatever meetings, with whomever, in order to get this land deal settled. The attorney was most gracious. He set up the meetings, squired Bob around, and readily owned up to the fact that his firm had originally made the mistake. It wasn't really him but someone else. It was someone who of course no longer worked there.

Now I guess the land we had owned for six years we now really owned. Hooray! And to think it only took us about five-and-a-half months to prove it.

The sale of the Inn and the purchase of Wind Chimes and that beautiful piece of land could now move forward, and it did. However there was still another catch.

Our attorney here in Marsh Harbour was holding a large sum of our money in an escrow account until he could determine how much property taxes we owed on the Inn.

We explained that we owed no taxes because we had purchased the Inn under the provision of the government's Hotel Encouragement Act. That meant that it was tax-free and would be for the next several years.

"Well, that exception was never formally filed, so I have no proof that it exists!"

He insisted that it was up to Bob to straighten it out. So, here we go again, with me wondering why in the world we were paying him if Bob had to do all the work.

Bob once again had to work with the attorney in Nassau. This time it only took three months because Bob found someone on staff who was more than willing to really work on our behalf. When she finally found the documents we needed, she sent them by FedEx so we wouldn't be delayed any longer. Bob was so pleased with her sincere efforts that he wanted the attorney to know what a good job she had done.. His only comment was, "She must have been working off the clock." The next day when Bob wanted to thank her again, he was told she no longer worked there.

Our attorney in Marsh Harbour saw all the written documentation but said he still couldn't release most of the money from escrow until the papers were properly filed with the government. Another seven months went by before he finally agreed to release those funds. He would see that we got some of them, but not all.

He had taken it upon himself to send the government $100,000, just in case we found out that we really did owe some taxes after all. Now it was up to Bob to try and get the government to reimburse us those dollars for "overpayment of taxes we never owed in the first place." Bob made one call to the Bahamian Tax Department—and only one—because the abrupt answer he received was "If it's yours, you'll get it." I can only tell you that as I'm writing this it hasn't happened yet, but Bob is working on it. I'm sure he will be successful and just as sure that it will take months. In the meantime I'm just staying out of his way.

Hopefully all these "horror" stories won't deter folks for looking for a vacation spot in the Bahamas, especially on Guana Cay. It is a delightful little island and even though there were times when we were really frustrated because it seemed like EVERYTHING was all *kerplunkeld* up, it eventually turned out all right. Nothing in all the governmental red tape stopped the sunrises, dulled the sunsets, quieted the slapping sounds of the waves, or stopped the gentle breezes. It is a wonderful place to be.

CHAPTER 43

Playtime

When we ran the Inn we met many second-home owners. They came for lunches, dinners, a swim in the pool or maybe just a drink or two. They not only were our guests but also could be thought of as friendly acquaintances.

Now that we are really retired and free from the burdens of business, we have found that those friendly acquaintances are now real friends. We have also found that we have time for many things. Bob goes to Nippers for coffee every morning and is supposed to come back with all the island news. Of course he never has very much to report—only once in a while is there a tidbit for him to share. I keep telling him that he had better come back with a lot of news or he won't be allowed to go there for coffee any more. That is a joke, of course !

After coffee he walks, and he walks all over the island. He is now up to over five miles a day and also up to the point where he doesn't even brag about it or need to take a nap when he gets home. In fact he volunteered to walk to the farthest end of the island at least twice a week to water the flowers for a second-home owner named Roger Dart, one of those former friendly acquaintances turned friend.

Santa Claus brought Bob everything a good fisherman would need, so he spends time stalking the bonefish that hang out right outside our cottage. He hasn't caught anything yet. At first he said it was because of our neighbor's dog.

Honey is a wonderful Golden Retriever, but every time Bob waded out to do a little fishing Honey jumped in and frolicked around wanting Bob to play. Of course the fish didn't hang around to watch.

Todd and Peggy are great neighbors and if they know it's Bob's' fishing time, they keep Honey in the house. There was a day when Peggy was painting inside so it wasn't feasible to keep the dog inside—he would certainly not have been much help. So Todd very nicely loaded Honey onto his golf cart and just drove her around for a while to give Bob a chance to fish. That tells you something about these delightful people as neighbors. And since Bob came in empty handed, it also tells you something about Bob as a fisherman. Just to be out there with all his gear "stalking" fish," as he calls it, seems to be a very relaxing hobby. Oh Lord, how I hope he catches one someday, and when he does I'll take tons of pictures so the kids will believe it.

There are many other things that keep Bob busy. There is always something to fix, something to connect, something to plan for or somewhere to give a helping hand. The most recent adventure was to help repair and widen the little road that winds through the Settlement.

He was right there bright and early and worked right along with men half his age. He didn't tote any wheelbarrows full of cement, but he sure did his share wielding a big old heavy rake. It was certainly interesting to watch the workers plugging away in a primitive sort of manner and to realize that over half of the workers were second-home owners. They were not only right in there busting their *bungies* with the local folks, but they had also been instrumental in raising the needed funds.

Our friend Ned sat and watched. It wasn't necessary that he pitch in. After all, he had been on the very first crew that built that tiny street over 40 years ago.

As usual the women took care of breakfast and lunch. Although we brought a lot of the goodies, the various eating places also donated food of all kinds. It was exciting to watch everyone working together.

All the kids from the Settlement were called over to write their names, add dates and handprints in the wet cement. Unfortunately, one gentleman thought their efforts were some sort of graffiti and raked them all out. Now the challenge was to get ALL those kids back for a repeat performance. Finding them and dragging them back proved to be one of the biggest challenges of the day. Fortunately they were all rounded up.

About two o'clock I figured Bob had had enough and so I decided to drag him home for a cool shower and a nice long nap. Needless to say he didn't object.

At first I was a little bit concerned about being bored without the Inn to tend to. I shouldn't have given it a thought. In fact there doesn't seem to be a day that isn't filled with things to do.

First, Quinn, the yoga expert who used to run retreats at Seaside, decided she'd love to have a few of us join her on her dock for morning exercises. She lives on Guana for most of the winter and her retreats are only two weeks in duration, so in the off times she was willing to work with anyone who would like to learn and become involved. Every morning except on Sundays we got together to participate and hopefully realize the benefits of yoga.

In the beginning there were only four or five of us, but as time went on the crowd grew and grew. There were a couple of mornings when our numbers were fourteen or fifteen and we were all stretched out, side by side, up and down the dock and around the edges. After a while when things settled down and folks had moved on, our solid group numbered around eight.

We met at 9:00 a.m. and for one hour I certainly tried to do my best. After the first few sessions I found the routine not too difficult and the rewards amazing. I seemed to be more balanced, more energized, in a happier frame of mind and really in touch with everything around me. However, there were a couple of balancing moves I just couldn't master. All my yoga mates would be standing on one leg, the other raised, hands out for the heron pose or up straight for what was called the tree. They would pose nice and steady while I flopped all over the place. Even practicing at the cottage or listening to advice from Peggy didn't improve my balancing skills. Finally I gave up. When Quinn would announce, "We will now go into our balancing pose," I would quietly mumble, "Go ahead— see if I care!" I learned a lot about myself— mostly positive aspects, but I also learned that as far as I was concerned what didn't creak, leaked.

When it was time for Quinn to return to the states, those of us who were really hooked continued with the morning sessions. We would gather on Peggy's dock and either JO or Peggy would lead us following the written notes from Quinn's sessions. A couple of times the notes blew off the dock and it was up to the group to remember the routine. Needless to say we laughed a lot, but we also managed to do most of the requirements. We also took the time at closing to express our gratitude for the world around us and for our many blessings, including the wonderful fellowship and caring friends.

That certainly gave me something real to look forward to. And with church on Sunday, my mornings were full. In fact Tuesday morning was extra full.

I remember when Norma first suggested we start a Texas Hold'em poker group. We would meet on Tuesdays at 11:00 a.m. and play until '1p.m. It sounded like fun but I never imagined just how much fun it would be. We thought of ourselves as the Great Guana Gambling Grannies, or the 4 G's. There were eight of us—all dear friends.

Peggy, my neighbor, was a rather laid-back and not too excitable player, except when she won. She was as always very steady and dependable.

Norma was the organizer who came up with neat ideas to enhance our time together. Most of the time Norma lost at the card table. I mean almost every week Norma lost. Even rotating the seats didn't help poor Norma. She would be holding what should have been a winning hand and damn if someone wouldn't have one just a little bit better.

There were two Barbaras. One took the game very seriously and was quiet while we played. She mentioned that she hoped no others would join because we wouldn't be able to tell if they were bluffing. I am terrible at shuffling, so Barbara would do that for me each time I was the dealer. She was really being helpful, but I suspect she was also guaranteeing that the cards were mixed up adequately.

The other Barbara talked constantly, amusing all of us. She really had and has outrageous stories to share. That is a trait everyone can enjoy whenever they are in her company.

Carol talked a lot also. However, she wasn't usually telling stories, just sort of chattering away. Most of the time I think she was talking to herself about her cards or who knows what. Sometimes she forgot just where we were. She might say something like, "Okay, we need three more cards on the table," and someone would answer, "Well hell, Carol you are the dealer." All that being said, she really is a sweetheart!

Bea, the oldest member of the group, is eighty-something but going on sixty. Hopefully we'll all be as young as she is when we are her age. We gathered at her house and she seemed to think that messing up her kitchen and spilling drinks on her special table gave her some sort of badge of honor. She somehow felt privileged.

Then there was Judy, who immediately took charge of the money, just as we all expected. You must have figured out by now that Judy the General usually is in charge. She collected our money, piled up the chips for each of us, counted at the end and always came out exactly right. She also made a chart reminding us that white chips were a nickel, blue ones were a dime, and the precious red ones were quarters. Maybe you can't believe that was a necessary for a group of grown-up women, but believe me it was! One day when someone asked about the value of the chips for about the hundredth time, Judy's response was immediate. Out of complete frustration she said, "Give me that damn chart because I am going to hang it around my neck so you can all see it plain and simple!"

The only thing I can report about my own involvement is that every once in a while I would announce that I wasn't going to look at my cards. And I wouldn't. I'd just follow the bidding, throw in my chips and win. Amazing. I didn't look at my cards and I won the pot. Most times when I did look, 'I lost. That must say something about my card playing ability.

All the pots seemed pretty small, so after three weeks of playing we decided to look up the betting rules. We had not been doing anything right. If some of us bet a nickel and then somewhere down the line the next person bet a dime, we'd say "So what? We already placed our bets." It took some real instructions before we figured out what "I'll see you," "I'll raise you," or even "I'll hold" or "I'll fold" meant. Once we got the betting down pat, the pots were bigger. But with a nickel, dime or rare quarter bet, how big could it get?

I printed out a paper that showed what hand would beat another and gave copies to everyone, but for some reason or other there was always amusing confusion. With our nickels and dimes we were just as serious as card players who bet hundreds and hundreds of dollars on a single hand.

The second week we got together, Judy came in with a big smile and a big jug of Bloody Marys. I remember that this was the Tuesday that both Carol and I came out winners, so we decided to spend it all on lunch. The following day there were a few things I needed clarified.

"Carol did we have another *Bloody Mary* when we went to lunch?"

"Yes, but when you wanted a second one I wouldn't let you!"

"Another question, did I pay for my own lunch or did you pay?"

"I don't think I paid, and I don't remember you paying. Maybe nobody paid!"

"One last thing, did you drive me home?"

"Let me think. I really can't remember, but I don't think so!"

"Well hell, Carol, remember it or not you must have. After all you had the cart.

And Barbara—fun-loving Barbara—went to the grocery store after the game to buy some ice cream. She couldn't decide what flavor she wanted so she bought a quart of every kind they had. Then on her way past the liquor store she stopped in and bought the biggest bottle of Kahlua they had. She couldn't figure out why because she didn't know anyone who really liked it, and she sure didn't.

After that Tuesday, any time one of us went into the grocery store and acted like we didn't know what we were there for (which happens anyway), someone on duty was bound to ask, "Been playing cards?"

Norma suggested that we pair up. From then on, one of the partners was responsible for bringing lunch, the other for bringing the drinks. The lunches varied with all kinds of dishes, some with a Bahamian touch, others with a Mexican flair, and of course some with the good old American touch. The food was marvelous and the drinks weren't bad either. It wasn't always Bloody Marys, but Mimosas, rum drinks, mystery fruit concoctions and coconut creamy things. Thankfully, there was only one choice at a time.

One Mimosas-Tuesday Carol announced she was going to have only one drink because she would be driving and would also be taking me home. At this point Peggy spoke up and said, "Don't worry, Carol. I brought you both here and I will bring you both back!"

It is just not possible to explain the entire scene, the fun, the hysteria or the blunders. If these games had been video-taped, I feel certain we could have transformed them into some sort of mini-series. If not that, then certainly we could have grabbed a spot or two on *America's*

Funniest Home Videos.

Even though the group is now scattered all over the states, we have already decided to begin our little poker club as soon as we return to Guana for the winter months. I had been thinking about bringing back t-shirts sporting "4G" logos for all of us. But remembering that never a Tuesday went by without a least a couple of drinks being spilled, I have changed my mind. I will buy us all sippy cups instead.

That isn't the only time I get to play cards. Every other Saturday night, at the little schoolhouse, there is a bingo game that I enjoy if nothing else is planned or gets in the way. You pay $1 for a card and if you win, half of the winnings is yours, and the other half goes to the school. It really is a fun way to raise money and sure beats all those raffles and bake sales under the fig tree. Just about everything the school needs is paid for by the parents or supporters. The teacher's' salary is the only responsibility that the government accepts, so that certainly leaves a lot to be desired. We play from 7:00 o'clock until 9:00 o'clock, but at 8:00 o'clock we take a snack break. That's the time when you can buy cookies, brownies, squares of macaroni and cheese or sandwiches that the parents have made.

The first night I played, Shannon saw Bob outside waiting for me. She ran outside shouting gleefully, "Mr. Bob, Mr. Bob! Miss Gerry just won $500 dollars!"

I had actually won $6.25.

She thought that was the greatest joke of all, and maybe she was right because I can't begin to tell you how many people with a smile on their faces asked me what I did with that $500.

On a good night they raise about $200, and a little more if the food sells really well. Maybe that 'doesn't sound like very much, but think about how many workbooks, reading books, or other items that money will buy. They were more than pleased.

When I am not doing yoga or gambling, there is plenty to do at the cottage. That dear little place needs some work and the obvious place to start is on the inside.

Our son-in law and a friend named Matt came down to replace three sliding glass doors and three sets of windows. They started on Monday and finished in time to catch the morning ferry on Friday. The way they worked was unbelievable—no one could believe how much they had accomplished in such a short time.

The sliders and the windows were all a different size than those that had been replaced, so there was a lot of inside painting that had to be done. At first I envisioned this effort would be a joint one, and in a way I guess it was. I painted and painted and to be of help, Bob either went to Marsh Harbour to buy more paint 'or went to the local hardware store to buy new paintbrushes. For some reason I ruined paintbrushes right and left. After a while Bob stopped buying what he called really good ones and just brought me back the 85-cent kind.

He helped in other ways. He even volunteered to make something good for the potluck supper and because he didn't know quite what it would be, he just decided on deviled eggs. Not a big gourmet surprise, but they were very good. He was very proud, and it freed my mind from fretting over what I should make. It also allowed me to continue painting without interruption. His biggest contribution, however, was his undying support. He cheered me on every step of the way.

"You do such a good job, honey!"

"Wow, Sweetie. Look how much you have done. 'You're moving right along!"

"You are such a good painter!"

"You are a much better painter than I am."

"I couldn't do it half as good as you're doing it!"

I guess he thinks he is the only one that ever read *Tom Sawyer*.

After the primer was all done and most of the topcoat finished, he decided to pitch in. He painted one half of a window, put down the brush, went into the other room and picked up the phone to call our son-in-law.

"Hey Scott, the inside painting is just about done."

" No, we didn't hire anyone, we just did it ourselves."

"It looks great. You should be proud of us!"

I guess he forgot how small the cottage is, because every word he said reached me. Of course those words prompted my reply, which was short and sweet:

"US? US? US? Who do you mean by US?" Looking at his grin, I knew I did not need to say another word.

The next time we return, it is the outside that will need our attention. Guess whose turn it will be to paint, and whose turn it will be to play Tom Sawyer?

CHAPTER 44
✑

Alone I Am Fine; With Sandra I Am Sad

I would stroll over to the Inn on a few occasions just to see what was going on. Usually there wasn't much of anything. With the exception of a security guard for the development company, no one else was around.

They had changed the dining room into a community room of sorts with a sofa, some chairs, and a decent size TV. They closed off the stairs that I had climbed so many times to serve our guests. Now there was a separate entryway for those stairs and the upstairs dining area was like a computer center where their employees all had their laptops. There was nothing so new or startling that I found it upsetting. It was only the quietness, the lack of fun, laughter, hustle and bustle that made it seem eerie. I would simply stroll back to the cottage pretty unaffected and not give it another thought. Then Sandra came to visit.

"Miss Gerry, could we please go over to the Inn?" she asked.

"Any special reason, Sandra?"

"No, just to look around and see what they have done."

So off we went. This time seeing the Inn was not so easy.

Sandra took a lot of time. She wandered through "her" kitchen, commented on any change no matter how small, and then began to cry.

"Miss Gerry, please Miss Gerry, offer those people a few dollars and tell them you want the Inn back!"

"Oh Sandra, it doesn't work that way."

"Well, it might if you just tried. I would come back. Glenn, Nora Mae, and even Renee would come back. We all want to come back. We were just talking about that the other day. See, you wouldn't have to worry about staff. We'd all be right here with you and ready to work."

I tried to help Sandra understand but it was difficult, though not quite as difficult as us saying goodbye at the end of that day. We hugged tightly. She cried a lot and I cried a little. It was the first time I had felt any sadness about not having Seaside as ours. I felt that sadness well into the next afternoon. It didn't leave me until I recognized that it wasn't really the Inn but Sandra that had captured my emotions. She has a position at Marsh Harbour where she works breakfast and dinner. She is closer to home and doesn't have to bother with the ferry any time she wants to do something on her days off. It is a really nice place but when I tried to point out all the positives she just kept saying, "It isn't the same, Miss Gerry. It just isn't the same!"

Aerial Shot of the Inn

I know she'll be back for another visit and I'll be glad to see her, but this time if we take a walk we'll sure as heck head away from Seaside

Village.

Some things change, and, just as in any place else, other things remain the same.

I see the same people jogging, riding their bikes, or out on the bay in their kayaks. There is the same staff at the grocery store and the same people singing and praying on Sunday mornings. The children who go to school in Marsh Harbour are on the early 8 o'clock ferry all spiffed up in their various uniforms and dragging their backpacks. The girls are doing homework, the boys are quietly fooling around, and the ferry captain is doing his best to maintain control. The ferries and freight boats run on schedule and usually are on time. When lobster season rolls around, the fishermen all gather on the dock waiting to load their boats and folks are there to see them off. Most are locals and they are all praying for a good haul and a safe return. Sometimes their husbands, brothers and sons are gone for weeks at a time.

The same second-home owners return in the late fall, early winter and hunker down until spring or the early months of summer. They greet each other like it is a family reunion.

There are months when the little Cay is full of tourists. Many of them are easily recognized because they come time and time again. The only time it is really quiet is in September and October when it is perceived to be high Hurricane Season.

The post office is now open for a few hours three days a week, and the police station still remains empty. Mostly things remain the same, but there have been some changes. Some changes are subtle, others more obvious.

We have a new little white fire station. The door hasn't had to be opened yet because thankfully there have been no calls for help.

Right at the end of the dock and straight ahead is the Art Bakery Café. It is a rather imposing place that is a new addition to the Settlement. In the beginning the plans called for a three-story building that certainly would have changed the entire complexion of the old and quaint "downtown." It would have dwarfed all the small one-story homes that had been there for years. The complaints about the proposed project were numerous.

"It will be so out of place!"

"It will be the first thing people see when they get off the ferry!"

"Hey, guess what? Everyone will think we have a Wal-Mart!"

In addition to all the hoopla, the new building would clearly not have been legal. According to Glenn, no three-story structures were allowed on Guana, so he went into action. His main complaint as Island Councilor was that the building permit had been issued in the first place, and he was determined to find out how that happened. All he could think of was that she surely knew somebody. And he was right! Finally he was able to determine just who that somebody was. After a couple of heated meetings, the plans were changed and only a two-story building was erected.

It is still pretty big compared to what surrounds it, but it is not that intrusive. In fact it is not a bad addition. It is bright, sunny, a pretty blue, and has a nice wrap-around porch with wicker tables and rocking chairs. It is good place to visit when you first get off the ferry or while you are hanging around waiting for the next one to come in. They have plenty of good baked goods, but even after two years there is still no art.

At first the Café was operated by the husband and wife who were owners. It didn't work out very well, simply because they weren't working out as a couple either. There had been several occasions when the husband left, stating that he was going away for good. He did that numerous times but would quite quickly return. But now that he really has been gone for a long time, people are assuming that this time he is gone for good.

A relative was hired to help run things, but that wasn't a very good alternative either. At first he was there working long hours and working hard, but after a while he kind of gave up. Instead of playing on the beach or in the sea, he wanted to go back home where he could play in the snow.

Jerry and Chorene are now running the Café, and we can already see the positive changes they are making. Remembering what a good job they did rescuing the Guana Beach Seaside Bar and Grill, I have no doubt that they will hang in there and make this new adventure work.

There have also been changes at that same Beach Bar and Grill that is now known as Grabbers. The new folks, Jimmy and Terry, are not just leasing this place, they are part owners and are on hand daily to run things. They have invested heavily, which has made numerous changes possible. Not only have there been numerous physical renovations and the addition of a gift shop, but there's also a new menu that includes such things as mussels, veal scaloppini, and other selections not usually found on Guana.

Blue Water Grill has also changed hands.

The young gentleman from New Jersey who originally signed a lease with the owner had a difficult time really making things work because any ideas he had were usually vetoed by the owner. In fact it seemed the owner actually tried to micro-manage all that went on, including personnel issues. Eventually he decided to go back home and open his own restaurant. He did exactly that and from all reports he is doing a booming business.

Now the owner had to look for someone else to sign a lease. He begged, pleaded and badgered Johnny from Nippers to step in and keep the restaurant open. It was hard for most of us to believe that Johnny would take on this challenge. We all believed that he had his hands full with Nippers. But those who really knew Johnny should have known better.

We no longer have The Blue Water Grill—we now have Docksiders!

Previously Blue Water had been decorated with seashells, sand dollars, and coral. All the tables had glass domes filled with sand and shells as centerpieces. There was netting decorated with starfish and that décor was carried throughout. When Johnny first took over he found the dining rooms and the inside porches completely bare. Everything was gone. He wasn't deterred—he would just start from scratch.

He and his family worked for days just getting ready to open for dinner at least a couple of nights a week. That would be the beginning schedule, but before long they were open for lunches and six nights a week for dinner.

They chose a nautical motif. When the owner discovered what they had planned, he strongly objected. "I don't want a nautical motif. That sounds tacky," he complained.

"Well, that is what we want and that's what it will be. I just want you to understand that as long as my name is on that lease, things will be done the way I say!"

That is really all it took. Someone who had the courage to tell it as it should be! Johnny will be in charge and will not stand for any interference.

The nautical theme is wonderful. They have hung blue and white striped curtains, sails to divide the eating spaces and carpeting on the inside porches, all of which help cut down on the noise level. There are new centerpieces on all the tables, delightful lamps strategically placed, and great boat pictures on the walls. I am not certain who in Johnny's family has the creative touch, but it certainly worked well. They have created a peaceful atmosphere, and when you combine that with soft music and superb food you really find yourself in an elegant dining situation.

In spite of all those efforts Nippers is still going strong. Bob continues to have coffee there every morning and gets a big kick out of Johnny when he makes the usual invitation announcements over the VHF. He starts out as he always did when inviting folks to join him at Nippers.

"This is Johnny," he shouts loudly and with an air of deliberate excitement." "Come play in the pool, watch the girlies, have a frozen nipper, walk the beach . . ." and on he goes, a little like a carnival barker. Then he changes.

"Good morning, this is Jonathan. I'd like to invite you to join us at Docksiders for a quiet elegant dinner. It is fine dining at its best. We ask that you please make reservations and dress appropriately. You don't have to come in a suit, but shoes and pants would really be appreciated."

Then he describes some of the enticing entrees. All this is said in a quiet gentlemanly voice and Bob swears that even his facial expressions change as he takes on the different persona'.

Bruce and Judy were somewhat is a tizzy. Bruce's daughter was coming to be married at High Rocks. And all the wedding reception plans had been developed weeks before with the folks in charge of Blue Water Grill. Even though Johnny promised to honor the contract they still wondered if he would be able to pull it off. In fact their acceptance of "Nippers" as the new face on the Blue Water Grill was lukewarm to say the least.

The morning following the reception, Judy got on the VHF and made the following announcement: "Anyone thinking about coming to the Bahamas to get married should really come to Guana. And for the reception you just have to make arrangements with Docksiders. They did a wonderful job. You couldn't find a better, more organized, elegant reception anywhere. They were great and it was great!!!"

Enough said!

There isn't much else for news or changes.

SGCRA was invited to attend the Small Island Developing States Symposium at the United Nations. They had several meetings and even had one of their discussions on a web cast. Some of the folks they met with were part of a Mangrove Action Project. Everyone involved was part of a group for Sustainable Development and Transparent Government. A team from SGCRA and their attorney traveled New York to make their case. I admire their dedication and really think their visit was good for public relations. However, I don't really expect to see a UN Peace Keeping Force converge on Guana Cay. Quite frankly I haven't much faith in the UN. I would much rather see them pay a little more attention to the slaughter of all the thousand of innocent people in Darfur. That personal opinion isn't meant to belittle the efforts of the SGCRA. I do wonder what they had hoped to accomplish and also wonder if their limited resources might not have been better spent on their ongoing court cases.

The first annual Guana Grand Prix was held just before folks were getting ready to pack for home. It was the inevitable result of two guys claiming each had the fastest golf cart on the island. David was the biggest bragger, so Dick just decided to challenge him. Planning for the big race began almost immediately, with Bruce being the real instigator. A track for the race was determined, but it would be held in an undisclosed location. Only those of us involved were to know since we would be someplace where we weren't supposed to be. There was a pace car, a large red strip across the road for the starting line, a green go flag, and a black and white flag to wave-in the winner.

Dave removed the top from his cart and Dick removed his muffler, both trying to gain an advantage. They wore goggles and screwy hats and acted out for those of us who made up the cheering squad. To make a long story short, Dick won hands down. In fact we waited patiently for Dave to round the corner. We all decided at that point that Dave would have to sit alone at lunch, and that he should also change his VHF call sign to "Loser-Loser."

The race lasted about ten minutes, the preparations a lot longer than that, and the celebration even longer, much too long in fact. We will repeat this Grand Prix next year, but this time we'll not hold it inside a gated community where we should not be. It will be held on the main road with everyone invited to watch. And I can bet you that it will be followed with some kind of potluck lunch and an afternoon of continued jeering and cheering!

I forgot to mention that Nora Mae gave birth to her fourth child. All of her children are bright and beautiful. Her oldest son earns high honors in every advanced class they have placed him in, and this new little guy looks like he'll follow right in line. With this new one Bob and I both know who the Daddy is. We would love to see him marry Nora Mae, or perhaps more to the point see her agree to marry him. It would be great when this little guy grows up, if he can proudly announce that he was one of the "in ones." I know it would be a little after the fact, but later is better than never.

Here we are, almost ten years later in that little two-bedroom cottage by the sea that we were searching for when we hit that bump in the road called Guana Seaside Village. Hopefully this dissertation has given you a glimpse of our adventures as innkeepers and a small picture of what life is like on the small Guana Cay. I can only hope that you enjoy reading about it as much as we enjoy living it.

Windy Hill South

Geraldine Sylvester

Geraldine Sylvester earned a degree in Social Science from the University of New Hampshire. She is the recipient of numerous awards and recognitions, including two honorary doctorate degrees. She and her husband Bob now divide their time between their homes in New Hampshire and Guana Cay in the Abacos, Bahamas. They have seven children and sixteen grandchildren.

Gerry's first book, *Windy Hill,* was published in 2003 and is still in print.

CPSIA information can be obtained
at www.ICGtesting.com
Printed in the USA
BVHW031252070819
555315BV00001B/11/P